MEDICINE IN THE BIBLE AND THE TALMUD

THE LIBRARY OF JEWISH LAW AND ETHICS
VOLUME V
EDITED BY NORMAN LAMM

President, and
Jakob and Erna Michael professor of Jewish philosophy
Yeshiva University

MEDICINE IN THE BIBLE AND THE TALMUD

Selections from Classical Jewish Sources

By

FRED ROSNER, M.D.

KTAV PUBLISHING HOUSE, INC.
YESHIVA UNIVERSITY PRESS
NEW YORK
1977

Library of Congress Cataloging in Publication Data

Rosner, Fred.
  Medicine in the Bible and the Talmud.

  (The Library of Jewish law and ethics; 5)
  Bibliography: p.
  Includes index.
  1. Bible—Medicine, hygiene, etc. 2. Talmud—Medi-
cine, hygiene, etc. 3. Medical ethics. I. Title.
R135.5.R67   296.1   76-58505
ISBN 0-87068-326-8

MANUFACTURED IN THE UNITED STATES OF AMERICA

שמע בני מוסר אביך

ואל תטש תורת אמך

משלי א׳ ח.

Dedicated to my parents,
Sara and Yehoshua Rosner,
who have given me so much,
in honor of their
golden wedding
anniversary

CONTENTS

Editor's Foreword

Many of the most important advances in contemporary medicine and medical technology have brought in their train agonizing moral problems. It almost seems as if every new scientific or clinical solution raises perplexing ethical questions.

Medical ethics has, indeed, become not only a live subject in the public forum, but a respectable branch of scholarship. Because the challenges thrown up by medical progress are universal, affecting all humans of every persuasion, it was inevitable that Jews—and others as well—would consult the Jewish tradition, with its millennial heritage of moral values and legal decisions. Not surprisingly, this tradition has, despite its ancient provenance, proven a rich mine for moral and juridical guidance.

Part of the explanation for this remarkable phenomenon lies in the characteristic Jewish interest in the healer's art. Some of the greatest sons of the Jewish people, since time immemorial, have been physicians, and some were quite distinguished. ("My grandfather, the doctor" is as apt a characterization of the historic Jew as the more well-known "My son, the doctor.") A number of modern scholars have written heavy tomes documenting the history of medicine amongst Jews, and these scholarly researches are an invaluable addition both to the history of medicine and to Jewish history.

The present volume, by Dr. Fred Rosner—a distinguished hematologist and Jewish scholar—has focused on specific subjects, pointing to the treatment of these themes in the Bible and the Talmud. The author has brought to this task both his professional medical knowledge and his considerable Jewish education, and the result is a book that is at once reliable and readable.

While Dr. Rosner does not directly address himself in this work to the problems of medical ethics, he does give the reader a feel for the medical interest and wisdom of the sages of the Jewish tradition. This, in turn, not only satisfies the student's healthy intellectual curiosity, but justifies the perplexed modern's quest for guidance of this same tradition, which embraces both value and fact, judgment and inquiry, ethics and science.

I trust that all who are attracted to the subject—whether they begin from an interest in the history of medicine or the Jewish tradition, or the current preoccupation with medical ethics—will find in this volume enough to stimulate their interest in the subject and encourage them to further reading and research.

NORMAN LAMM
Editor

April 25, 1977

Preface

There are many ways to approach the subject of biblical and talmudic medicine. One method is to study the Bible sequentially and identify medical passages and diseases. For example, in the first chapter of Genesis, paramedical topics such as the creation of man and the creation of life and death are mentioned. Later in Genesis, the Bible relates that when Abraham came to Egypt he told Pharaoh that Sarah was his sister and not his wife. As a result, Pharaoh took her, and God afflicted Pharaoh and his family with a mysterious disease (Gen. 12:17). What was this sickness? A systematic study of this passage in the Pentateuch, based upon all available source materials, including commentaries on the Bible from ancient, medieval, and more modern times, as well as recent archaeological and manuscript discoveries, might shed some light on the nature of Pharaoh's affliction.

Later yet in the Book of Genesis we are told that Sarah, at the age of ninety years, gave birth to Isaac. How was this possible? Did her menses return? Was this event purely a miracle? What were the medical circumstances surrounding the birth? Another incident concerns the Patriarch Abraham's nephew, Lot, who protected two angels in Sodom against physical harm at the hands of the inhabitants of that city. The angels afflicted the wicked people with blindness (Gen. 18:11). What kind of blindness was this? Was it trachoma? Was it physical, mental, or psychological blindness? Was it temporary or permanent? These questions cannot be answered with any degree of certainty.

Some illnesses are clearly stated. For example, when God came to visit Abraham following his surgery (Gen. 18:1), it is clear that the operation was a circumcision. Not so clear, however, is the meaning of the disease *zara'at* to which large sections (chap. 13:1 ff.) of the Book of Leviticus address themselves. Although commonly translated as leprosy, there is serious doubt in the minds of many as to the validity of this interpretation. Some consider *zara'at* to be elephantiasis; others syphilis, and yet others "a malignant disease of the skin." At least two biblical commentators consider *zara'at* to be a social disease and not a medical condition at all. To fully examine such a subject requires an in-depth investigation

xi

of the medical, historical, and linguistic aspects of *zara'at,* with a search of citations in the Bible, the writings of ancient and medieval Jewish and non-Jewish scholars, and perhaps even the paleontological evidence, if any, to arrive at the proper meaning of *zara'at.*

The above chronological methodology of the study of biblical and talmudic medicine represents only one approach. Another approach is to seek information in the Bible and Talmud concerning specific topics, subjects, or disease entities. For example, the ophthalmologist interested in Jewish medical history may ask himself: Where are eye illnesses discussed in the Bible and/or Talmud? Which eye illnesses are described? What is stated about them in terms of diagnosis, treatment, cause, prevention, etc.? Or, one can seek information about diabetes, gallstones, jaundice, anemia, arthritis, or a variety of specific disease entities or symptoms. What do the Bible and/or Talmud say about each of these?

Another approach is to seek material in the Bible and Talmud about individual body organs, such as the heart, the brain, the kidney, and others. A variety of broader subjects, such as air pollution, legal medicine, dietetics, anesthesia, general surgery, and many more, can also be looked for in the Bible and Talmud. Finally, the Talmud contains sayings and teachings by sages who were physicians as well as talmudic scholars. An in-depth study of one or more such physicians is certainly a desideratum.

The present book offers examples of all these categories. A general introduction to biblical and talmudic medicine by Suessman Muntner is provided, as well as a brief biography of Julius Preuss and a description of his classic *Biblisch-Talmudische Medizin.* Anatomic organs are represented by chapters on the heart, spleen, and gallbladder. The specific disease entities discussed are hemophilia, rabies, gout, sunstroke, *kordiakos,* scurvy, and *yerakon.* Specific medical topics derived from biblical and talmudic sources are sex determination, suicide, snakes and serpents, dolphins, the biblical quail incident, anesthesia, artificial respiration, and "forensic" medicine. One chapter is devoted to the medical life of the most illustrious of all the physicians in the Talmud, Mar Samuel. Finally, a section on ethics and prayers for the Jewish physician presents chapters on the physician and patient in Jewish law, visiting the sick (*Bikkur Holim*), the Oath of Asaph, the physician's prayer attributed to Moses Maimonides, and the therapeutic efficacy of prayer.

The various selections comprising this work represent only a small portion of the voluminous literature about medicine contained within the Bible and Talmud and other ancient Hebrew writings. Much work is yet required for this rich treasury of source material on medicine to be brought to the attention of the reader of English.

The chapter entitled "Medicine in Ancient Israel" was written by the late Suessman Muntner, professor of the history of medicine at the Hebrew University, director of the Gallery of Medicine of the Jerusalem Academy of Medicine and the Israeli Medical Association, and co-founder and editor for many years of the Israeli medical-historical journal *Korot*. Professor Muntner, a recognized authority on Jewish medical history, edited from manuscripts and published most of the medical writings of Moses Maimonides, and wrote extensively on ancient and medieval Hebrew medicine. I was privileged to collaborate with Professor Muntner in the English translation of several of Maimonides' medical works. "The Oath of Asaph," which appears in this book, was also a collaborative effort between Professor Muntner and myself.

I am indebted to the editors of the following journals for permission to reprint various letters and articles: *American Journal of Clinical Nutrition, Anesthesia and Analgesia, Annals of Internal Medicine, Bulletin of the History of Medicine, Clio Medica, Intercom, Israel Journal of Medical Sciences, Jewish Observer, Journal of the American Medical Association, Journal of the History of Medicine and Allied Sciences, Journal of Religion and Health, Medical History, New York State Journal of Medicine,* and *Tradition*. Several of the chapters in this book have not been published elsewhere. Mrs. Sophie Falk and Mrs. Miriam Regenworm typed the manuscript, and for this I am grateful.

Fred Rosner, M.D.

New York
1976

Part I
General
Introduction

Medicine in Ancient Israel

by Suessman Muntner

The Biblical Era (ca. 1500–300 B.C.E.)

"The history of medicine is part of the story of human civilization. We must remember, however, that every civilization is the result of a long evolutionary process. By the time we first encounter it in writings or other concrete evidence, it has already gone through a course of evolution which is hardly ever a purely esoteric one. At some time or other in its history every people must have made contacts with other groups, contacts which of necessity resulted in an exchange of culture traits. . . . In each case under study, it is the scholar's task to determine and to demonstrate which traits were original with the Hebrews and which were derived from other civilizations."

While this statement from Julius Preuss's introduction to his classic work, *Biblisch-Talmudische Medizin,* is applicable to all cultures, it is of particular relevance to the history of oriental civilization.

The thought patterns of occidental civilization have been basically influenced by the mentalities of two peoples: the ancient Greeks, with their lucid reasoning and logical approach to scientific problems, and the People of the Book, with their intuitive ethical teachings, their timeless moral laws, and, last but by no means least, their ethically based health rules.

The People of the Book originated in the land of Mesopotamia (Ur Kasdim, Chaldea). This people, known as the people of the Hebrews (from *'ever ha-nahar*—"from the other side of the River [Euphrates]"), first moved to Canaan, and later spent 430 years in servitude in Egypt, where it came to know not only the civilization of the Egyptians but also their cruelty, especially to those whom they considered their inferiors. After their deliverance from Egypt, the Children of Israel returned to Canaan (around the thirteenth century B.C.E.), where, (except for seventy years spent in exile in Babylonia—fifth century B.C.E.), they lived as a free nation and remained until the year 70 C.E.

3

Canaan lies at the crossroads between two continents—Africa and Asia —and two civilizations—those of ancient Egypt and Assyria-Babylonia. Through its access to the Mediterranean Sea it was linked with the continent of Europe. As a result, the Hebrews were not only "midway" between two highly advanced civilizations but also natural "middle-men" for the transmission of cultural and material values from one country to another. Later, in similar fashion, the Jews were to introduce the medical skills of the ancient Greeks to the Arabs, and those of Eastern Arabia to the Western Arabian peoples. It was the Jews, too, who eventually carried the medical attainments of the medieval Arab world to the continent of Europe.

The Bible was not created in a vacuum but drew on sources from surrounding cultures. In the same manner, the people of Israel cannot be viewed outside the context of neighboring civilizations. From the time they first became a people until the destruction of the First Temple in the year 586 B.C.E., the ancient Israelites were constantly under the influence of the civilizations of the "Land between the Rivers" (Sumeria, Akkad, Assyria, Babylonia), of ancient Egypt, and of the Canaanitish peoples. The crucial point here is not what cultural values or inspiration Israel drew from its neighbors, but the way in which it assimilated these acquisitions spiritually and morally.

*   *   *

Our main historical sources for the study of medicine in the so-called biblical era are the Bible, which was written in the Hebrew language, and archaeological findings made in Palestine.

Although the Bible is not a medical text, its historical accounts, laws, and precepts, and even its wording, yield an abundant harvest of information concerning the structure of the human body, diseases, injuries, cures, and, above all, preventive and sanitary procedures. The material contained in some portions of the Pentateuch (such as chapter 13 of the Book of Leviticus) is so factual that even the sophisticated present-day student cannot help but be amazed at what he reads there. Especially the sanitary regulations of cleanliness and purity, such as the prohibition against the consumption of blood and quarantines for infectious diseases, are unique and do not occur in the codes of the civilized nations of antiquity that surrounded the Land of Israel. Other references, again, despite the thorough and detailed descriptions they present, are difficult to correlate with modern diagnoses and terminology.

The Pentateuch contains directives not only for the quarantining of persons suffering from infectious ailments, but also for the disinfection of contaminated household furnishings by burning or incineration, and for the fumigation of contaminated homes.

According to biblical precept, all the clothing of soldiers returning from battle, and their gear of leather, goat's hide, or wood, had to be disinfected. Vessels or objects of gold, silver, copper, iron, tin, or lead—"everything that may abide fire" (Num. 31:23)—had to be put through fire. Objects that could not stand fire were immersed in boiling water. The clothing or objects could not be brought into the camp or used until seven days after disinfection (Num. 31:22–24; Lev. 14:35–45).

As part of his sanitary gear, every soldier had to carry in his belt a small shovel or paddle, "and it shall be, when thou sittest down abroad, thou shalt dig therewith, and shalt turn back and cover that which comes from thee" (Deut. 23:13–14). This procedure was intended to help prevent pollution of the air and the spread of intestinal infections.

The warning in Leviticus 18:3, "After the doings of the land of Egypt . . . shall ye not do," refers not only to human relations, particularly with inferiors ("Remember that thou thyself wast once a slave to Pharaoh in Egypt"), but also to the health regulations which the ancient Egyptians did not observe. Among the health measures enumerated in the Bible are the careful inspection of all meat (*kosher* vs. *trefa*), and sanitary regulations with regard to burial, dress, housing, etc. The enforcement of the sanitary laws (quarantine, sterilization of utensils, fumigation of homes, etc.) was entrusted to the priests, but not the actual treatment of the sick. There were physicians ("Is there no balm in Gilead? Is there no physician there?"—Jer. 8:22), pharmacists (Exod. 30, Neh. 3), male nurses (*toflim*—in the Book of Job), and midwives (Exod. 1). There is mention of a midwife also in the story of Tamar's pregnancy, which resulted in the birth of twins (Gen. 38:27–30). The birth was accompanied by a *prolapsus mani* (*nethinat yad:* "And it came to pass, when she travailed, that one put a hand . . ." Gen. 38:28).

Biblical medicine was also aware that certain diseases could be communicated (*nega'*) to others through utensils or through a third person.

Social hygiene laws included regulations applicable to sex relations, family life, clothing, and diet. While hospitals were apparently unknown in biblical times, there is a reference in the Second Book of Samuel (15:17) to a *Bet Merḥak,* lit. "house of distance" ("and they tarried in *Bet-Merḥak*"), which probably was a sort of "isolation ward" outside the city limits. All these health rules were intended to ensure the survival of the people.

While the practice of embalming the dead after the manner of ancient Egypt was not customary in Israel, it was not explicitly prohibited by biblical law (see the account in Gen. 50 of the embalming of Jacob and Joseph by Egyptian physicians). The circumcision of all male infants, which has been practiced by the Jewish people ever since the days of Abraham, was not an exclusively Israelite procedure. Zipporah, the heathen wife of Moses, circumcised her son to save his life (Exod. 4:25), performing the operation with a "flint" (*zur*). In one of the tombs of Zakkarah, near Cairo, a picture was found showing a circumcision performed with a knife. The Book of Joshua (5:2–3) relates that Joshua circumcised the Children of Israel with "knives of flint" when they entered the land of Canaan.

Among the diseases mentioned in the Bible are plagues, heat-stroke (2 Kings 4:18 ff.), epilepsy ("the saying of him who . . . sees the vision of the Almighty, *fallen down, yet with opened eyes*"—Num. 24:4), jaundice (*yerakon*), edema (*bazeket*), hemiplegia (*shituk:*—Jeroboam's "hand, which he put forth . . . dried up so that he could not draw it back to him"—1 Kings 13:4), pemphigus (*shekhin poreah avabu'ot:* "a boil breaking forth with blains"—Exod. 9:9), leishmaniasis, or oriental boils (*apholim:* "the boil of Egypt"—Deut. 28:27), consumption (*shahephet:* "even consumption and fever"—Lev. 26:16), pestilence (*dever:* "The Lord will make the pestilence cleave to thee"—Deut. 28:21), osteomyelitis (*rekev 'azamoth:* "envy is the *rottenness of the bones*"—Prov. 14:30), menorrhagia, gonorrhea, leucorrhea, etc. (*zav:* lit. "flow"—Lev. 15), and lumbago (*shivron motnayim:* "with the *breaking of thy loins*"— Ezek. 21:11).

The plague which befell the Children of Israel when they committed harlotry with the daughters of Moab (Num. 25) is referred to as *magefah,* a term denoting "plague," "epidemic," or "infectious disease" in general. Presumably this particular "plague" was a venereal disease, probably one resembling syphilis. *Beyel* (the yaws) is still endemic among nomadic peoples in the Middle East today. The epidemic described in the biblical account claimed twenty-four thousand lives.

The fifth chapter of the First Book of Samuel tells of an epidemic which must have been bubonic plague, for it was brought about by "emerods," i.e., rodents, which, as we know today, carry the disease. An outbreak of what probably was dysentery (2 Kings 19:35) claimed 185,000 victims among the soldiers of King Sennacherib of Assyria (cf. also Herodotus II. 141).

As regards diseases of the eye, the Book of Genesis (29:17) relates that Leah had "weak eyes," meaning that she was suffering from *blepharitis ciliaris,* an inflammation of the eyelids. The Book of Leviticus (15:3–6) alludes to *ophthalmia gonorrhoica.* The terms *sanverim* (Gen. 19:11) and *'averet* (Lev. 22:22), translated in the standard English version as "blindness" and "blind," respectively, both refer to amaurosis—blindness without visible organic change, caused by disease of the optic nerve. "Blindness" in the sense of lacking insight or understanding is termed *'ivaron* ("The Lord will smite thee with madness, and with blindness, and with astonishment of heart"—Deut. 28:28). *Dok* or *tvalul* (Lev. 21:19) refers to coloboma.

Other diseases mentioned in the Pentateuch are hydrocele or hernia (*shavur: "broken"*—Lev. 22:22), harelip (*haruẓ:* ibid, testiculus privativus (*paẓu'a daka:* Deut. 23:2), and mental disturbances like madness (*shiga'on*), bewilderment (*timahon*), and horror or "appalment" (*shimamon*).

Remedies and treatments mentioned in the Bible include washings, baths, orthopedic bandages, ointments, and herb medicines.

However, the main emphasis is not put on therapy but on preventive medicine and physical and mental hygiene as applied to the individual, the family, the people, and society in general. Prominent in biblical law are methods of diagnosing infectious diseases, the prevention of epidemics, and the introduction of a weekly day of rest not only for each Israelite but also for aliens living in the land of Israel, as well as for servants and even domestic animals. Master, servant, and cattle alike were subject to laws of labor hygiene. There were also Sabbatical and Jubilee years when oppressive debts were canceled and the soil was allowed to lie fallow.

In the Israelite monotheistic conceptual scheme described above, there was no room for "healers." Only God could "heal" sickness. In Israel there were only "helpers" who treated patients. Those physicians who called themselves *rofé* (lit. "healer") were foreigners, as a rule, and are mentioned in a derogatory fashion only. Thus we are told of the Egyptian physicians who embalmed Jacob (Gen. 50), and of the physicians in Gilead (Jer. 8:22) who apparently could not heal the sick. Hosea (5:13) has "Ephraim turn to Assyria and King Yarev for a cure," without results. The Book of Job (13:4) calls the idolatrous doctors "physicians of no value." It is said disparagingly of King Asa of Judah

(2 Chron. 16:12) that he sought healing not from God but from (foreign) physicians. Although nearly all the prophets knew how to apply remedies, they were never accorded the designation of *rofé*. They were not healers; they merely treated the patient. God alone could "heal" sickness. It was God who "healed Abimelech" (Gen. 20:17). When his sister, Miriam, was stricken with leprosy, "Moses cried to the Lord, saying: *'Heal her now,* O God, I beseech Thee' " (Num. 12:13). God Himself tells the Children of Israel in the wilderness, "I will put none of the diseases upon thee which I have put upon the Egyptians; for *I am the Lord Who heals thee*" (Exod. 15:26). In the thirty-second chapter of the Book of Deuteronomy (v. 39) Moses proclaims in the name of God: "I kill, and I make alive; *I have wounded, and I heal . . .*" Similar statements occur in Job 5:18 ("He wounds, and His hands make whole"), Isaiah 19:22 ("And the Lord will smite Egypt, smiting and healing"), Isaiah 57:18 ("I have seen his ways, and will heal him"), Isaiah 57:19 ("Peace, peace to him that is far off and to him that is near, says the Lord, who creates the fruit of the lips; and I will heal him"); Jeremiah 30:17 ("For I will restore health to thee, and I will heal thee of thy wounds, says the Lord"), Jeremiah 33:6 ("Behold, I will bring it healing and cure, and I will cure them"), 2 Kings 20:5 ("Behold, I will heal thee"), 2 Kings 20:8 ("What shall be the sign that the Lord will heal me"), Hosea 6:1 ("Come and let us return to the Lord, for He has torn, and He will heal us, He has smitten and He will bind us up"), Psalm 103:2–3 ("Bless the Lord, O my soul . . . Who heals all thy diseases"), Psalm 107:20 ("He sent his word and healed them"), 2 Chronicles 30:20 ("And the Lord hearkened to Hezekiah and healed the people"), etc. Wherever mention is made of a "cure" in the positive sense of the term, what is meant is a *vis medicatrix naturae* deriving from Divine power. Since God Himself is called a *rofé* ("healer"), it would have seemed presumptuous to the medical experts of the biblical era to claim that title for themselves.

The remedies and cures described in the Bible are all rational in character, except for the brass serpent which was employed to heal dangerous snakebites (Num. 21:9), but which, we are told (2 Kings 18:4), was destroyed by King Hezekiah, much to the gratification of the sages of his day (*Berakhot* 10b). There is no reference in the Bible to any of the remedies used in the so-called dung pharmacopeias. Incantations and exorcisms such as were in vogue at the time and are still practiced in some parts of the world today were frowned upon. Anyone who consulted exorcists was cut off from the community (cf. "Turn not to the ghosts,

nor to familiar spirits; do not seek them out to be defiled by them"—
Lev. 19:31; "And the soul that turns to the ghosts and to the familiar
spirits . . . I will . . . cut him off from among his people"—Lev. 20:6).
The exorcists themselves were to be stoned to death ("A man also or a
woman who divines by a ghost or a familiar spirit shall surely be put to
death; they shall stone them with stones . . ."—Lev. 20:27). Elsewhere
in the Book of Leviticus (18:1–5), the Lord tells Moses to command the
Children of Israel to keep away from alien practices so that they may
live. It is in character with this principle that the Bible has been called
the Tree of Life (*Ez Ḥayyim*). The Book of Deuteronomy (18:10–12)
brands any kind of magic as an "abomination to the Lord." Even such
magic cures as were applied in hopeless conditions, such as dangerous
snakebites, were simply an expression of man's hope for healing from
God. These procedures would take the form of incantations, amulets, and
charms, but were never permitted to degenerate into the cruel or obscene
excesses which were by no means rare among the other peoples of the day.

Among the therapeutic procedures listed in the Bible were washings,
anointment with oils, wine, balm, compresses, squeezing of abscesses to
remove pus, and baths at spas, especially in the treatment of skin diseases
(2 Kings 5:6–14). Chapter 16 of the First Book of Samuel describes the
beneficial effect of music on King Saul, who was suffering from melan-
cholia. Elsewhere we read of exposure to sunlight (*shemesh ẓedakah
marpeh bi'khnapheha;* lit. "the sun of righteousness *and healing in its
wings*"—Mal. 3:20), bandages for bone fractures ("I have broken the
arm of Pharaoh . . . and it has not been bound up to be healed, to put a
roller, that it be bound up and wax strong . . ."—Ezek. 30:21), and
potions (*shikui*) (Prov. 3:8). Among the medicines mentioned are
olibanum, galbanum, various sorts of oil, mandrake, balsamodendron,
laudanum, tragacanth (*nekhot*), soda, borax, absinthium, "gall and wormwood" (Deut. 29:17), sweet cinnamon, sweet calamus, and cassia.

A case of resuscitation by mouth-to-mouth breathing is described in I
Kings 17:17 ff. in the account of Elijah's revival of a child that had been
given up for dead.

One might even contend that the method employed by Moses to sweeten
the bitter waters of Marah (Exod. 15:22–25) was an early instance of
desalination.

Of the 613 biblical commandments and prohibitions, no less than 213
are health rules imposed in the form of rigorously observed ceremonial
rites.

The significance attributed to blood as the vehicle of the soul might be traceable to Sumerian influence.

If one were to attempt to place biblical medicine into a definitive category, one might class it as representative of the *pneumatic* school (cf. "all in whose nostrils was the breath of life . . . died"—Gen. 7:22).

Although, as we have pointed out elsewhere, the Bible was not intended as a medical reference text, it contains a specialized nomenclature for certain diseases and parts of the human anatomy.

The Hebrew terms for most physical ailments are patterned almost exclusively on the verb roots *pa-'elet* or *pa'alat:* e.g., *daleket* (inflammation), *sapaḥat* (lit: "scab"; psoriasis), *gabaḥat* (loss of hair, dandruff), *karaḥat* (alopecia), *ẓara'at* (leprosy), *baheret* (leukodermia, vitiligo, piebald skin), *yabelet* (acne), *'aẓevet* (neuritis), *saretet* (incision), *shaḥefet* (tuberculosis), etc.

The Hebrew terms for nervous and mental conditions are patterned on the verb root *pi'alon:* e.g., *deavon* (regret), *ḥipazon* (overhasty judgment); *kilayon* (sense of impending death), *'iẓavon* (depression), *'ivaron* (mental blindness); *shivaron* (lumbago), *shimamon* (stupor), *shiga'on* (hallucination), *shikaron* (intoxication), *timahon* (bewilderment), etc.

The Hebrew terms for trauma (injuries or wounds) are patterned on the verb root *pa'ul:* e.g., *shavur* (hernia by trauma), *ḥaruẓ* (maimed), *ma'ukh* (bruised, crushed), *natuk* (severed), *raẓuẓ* (shattered), *ẓarua* (infected), *paẓu'a* (injured), *karut* (castrated), etc.

Hebrew terminology for physical deformities or handicaps is patterned on the *pi'el* verb root: e.g., *iter* (paralyzed), *ilem* (dumb), *gibe'aḥ* (baldheaded), *gibben* (hunchbacked), *giddem* (chopped off), *gimgem* (stammering), *'iver* (blind), *ḥeresh* (deaf), *pisseaḥ* (lameness), etc.

While most Hebrew words are based on three-consonant roots, many anatomical terms in that language are built on the ancient two-letter root *Pal:* e.g., *gan* (alleg. term for vulva), *gid* (nerve, sinew), *'or* (skin), *rok* (saliva), *shok* (thigh), *ris* (eyelash), *kis* (scrotum), *shet* (buttocks), *ḥek* (bosom), *dam* (blood), *lev* (heart), *peh* (mouth), *shen* (tooth), *ḥekh* (palate), *aph* (nose), *'ayin* (eye), *rosh* (head), *ruaḥ* (breath, spirit), *guph* (body), *gav* (back), *lo'a* (throat), *moaḥ* (brain), *shad* (breast), *dad* (nipple), *yad* (hand), *kaph* (palm), etc.

Since most of the medical terminology found in the Bible has been translated by non-physicians, there frequently is some confusion with regard to the real meaning of some terms. One case in point is the Hebrew *ẓara'at* (efflorescens), which actually does not refer to one specific diagnosis but covers a wide variety of infectious and noninfectious skin ailments. The fault lies in the original Septuagint version, which renders *zara'at* throughout as "leprosy." Actually, the ancients used the term "leprosy" not for the disease known by that name nowadays, but to denote the condition to which modern medicine refers as "psoriasis." The term *zara'at* can denote many different conditions, depending on the combinations in which it is used. Thus *neg'a ha-zara'at* is an infectious skin disease—perhaps yaws; *zara'at 'or ha-basar* (Lev. 13:43; usually rendered as "leprosy in the skin of the flesh") is *ulcus durum penis; zara'at porahat* (Lev. 13:42) is leishmaniasis; *zara'at noshenet* (Lev. 13:11) is chronic syphilis (yaws et al.); *zara'at ha-rosh* is trichophytia; *zara'at mameret ha-beged* is a fungus growth that can be transferred to clothing; and *zara'at ha-bayit* is a saprophytic contamination of dwellings. In some instances the term *zara'at* used by itself does have the meaning of "leprosy." Thus, *zara'at ha-mezah* is lepra leonina.

It is only natural that in the course of the thousand-year period covered by biblical medicine certain variants should have been introduced. According to chapter 10 of the Book of Jubilees, a pseudepigraphical work, Noah wrote a medical textbook which he passed on to Shem, his first-born son. Shem, in turn, handed the book down to Abraham, who, according to *Baba Batra* 16, could cure various diseases by the use of a precious stone. These medical skills were handed down by word of mouth through the generations. Enriched by Moses with the medical knowledge he had acquired in Egypt, the tradition eventually passed to King Solomon and to all the generations that followed.

Medicine in the Talmud (ca. 200 B.C.E.–700 C.E.)

The geographic setting of the talmudic era—the "era of the Oral Tradition"—comprises not only the Land of Israel but also Israel's neighboring countries where Jews resided.

Concerned that the Oral Tradition should not be lost as a result of the loss of Jewish statehood (70 C.E.) and the subsequent wide dispersion of the Jews, R. Judah the Prince committed the entire Oral Law to writing. This monumental work, which was finished in the second century of the common era, is known as the Mishnah. Later generations of sages (third–sixth century C.E.), living in Mesopotamia and in the northern part of Palestine, added supplements and commentaries, which, together with the Mishnaic text, form the Talmud. The term is applied to two distinct com-

pilations—the Babylonian Talmud and the Palestinian (or Jerusalemic)
Talmud.

This era, along with the period immediately preceding, was marked
by momentous changes in the course of Jewish history. In the fifth century
before the common era, a part of the Jewish people had returned to Palestine from Babylonian captivity. Around the year 300 B.C.E. the influence
of Hellenic civilization first made itself felt in Palestine. This development
was followed by the revolt of the Maccabees against foreign domination,
which resulted in the formation of the Second Jewish Commonwealth.
There arose a number of parties—the Pharisees, the Sadducees, and the
Essenes, the latter being precursors of the early Christians. The second
fall of Jerusalem, in the year 70 C.E., resulted in the dispersion of the
Jews to many lands in Asia, Africa, and Europe. From that time on the
Written Law and the Oral Tradition became the "portable" spiritual home
of the Jews, replacing the physical homeland they had lost. Jewish life in
exile centered around the "houses of study" (*batei midrash*) and the
"houses of assembly" (*batei k'nesiyot,* which came to be called "syna-
gogues"). Much attention was given to the study and dissemination of
Jewish law and literature, and to the search for truth. Last, but by no
means least, these endeavors included also the arts of medicine.

Our literary sources for this period are the Apocryphal writings, Greco-
Roman works of Jewish and non-Jewish authorship, the two talmudic
codes, and midrashic literature. All these works are no more medical texts
than is the Bible. The Talmud is a compendium of commentaries and
elaborations on biblical teachings—legal, theological, philosophical, ethical, historical, mathematical, scientific, and folkloric. It also includes discussions of medical problems. Tractates like *Ḥullin, Bekhorot,* and *Nega'im*
are replete with such material. According to some accounts, there had
been medical texts and even a pharmacology of sorts at the time. However, these were apparently no longer known to the sages of the Talmud
(*Pesaḥim* 30a, *Yoma* 38b).

Medical problems, particularly those relating to anatomy and pathology,
take up considerable space in the Talmud because of their role in the
observance of the dietary laws and the health rules set down in the Bible.
After ritual slaughter, animal cadavers were subjected to anatomical and
pathological examinations to determine whether they were *kasher;* that
is, whether they had been healthy and not rendered *trefah* (unfit for consumption) by worms, infectious disease, or ptomaines (poisons found in
decaying animal matter), etc. In addition, physiological studies and ex-

periments were conducted with sick animals before as well as after slaughter. In those days, postmortem examinations were also performed on human cadavers. We find that the sages of the period did not believe in humoral pathology but rather in a sort of "solidary" or anatomical pathology.

The Talmud reflects the influence of Greek, Babylonian, and Persian medicine, including some elements of superstition (e.g., the evil eye, amulets, angels, etc.).

In chapters 34–38 of his "Book of Proverbs," Jesus Ben-Sira (ca. 150 B.C.E.) dwells at some length on the importance of medicine and the role of the physician, who is sent by God and on whom he lavishes praise. The Essenes, a splinter group which had broken away from the Pharisees, and which was active shortly before and after the advent of Christ, concerned themselves not only with moral and religious questions but also with medical problems and procedure. The very name of this sect "Assia," is derived from the Aramaic *assia,* a term denoting "helpers," i.e., physicians or "therapists." The Essenes lived in small monastic groups, devoting their time to handicrafts and to the healing of the sick. Philo of Alexandria made a study of this sect and stressed the kinship of the Essenes with the magicians of Persia and Chaldea and with the gymnosophists, a Hindu sect of ancient India.

The historian Josephus praised the altruism of the Essenes and their high ethical ideals. He reported that they would gather herbs and roots, which they would employ in the treatment of the sick. However, they considered these physical remedies merely as aids in their efforts to bring about cures by supernatural means. Their main remedies consisted of prayer, mystic incantations, and amulets. They were convinced that faith could cure not only remediable physical ailments but also handicaps then considered incurable, like insanity, blindness, deaf-and-dumbness, and lameness. The principal object of the Essene therapeutic procedures was to bring the patient's soul nearer to perfection and to make it receptive to the truth of God. Many of the teachings of the Essenes were adopted by the early Christians.

Jewish physicians who had received their training in Alexandria concerned themselves with both theory and practice. While the Jewish doctors of the time, unlike their Egyptian counterparts, did not "specialize" in any one field, a distinction was made between the *rofé* (as above) or "general practitioner," and the *umman,* or "surgeon." Talmudic literature lists a large number of Jewish physicians by name. Tractate *Bekhorot* of the

Mishnah mentions Theodos, a noted physician who hailed from Alexandria. Galen tells of Rufus Samaritanus, a Jewish physician who was active in Rome during the first and second centuries of the common era. Aulus Cornelius Celsus, the Latin encyclopedist (first century C.E.) refers (bk. V, chap. 19) to ointments prepared by Jewish physicians. Similar references are found in the writings of authors like Marcellus Empiricus, Aetius of Amida, and Paulus of Aegina. In his encyclopedic *Natural History* (37:60:10) Pliny the Elder writes of a "Babylonian physician" named Zechariah, who must have been a Jew, and who wrote a medical text which he dedicated to King Mithridates. The Emperor Mark Antony requested R. Judah the Prince to send him a physician from among his disciples to attend to his personal slaves. St. Basil (ca. 300 C.E.) employed a Jew named Ephraim as his personal physician. A campaign was waged against Jewish physicians by St. John Chrysostom (ca. 347–407 C.E.). St. Jerome (ca. 380 C.E.) and the Emperor Theodosius (438 C.E.) both barred Jews from employment as town physicians. At the same time, Gelasius, bishop of Rome, had as his personal physician a Jew named Telesinus, whom he called the "friend of his soul." With the rise in hostility against both Jews and Christians in Alexandria, Jews began to translate Greek medical texts into Hebrew. Fragments of these very early translations have been preserved only in the manuscript of Asaph HaRofe. Although there is no specific mention of individuals who did so, it may be assumed with almost complete certainty that a number of Jewish medical practitioners went to Edessa (now Urfa, Turkey), Nisibis, and Gondisapur, where they helped preserve Greek medical lore by translating it into Syriac-Aramaic.

It was agreed that physicians had a right to adequate payment. According to tractate *Baba Kamma* 85a, "A physician who works for nothing is worth nothing." Elsewhere in this tractate (85a) patients are advised not to consult a transient physician from abroad because such a person would not have the needed knowledge of local environmental and climatic conditions. Each locality had its own physicians, who were charged with the responsibility of assessing damages due to accident victims, or of examining individuals sentenced by law to corporal punishment to see whether they would be able to stand the flogging (*Sanhedrin* 78a, *Makkot* 22b). Each physician had to have a license from the local court of justice to treat the sick (*Baba Kamma* 85a). Many Jewish patients were in the habit of consulting the physician at his home rather than in the marketplace or in special shops, as was the custom in Greece and elsewhere. As a result, a special law was enacted prohibiting a landlord from renting an apartment to a physician without the consent of his prospective neighbors, who might be disturbed by the moans of the sick (*Baba Batra* 21). A great many Jews entered the medical profession since Jews were forbidden to dwell in a city, town, or village in which there were no physicians (*Sanhedrin* 17b).

It seems that the Jewish physicians in Palestine and Babylonia were organized and had their own emblem—a *haruta,* the branch of a palm or peach tree. The "balm" extracted from the *haruta,* which is mentioned by a number of Greek and Roman authors, was considered the most effective remedy for slow-healing wounds and was therefore a much-sought-after export commodity, considered worth its weight in gold (Pliny, *Natural History* XII, 54).

Many of the talmudic sages were accomplished physicians. Among the sages who practiced medicine were R. Ishmael ben Elisha, R. Hanina ben Dosa, R. Hanina bar Hama, Joseph HaRofe of Gamla, Tuviah HaRofe of Modiin, Benjamin, etc. The Babylonian *amora* Samuel, often called "Mar Samuel" (ca. 165–257), was an outstanding physician, who had considerable knowledge of pharmacology and anatomy and for a time was personal physician to King Sapor I of Persia. Following are some of his utterances, which are recorded in the Talmud:

> Washing one's hands and feet in the morning is more effective than all the *collyria* [lotions] in the world. [*Shabbat* 108a]

> A change in habit is the start of illness. [*Ketubot* 100a]

> Drink only water that has been boiled first. [*Terumot* 8]

> One who fasts to excess is called a sinner. [*Ta'anit* 11a]

Mar Samuel also ruled that it was permissible to violate the Sabbath for the sake of a woman in labor, regardless of whether she requested it or not. He stressed the need for strict cleanliness in all persons and objects coming in contact with the *os uteri* during childbirth (*Shabbat* 29a).

In addition to their practical activities, the rabbi-physicians of the Talmud kept at their theoretical studies and experiments. The disciples of R. Ishmael Ben Elisha boiled the skeleton of a human cadaver for their experiments (*Niddah* 30b, *Bekhorot* 45a); they used a human scalp for

teaching purposes (*Abodah Zarah* 11b, *Hullin* 123a). Mar Samuel col-
lected human bones for similar purposes. The physicians were their own
pharmacists, compounding simple remedies for use with their patients.
Among the remedies mentioned in the Talmud are various powders,
potions, balm, juices, plasters, compresses, *collyria* (lotions), and incenses.

Surgeons were assigned operating rooms (*beta de sha'isha*). Mention is
made of anesthetics (*samei de shintha;* lit. "sleep-inducing drugs"). The
Talmud contains accounts of a splenectomy (*Sanhedrin* 21b), a trepana-
tion (*Hullin* 57a), and amputations (*Gittin* 56a). There is reference also
to a Caesarean section, but the text does not specify whether the mother
was living or dead at the time of the operation. In general, the rule was
that the mother's life took precedence over the life of her unborn child.
Accordingly, it was considered permissible, in such critical situations, to
remove the fetus by morcellation (*Tosefta Yebamot*).

Surgeons wore special "surgical" aprons (*Kelim* 26:5). There were
needles and instruments for venesections (*Shabbat* 108b). *Baba Kamma*
(85a) mentions the use of anesthetics. There are references even to plastic
surgery and to catheterizations of the throat (*Hullin* 43b). In the same
tractate (54a) there is a statement to the effect that when a surgical wound
is sewn up, the lips of the wound are renewed. *Kelim* 12:1 describes an
operation for rectal prolapsus, Tractate *Sanhedrin* (129b) gives directions
for the application of cupping glasses and bloodletting. *'Abodah Zarah*
(129a) contains a description of a procedure to make an artificial anal
opening for an infant born without an anus. There are references to amputations of limbs and various types of prostheses.

The Mishnah and the two talmudic codes list a number of individuals
who were medical theorists but not practicing physicians, like R. Yohanan
(*Hullin* 93b) and R. Yehuda (ibid., *Gittin* 46b). Other sages are described
as pure natural scientists (*'askan bi-d'varim*) (*Hullin* 57b). In this category are men like R. Hanina, Rabbina (*Hullin* 51a), and Rav (Abba
Arikha). Rav, who spent eighteen months with a shepherd to conduct
experiments on eye diseases with sheep, asserted that the arteries (note
that this designation is derived from *arteria,* a Latin term for "windpipe")
did not contain air but blood (*Hullin* 57b). R. Joshua Ben Levi, a Palestinian *amora,* studied the anatomy of the testicles, and R. Hananiah
examined the structure of the quadrigeminal body of the brain of fowl.
R. Tarphon held at one time that hysterectomies were always fatal, but
revised his judgment after consulting with experts who had been fattening
sows in Alexandria by spaying them. Baba Ben Buta, who studied egg

whites, was once called upon in a criminal court case to differentiate between albumen from a hen's egg and a specimen of seminal fluid from a human male. Theodos the Physician was able not only to tell the difference between human and animal bones, but also to establish whether two bone specimens came from the same cadaver or not (*Nazir* 52a). R. Simon Ben Ḥalafta experimented with hens and ants (*Ḥullin* 57b), and R. Assi, with young ravens.

At the time physicians generally agreed with Aristotle's doctrine that the heart was the seat of the soul, Jewish physicians believed that the blood is the bearer of it.

Considerable familiarity with anatomy was a sine qua non for the enforcement of the *kashrut* laws. Accordingly the Talmud contains numerous references not only to the outer parts of the body but also to sinews and to internal organs, such as the esophagus, windpipe, lungs, pleura, heart, liver, spleen, kidneys, intestinal segments, genital organs, cerebral meninges, etc. Blood is viewed as the essential element of life. The muscles are referred to by the general designation *basar* (flesh). There are references also to sinews (*giddim*), nerves, and blood vessels. According to the Talmud, the human body consists of 248 different bones and 365 sinews (arteries), the latter, it is pointed out, corresponding to the number of days in the solar year. There are frequent references to a little bone named *luz,* which can never die. In all likelihood this is not a bone at all, but the male seed, which is said to have remained alive since the days of Adam.

While there seem to have been no hospitals at the time, there were synagogue halls in which the sick could stay. Moreover, there were "houses set apart" for lepers, just as there had been in the days of the Bible (2 Kings 15:5, 2 Chron. 26:21). As indicated earlier in the present study, there were also "operating rooms" (*batei shayish*) with marble-paneled walls. We are told that the Temple in Jerusalem had a separate section where priests would be examined for physical fitness to perform their sacred functions. Disciples of R. Ishmael made a study of a human skeleton (*Bekhorot* 45a). Others studied embryology with a view to finding out at what point the embryo is fully developed and at what stage sex differences first become discernible (*Niddah* 25a).

R. Judah knew that the brain was the seat of thought and logic (*Yebamot* 60a). Unlike Galen, the Talmud gives the correct number of pulmonary lobes in the human lung (*Ḥullin* 47a). The same tractate contains a description of the various parts of the respiratory system (*Ḥullin*

18b, 19a, 21a, 46b). Rav Hisda noted the presence of accessory muscles near the psoas and described striated muscles (*Hullin* 59a). The sages also knew that the layers of tissue making up the inner organs were lined with a serous membrane and with a muscular membrane (*Hullin* 43a). Tractate *Hullin* includes descriptions also of the pleura, the mediastinum (*Hullin* 47a), and the nervous system, with particular attention to the spinal cord, starting with the foramen magnum and ending with the cauda equina (*Hullin* 45a).

The rabbis had a surprisingly extensive knowledge of the physiological aspects of menstruation (*Niddah* 4, 24b).

A method was devised for estimating the quantity of blood in the body of a patient (*Pesahim* 19a, *Tosefta Oholot* 3).

Rav Ulla studied pathological cavities of the lungs, and Abba Shaul studied the bones of exhumated human cadavers (*Niddah* 25a). Numerous diseases of the lungs, liver, and internal organs were attributed to "worms" (*Hullin* 48a, *Shabbat* 109b). Other ailments were ascribed to a salt deficiency in the body (*Erubin* 83a). Dehydration, it was stated, caused digestive disturbances (*Shabbat* 41a), fear caused palpitations and an accelerated pulse rate (*Sanhedrin* 100b), falls from high places could give rise to fatal internal hemorrhages (*Hullin* 42a), injuries to the spine or the spinal cord resulted in paralysis (*Hullin* 51a), and stoppages in bile flow brought on jaundice and hydropsia. In some instances hemophilia would be discovered in newborn infant boys at the time of circumcision. Circumcision would then be forbidden in the case of all male infants subsequently born to such a family. It was known, too, that this condition was transmitted through the female parent (*Yebamot* 64a, cf. *Hullin* 47b).

The sages of the Talmud knew that certain illnesses could be transmitted through tainted foods and sweets, bodily discharges, beverages, clothing, bath water, and air (*Ketubot* 20a, 77a; *Berakhot* 25a et al.). Animals and insects, especially flies, are frequently named as carriers of communicable diseases. The rabbis also knew that plagues could be disseminated by way of contaminated water, and Mar Samuel stated that diseases could be spread from country to country by way of traveling caravans (*Ta'anit* 21b).

There is considerable discussion on the etiology of disease in general. The Talmud attributed many diseases to colds (*Baba Mezia* 107b). Mar Samuel attributed the cause of diseases to bile (a "humor" of the body) and the air, respectively. The most widely held view, however, was that "blood is the chief cause of disease" (*Baba Batra* 55b).

R. Ulla differentiated between cavities and ulcerations (bronchiectasies of the lung) (*Ḥullin* 47b). A distinction was made between the pleura pulmonalis and pleura pectoralis (ibid.). Rabba described a croupy inflammation of the lung (*Ḥullin* 46b). Hemoglobin studies were made of the venous blood of menstruating women (*Niddah* 19a). The sages knew that a mixture of blood samples in some instances from two different individuals could be expected to clot, whereas mixtures of blood and water would never coagulate. (Mishnah *Ḥullin* 6:5; ibid. 87b). R. Simeon Ben Eleazar disagreed with Hippocrates and Galen, who claimed that any injury to the Achilles' tendon was fatal. The scholars of the Talmud also did not consider the removal of the spleen dangerous to life (*Ḥullin* 42b, 54a; *Abodah Zarah* 44a; *Sanhedrin* 21b). Cholelithiasis and cirrhosis of the liver (*keshita*) were known (*Ḥullin* 49a), as was filariasis (*ra'athan*) (*Ketuboth* 77) and a treatment for the last-named condition. There is mention also of other diseases, which are attributed to worms (*Gittin* 70a).

Instructions concerning the treatment of patients, isolation in cases of infectious disease, visits to the sick, and the doctor-patient relationship are found scattered throughout the Talmud. It was generally agreed that it was not up to men to judge or punish physicians for failures or mistakes in the treatment of patients, since that was the prerogative of God alone.

Among the treatments mentioned are diets, warm and cold compresses, sweating cures, rest cures, sunbaths, change of climate, hydrotherapy, psychotherapy, massages, and exercises (*Shabbat* 40a, *Gittin* 70b). Constipation was treated with herbs (*'Abodah Zarah* 11a); in stubborn cases, purges would be administered, unless the patient was pregnant (*Pesaḥim* 42b). The rabbis of the Talmud knew of the analgesic and hypnotic properties of opium and cautioned against overdoses of this drug (J.T. *'Abodah Zarah* 11).

However, the main contribution of talmudic medicine, like that of biblical medicine, consists not so much in the enumeration of therapeutic methods as it does in measures of preventive medicine, as expressed in its health rules, which were all based on religious and ethical principles. A tenet that recurs throughout talmudic literature is that "physical cleanliness is conducive to spiritual purity" (*'Abodah Zarah* 20b; J.T. *Shabbat* 1:3). The health rules stated in the Bible and the Talmud were applicable to city planning, personal hygiene, social relationships, agriculture, and climatic conditions. Even in biblical times the Jews knew about the preventive significance of isolation and of the disinfection of clothing and objects by washing, fumigation, or fire in cases of communicable disease. One passage in tractate *Zebaḥim* (95a) tells of a disinfectant made of seven ingredients. The public was advised to avoid crowds and narrow streets during epidemics (*Baba Kamma* 60b). Flies were to be avoided as carriers of disease (*Ketubot* 77a). It was forbidden to dig wells near dumps and cemeteries (*Tosefta Baba Batra* 1). Water that had been left standing uncovered was considered unfit for human consumption, and water suspected of being contaminated had to be boiled before use (*'Abodah Zarah* 27b). It was forbidden to live in a city where there was no physician or no public bath. It was not permitted to wear the same clothing in the dining room that one had worn while preparing the food in the kitchen. The food itself had to be served fresh and in clean dishes, and meat had to be cooked sufficiently to destroy any parasites it might harbor (*Sanhedrin* 9a). Clean air and sunlight were considered the best cure for disease (*Ketubot* 110b). It was stressed that kissing on the lips should be avoided and kissing confined to the back of the hand in order to prevent the spread of infections.

It is surprising to note that talmudic pathology seems to have had no impact on medieval medicine, not even on the great Jewish physicians of the Middle Ages, such as Moses Maimonides and Isaac ben Solomon Israeli (I. Judaeus), who were thoroughly familiar with the Talmud. Medieval medicine was so completely under the spell of Galen that anything he ever said about medicine was accepted as infallible, while the health rules of the Talmud were ignored. In fact, the indiscriminate use of medication recommended by the Talmud for internal use was frowned upon, since it was believed that these drugs and compounds might not have the same effect in every country and in every age. The Talmud was regarded as a purely religious code and not as a medical treatise of any kind. As a matter of fact, the *Tosafot* commentators questioned the validity of the ancient health theories of the Talmud and decided that they were outdated (*Tosafot, Mo'ed Katan* 13) as were, in their opinion, the remedies prescribed in the "Six Orders of the Mishnah." In support of this view, the author of *Kessef Mishneh,* a commentary on Maimonides' *Mishneh Torah, Hilkhot Deot,* cites the fact that the medicines and personal habits in Babylonia, where most of the sages of the Gemara resided, were different from those in other lands (chap. 4:18). In the same vein, the author of *Meginei Erez* states (*Or-Ḥayyim* 173): "We have seen mentioned in the Gemara many things which are dangerous. They are no longer effective today because conditions and ways of living have changed." And R. Yehuda Segal (Minz), in his *Yalkut,* asserted that "one should not try any of the medicines, prescriptions, or exorcisms recommended in the Talmud because no one today knows how they should be applied. If they should be tried nevertheless, and found ineffective, the words of our sages would be exposed to ridicule."

Julius Preuss
and His Classic
Biblisch-Talmudische Medizin

The oldest known Hebrew medical writing is that of Asaph, which dates from the seventh century.[1] Since the ancient Hebrews left us no specific medical texts, our only sources of knowledge on this subject are the medical and hygienic references found in the Jewish sacred, historical, and legal literatures.[2] It is from these that the fragments of our knowledge of their medical views and practices have been gathered. The difficulty has been great, for the material is scant and its meaning often uncertain; the period which these sources cover is very long. Much of the material is "popular medicine"; most, if not all, was transmitted by laymen.

The first systematic studies of the medicine of the Bible were published early in the seventeenth century, among the first fruits of the study of the Bible awakened by the Reformation. The earlier books dealt only with the Hebrew and Christian Bibles (with the single exception of the dissertation of Gintzburger of 1743). It was not until the nineteenth century that studies included the Talmud and other ancient Hebraic writings.[2]

The literature that has grown up during the past three centuries is very extensive; much of it deals with special subjects, much embraces studies limited to single works such as the Talmud. As would be expected, these studies reflect the scientific spirit of their period, the uncritical or critical attitude of the biblical scholars, and the current views on medicine.

The writers have, for the most part, been biblical students; others were students of medical history; there are a few who were both.

Thus, for instance, of the two most important works on biblical and talmudical medicine until recently, one, published in 1860, was by Wunderbar, a layman, and the other, which appeared in 1901–3, was by Ebstein, a great physician, but unfamiliar with the Semitic languages and literatures. What this means can hardly be appreciated by someone who knows nothing of the Hebrew or Arabic tongues—their briefness, conciseness, and force.[3] It was not until the publication of Julius Preuss's *Biblisch-Talmudische Medizin* in 1911 that we acquired a reliable, comprehensive, and scholarly exposition of the subject by an author who was both a first-class physician and a thorough Semitic philologist, and who had made the history of medicine his life's study.[3]

Julius Preuss (Fig. 1) was born on September 5, 1861 in the small village of Gross-Schoenbeck near Potsdam in Uckermark, Germany.[3-17] His was the only Jewish family in the village. Young Preuss attended the public schools in the town of Angermunde and then entered the *Gymnasium* in Prenzlau, where he distinguished himself by his brilliant scholarship. Upon graduation, he went to study medicine at the University of Berlin. There he completed the course of study in 1886. Preuss's doctoral thesis was entitled "Concerning Syphilis as the Etiology of Tabes Dorsalis and Dementia Paralytica." The newspapers contained an interesting account of the brilliant young doctor, who achieved the rare feat of having passed Rudolph Virchow's examination with the highest marks.[3,15]. Virchow, the founder of cellular pathology, was a highly versatile personality, known for his uncompromisingly exacting standards. He paid Preuss the extreme compliment of telling him that his way of thinking was that of a true physician: "sie koennen medizinisch denken." Preuss returned to his native town to practice medicine, but in 1891 went back to Berlin, where he was a general medical practitioner and where he studied and wrote.

According to Muntner,[4,6] Preuss lived in an age which saw the resurgence of the critical approach in scientific as well as historical research. He was a part of the century which gave to the Jewish world Solomon Judah Rapoport (1790–1867) and Leopold Zunz (1794–1886), the pioneers of the "Science of Judaism"; the literary historians Leopold Dukes (1810–1891) and Abraham Berliner (1833–1915); scholars like David Cassel (1818–1893), Abraham Geiger (1810–1874), Moritz Guedemann (1835–1918), David Kaufmann (1852–1899), Mayer Moritz Kayserling (1829–1905), Isidore Loeb (1839–1892), and, of course, Heinrich Graetz (1817–1891), the author of the classic history of the Jews. Towering above all these luminaries was Moritz Steinschneider (1816–1907), the orientalist and bibliographer, who, in addition to other ancient source material, unearthed a wealth of data on the history of Jewish research in the sciences, including medicine.

Historical literature in the field of medicine could boast of a number of impressive works, including those of Haeser, Henschel, Neuburger, and Pagel. Sadly lacking, however, was reliable and critical research in the field of Jewish medicine. To be sure, continues Muntner, there was no dearth of general essays on medicine in biblical and even talmudic times, but most of these were superficial, unscientific, and occasionally, like those written by Carmoly (1802–1875), of dubious authenticity. Even the few outstanding works that appeared, such as those of Bergel, Holub, Rabinowitz, Wunderbar, and Ebstein, fell far short of the analytical approach which characterized the writings of Julius Preuss.[4]

Preuss was a physician of fine training and wide experience, a learned scholar in Hebrew literature as well as in medical and general history. He studied Talmud with Rabbi Biberfeld and the famous Rabbi Ritter, later Chief Rabbi of Rotterdam, never having attended a Jewish school in his youth. Preuss's unusual Hebraic background, his vast knowledge of Jewish thought and Hebrew literature, and his scientific method make his book *Biblisch-Talmudische Medizin* the authoritative work on the subject to this very day.

In 1961, to commemorate the one-hundredth anniversary of the birth of Julius Preuss and the fiftieth anniversary of the appearance of his magnum opus, a variety of meetings and lectures were held, and numerous articles and essays published.[5-11] Leibowitz decries the lack of detailed information concerning the life of Preuss.[7] He points out that Rabbi Joseph Carlebach, last Chief Rabbi of Hamburg and son-in-law of Preuss, said that Preuss used to read the Book of Psalms and study the Mishnah when he traveled to and from his patients in neighboring towns, so that after a while he learned them by heart. Preuss turned to the renowned Rabbi Hildesheimer for Judaic legal opinions concerning medical matters, such as remuneration for Sabbath visits to the sick. Preuss's return to Berlin in 1891 was precipitated either by his desire to be surrounded by learned scholars and academicians[3] or by the great difficulties in the observance of traditional Judaism which he encountered in his small native village.

Preuss was a very successful physician, and his practice grew considerably. He married Martha (Rachel) Halberstadt from Hamburg late in 1899 or early in 1900. His wife, Martha, was an enormous help to her husband, proofreading all his writings and assisting in any other possible way. The Preusses had three children, two daughters and one son. One daughter and her husband, Rabbi Carlebach, were killed in the Holocaust of World War II; two of their daughters now reside in Israel, one son lives in England, and one son lives in New York. A second daughter of Preuss, married to Felix Goldschmidt of Jerusalem, died in 1966 leaving five children, all residing in Israel. Julius Preuss's son, Jacob Preuss, lives with his wife in Herzliya, Israel. Their four children are also residents of the Jewish state. Julius Preuss's wife died in Israel in 1960.

Preuss himself became ill in 1911 when his *Biblisch-Talmudische Medizin* first appeared, although he had already written to Immanuel Löw in 1898 expressing his fear that he would not be able to complete his work because of ill health (Fig. 2). His illness is variously described as "a lung abscess which probably could have been controlled by chest surgery and/or antibiotics which were not available in his lifetime," [7] or "cancer of the throat, complicated by tuberculosis and bronchiectasis." [4] Details of his fatal illness are described by Leibowitz.[7] Preuss died on September 23, 1913, at the young age of fifty-two, and was buried in the Adath Israel cemetery in Berlin. He was not eulogized at his funeral, in accordance with his own wishes. In his last will and testament, dated May 18, 1905 (Fig. 3), Preuss said, in part: "no one should deliver a funeral oration, memorial address or the like for me, not at home nor at the cemetery, not at the interment nor later, not a paid speaker nor anyone else. No one should be motivated to fast on the day of my death . . . the grave should not be preserved with any type of ornament or ivy or the like." His tombstone bears the simple epitaph: *Rofé, velo lo*—"physician, but not for himself." The humility of Preuss is also exemplified by the title which appears beneath his name in all editions of his book: Julius Preuss, *Arzt in Berlin,* "physician in Berlin." Lengthy eulogies did appear in the press, however, following Preuss's death, including those by Karl Sudhoff (*Münch. Med. Wchschr.* Jan. 13, 1914), Edward Biberfeld (*Der Israelit.* Oct. 1, 1913), Joseph Carlebach (*Jüdische Presse,* 1913, p. 397), David Macht,[3] and many others.

Sudhoff said the following about Preuss:

> In the 1 hour we were together, Preuss permitted me, the non-Jew, to see so deeply into his soul, that I knew his hope was to be a classical philologist—this man, whose practical course of life made his dream impossible because he was a Jew. He had become a physician and his remarkable talent for historical and philological investigation directed him to the study of the history of his specialty as an avocation, and in particular to that branch which inevitably attracts every Jewish physician of the old stamp, namely, Biblical and Talmudic medicine.
>
> . . . Julius Preuss never lacked in his work either the inspiration or the devotion so essential to thorough accomplishment. But from inspiration he derived only the incentive which spurred him on to the mastery of difficulties. Never did he permit it to obscure his his-

torical judgement in its incorruptible service toward the establishment and enunciation of truth. Cool to the very heart, he was; love of the people of Israel did not cloud his view. Enthusiasm for their superior viewpoint did not make him see the straight line as crooked. For these very reasons, Dame History has laid laurels upon his grave, as a memorial to him, the master of historic criticism . . .[15]

The original manuscript of Preuss's magnum opus is today housed in the manuscript and archives section of the Hebrew University library (Ms. Var. 443 #13–14) in Jerusalem (Fig. 4). In the Friedenwald Collection of Medica-Judaica in the same library, one finds an item called "Notes on Preuss" (rare book division, Fr. 812B), in which the late Dr. Harry Friedenwald of Baltimore took copious notes in English on Preuss's book, chapter by chapter. Interesting is Friedenwald's assertion near the end of his notes: "I find no chapter on senility in Preuss, not even a paragraph."

Preuss's writings on biblical and talmudical medicine began with an article entitled "Der Arzt in Bibel und Talmud" (The physician in the Bible and Talmud), which was published in 1894 in the prestigious *Virchow's Archiv* and was soon reprinted in Hebrew translation in the periodical *Ha-Me'assef*. Numerous other essays on various aspects of biblical and talmudical medicine followed in a variety of scientific and literary journals. A complete bibliography is found at the end of this chapter. The two previously published bibliographies of Preuss's writings [2,4,11] are incomplete and contain several errors. Both Friedenwald [2] and Muntner [4,11] cite an anonymously written English article entitled "The Medicine of the Bible," published in *Medical Magazine* (London), 23, no. 4 (April 1914): 232–44. It seems highly unlikely that Preuss wrote this paper, since Preuss did not write in English [17] and the article was published a year after he died. Copies of several unpublished articles of Preuss, kindly supplied to me by Mr. Jacob Preuss of Herzliya, Israel, are also included in the bibliography. The article entitled "Ueber die Veranderungen der Zähne bei der Kieferrachitis des Schweines" (Concerning changes of the teeth in rickets of the jaw in the pig), published in the *Archiv fur Wissenschaftliche und Praktische Tierheilkunde* (Berlin), 35, no. 6 (Sept. 27, 1909): 561–81, was written by a veterinarian, Dr. Julius Preuss, but he is not the same Julius Preuss of *Biblisch-Talmudische Medizin* fame.[17]

Preuss's book is not without imperfections. Gordon points out that the Jerusalem Talmud was not compiled by R. Yoḥanan, as Preuss asserts, because many sages therein lived much later than R. Yoḥanan.[5] Rav Ashi is also not the last of the compilers of the Babylonian Talmud, as stated by Preuss. The listing of physicians of the Talmud enumerated by Preuss is incomplete. Numerous other "minor" criticisms are cited by Gordon. For certain errors, Preuss cannot be faulted. For example, he states that the earliest Hebrew medical writing is that of Donnolo from the tenth century. Recent research by Muntner has shown that the text of Asaph HaRofe antedates Donnolo by several centuries.[1] The indices in Preuss's book, particularly the general index, are very sparse.

In preparing an English translation of Preuss's classic book, I too have found numerous minor errors. For example, in chapter 12, Preuss states that tractate *Negaim* has ten chapters whereas in fact there are fourteen. In chapter 17, he erroneously attributes a talmudic statement to R. Akiba instead of R. Eleazar, and in chapter 6, he does the reverse. In the first appendix to chapter 5, Preuss gives the dates of birth and death of Maimonides as 1131 and 1205. The correct dates are 1135 and 1204. In chapter 4, Preuss incorrectly speaks of the "daughter" of the Shunamite woman instead of her "son." He says the Hebrews have no word for coughing like the *su'al* of the Arabs; yet he overlooked the Hebrew word for cough, which is *she'ul*. He says that *yerakon* and *shiddafon* always occur together in Bible and Talmud. There is an exception, however, in Jeremiah 30:6. Numerous other minor errors of this nature could be cited. Furthermore, there are more than a score of incorrect bibliographic citations from Bible and Talmud (for example, Eccles. 13:2 instead of 12:2 and Gen. 32:36 instead of 32:25). These amount, however, to less than a fraction of one percent of the many thousands of references which Preuss quotes.

The above shortcomings do not detract from the classic and enduring value of Preuss's work. Every major medical library, public or private, possesses at least one copy of *Biblisch-Talmudische Medizin*. The creation of the State of Israel in 1948 and the renaissance of the Hebrew language have awakened new interest in biblical and talmudical writings. The grandeur of Preuss's contribution to medical research from Bible and Talmud is being more and more appreciated by modern scholars. An updating and revision of Preuss's magnum opus with correction of errors, remains a desirderatum to this very day. Only four pages of Preuss's work (p. 515–19)[18] and a few excerpts[19] have ever been published in English translation. The inaccessibility of Preuss's classic book to the non-German reader has now been overcome with the imminent publication of an English translation. Karl Sudhoff, the most illustrious figure in the field of the history of medicine during the era of Preuss, hailed Preuss's work as one of the most important contributions to the history of medical scholarship in the preceding half-century.[15] Nothing has happened in the nearly seven decades since then to change that assertion. It remains an indispensable work for the student of Hebrew medicine.

I would like to call attention to several little known yet important articles of Preuss which antedated his biblical-talmudical compositions The first, which was never published, was written in 1885 and is entitled "Ueber Untersuchungen des Blutes Zu Diagnostischen Zwecken" (Concerning the examination of blood for diagnostic purposes). In this paper, Preuss gathered material from the major books and medical journals on pathology, therapy, and diagnosis. His purpose was to provide practical diagnostic guidance to the practicing physician about bleeding from any body orifice, including the mouth, nose, urethra, anus, vagina, navel, and venipuncture site.

This lengthy paper already shows the systematic organization of source material and its presentation in a clear and lucid manner, qualities characteristic of Preuss's subsequent writings, including his classic *Biblisch-Talmudische Medizin*.

Another major but little known article of Preuss, entitled "Vom Versehen den Schwangeren," was published in two different periodicals in 1892 (see bibliography). In this detailed critical-historical study with 211 references, Preuss discusses the possible effect of a woman's psychic or psychological impressions during coitus on her child. Can such psychic influences partially or completely alter the development of the unborn fetus?

This erudite paper was published in 1892 and already clearly demonstrated the depth and precision with which Julius Preuss approached a subject. His scholarship was extraordinary, and it was the lucidity of his presentation that made Rudolph Virchow say of him, "he knew how to think medically."

Another brief article, entitled "Zur Pathologie der Zunge" (On the pathology of the tongue) describes two patients, one of whom was a baby with a tumor of the lingual frenulum, and the other a woman with chronic superficial glossitis.

Other unpublished articles by Preuss include papers on quackery and secret remedies, domicile, hygiene, the position of the woman in Judaism, and the duty of Jewish physicians (see bibliography).

I will now give a brief description of Preuss's classic *Biblisch-Talmud-*

ische Medizin, a book which has indelibly recorded his name for posterity as a giant in biblical and talmudic medical scholarship. Muntner seems fully justified in calling Preuss "the father of Hebrew medical research."

Preuss's book was originally published in Berlin by S. Karger in 1911; it was reprinted unchanged in 1921 and 1923 by the original publisher and in 1969 by Gregg Publishers in England. In 1971, the Ktav Publishing Company in New York reprinted the book unchanged for the fourth time, but added an introduction, biographical sketch, and bibliography of Julius Preuss by Suessman Muntner, and a Hebrew and Aramaic register, which had been prepared in handwritten copy by Adolph Löwinger several years after the original 1911 publication. An English translation of this register, by Samuel Paley, is also included.

Preuss's classic book is an anthology of all his articles published over many years in a variety of scholarly journals (see bibliography), beginning with his pioneering study entitled "Der Arzt in Bibel und Talmud" which appeared in *Virchow's Archiv.* in 1894. In the preface to his book, Preuss points out that the number of commentaries, textbooks, and individual works on the Bible is greater than the number of letters contained in the Bible. Preuss's book, covering the entire subject of biblical and talmudical medicine, is the first composed by a physician in which the material is derived directly from the original sources. Wunderbar, who completed his *Biblisch-Talmudische Medizin* in 1860, was a layman. Ebstein, whose writings appeared in 1901 (*Die Medizin im Alten Testament*) and 1903 (*Die Medizin im Neuen Testament und im Talmud*), was dependent upon the use of available fragmentary translations. Other works concerning the totality of biblical-talmudical medicine did not exist.

In chapter 1, entitled "The Physician and Other Medical Personnel," Preuss defines the term "physician," *rofé* in Hebrew and *asya* in Aramaic. He describes the position of the physician in antiquity, his fees, and his responsibilities to his patients. In Judaism, a physician is regarded as a messenger of God. If he intentionally injures a patient, the physician is obviously liable; otherwise he is held blameless. Physicians served as expert witnesses in civil court cases and in the evaluation of a criminal in terms of his capacity to tolerate disciplinary flogging. The physician was, and still is, consulted regarding the severity of an illness which involves the need to desecrate the Sabbath or the Day of Atonement for the patient.

Preuss describes the education of a physician in ancient times, which was accomplished either by the apprenticeship method or in official schools of medicine. He also lists some of the physicians mentioned in the Talmud, such as Theodoros, Tobiya, Bar Girnte, Bar Nathan, R. Ammi, and, of course, Mar Samuel, the most illustrious of all.

In chapter 2, Preuss describes the anatomy and physiology of the various body organs and limbs as mentioned in the Bible and Talmud by dividing them into external organs (head, face, chin, neck, shoulder, axilla, elbow, forearm, hand, fingers, thumb, fist, nail, foot, heel, toes, knee, thigh, hips, back, and abdomen), organs of sensation (eye, nose, ear, skin), and internal organs. The latter include organs of the digestive system (lips, teeth, esophagus, stomach, liver, gallbladder, and spleen), respiratory system (lung and voice box), circulatory system (heart and aorta), genito-urinary system (kidneys, urinary bladder, and male and female genitalia), and nervous system (brain and spinal cord). Preuss attempts to identify the 248 limbs mentioned throughout early Jewish writings, which are said to correspond to the 248 positive commandments of Judaism.

In chapter 3, Preuss begins by defining a patient. He then discusses the belief in ancient Judaism that demons cause illness. For example, the Talmud states that a mad dog is possessed by an evil spirit. Preuss talks of astrology and the evil eye, of magic and incantations and amulets to ward off disease. Astrological reasons were especially decisive for the selection of days appropriate for bloodletting, not only in talmudic times, but throughout the centuries and millennia. Rarely found in talmudic writings is the medieval concept of the four body humors (black bile, yellow bile, phlegma, and blood), whereby diseases are thought to occur by a dysequilibrium of these humors, with one or the other predominating in the body or in a specific organ.

The fourth chapter, called "Sicknesses and Their Treatment," begins with a lengthy discussion of plague, or pestilence. Preuss lists all the epidemics described in the Bible and Talmud, and concludes that it is not possible, because of the dearth of symptomatology mentioned, to establish with certainty whether or not the biblical and talmudical diseases referred to as *magefa, deber, nega,* or *negef* represent bubonic plague, cholera, dysentery, typhus, or some other epidemic illness. *Askara* seems to be epidemic diphtheria since it primarily afflicts children, and the major symptoms are referable to the throat.

Preuss discusses acute and chronic fevers and describes various remedies, mostly from folk medicine, for quotidian, tertian, and quartan fevers. He also lists the causes and remedies for hydrops (dropsy), podagra (gout), heatstroke, and *yerakon,* which is the biblical and talmudical expression for jaundice and/or anemia.

Biblical and talmudic descriptions of lung maladies, such as perforations, defects, lumps, cysts, fistulae, and adhesions, as well as citations of digestive tract illnesses, such as dysentery, colic, bulimia, hemorrhoids, and intestinal worms, are provided by Preuss in this chapter. Finally, the five types of heart ailments are discussed: pain, weakness, heaviness, palpitations, and pressure of the heart.

Chapter 5 is devoted to surgery and deals primarily with injuries and malformations. Preuss begins with a discussion of surgical instruments, such as the small drill for opening the skull, the knife for circumcision, needles to remove splinters, and others. He then describes various types of injuries, such as sword or other stab or puncture wounds, burn wounds, broken bones, dislocations and sprains, and amputations for gangrene. Also described are injuries inflicted by animals, such as the bite of a mad dog, snake bites, insect bites, and worm infestation. The signs of a mad dog mentioned in the Talmud are as follows: its mouth is open, its saliva is dripping, its ears flag, its tail hangs between its thighs, and it walks on the edge of the road.

There are two appendices to this chapter. The first deals with circumcision. Preuss discusses some of the boundless literature on the theories of the origin of circumcision, the covenant of Abraham, the importance, technique, and timing of circumcision and reasons for its postponement, i.e., illness, the instrumentation used, and circumcision practiced by other peoples. Astounding is the recognition by the sages of the Talmud of a bleeding disorder, probably hemophilia, and its genetic transmission. The Talmud rules that if two children of a woman exsanguinated as a result of circumcision, the third child should not be circumcised. Furthermore, if two sisters each had a son who died of bleeding following circumcision, then the third sister should not circumcise her son. Although later Jewish codes assumed that hemophilia can also be transmitted through the baby's father, the second-century Talmud correctly recognized the sex-linked nature of this disease, i.e., only males have the disease but females are carriers and transmit it to their male offspring.

The second appendix deals with bloodletting, either for therapeutic reasons or as a preventive measure. The Talmud discusses the frequency, amount, site of bloodletting, and the instrumentation used, including a lancet, a nail or other pointy objects, and cupping glasses. Dietary factors in relation to bloodletting are considered important. Mar Samuel said that a person to be bled should be fasting; after the bloodletting, the patient should tarry a little, then arise and eat a little before going out. The consumption of nourishing foods after bloodletting is essential. Venesection on animals is also discussed.

Surgery on the eye is not at all considered in the Bible or Talmud, but eyeglasses, eye prostheses, artificial eyes, and eye makeup are described in some detail.

In chapter 7, which deals with dentistry, Preuss discusses toothaches, cavities, loose teeth, and artificial teeth. Sour fruit is said to be good for toothache. The vapors of a bathhouse are harmful to the teeth. Vinegar causes loosening of teeth. Preuss points out the emphasis which oriental people place on beautiful teeth.

In the very brief chapter on otology, Preuss describes anatomical defects of the ears, piercing of ears, and other injuries, whether intentionally inflicted or not, pain in the ear, remedies for ear ailments, and deafness and its causes.

In an equally brief chapter on disorders of the nose, Preuss describes various abnormal shapes and disfigurements of the nose, as found in the Bible and Talmud, mostly secondary to leprosy. Nasal polyps are discussed, as well as remedies for nosebleeds, mostly from folk medicine.

Chapter 10 is devoted to neurological disorders. About a third of the chapter deals with epilepsy and hysteria. Love-sickness was thought in antiquity to be a type of hysteria. Also discussed in this chapter are headache, plethora and migraine, paralysis, strokes (apoplexy), sciatica, and the tremor of old age. The Talmud recommends that one rub the head with wine, vinegar, or oil to treat a headache. Numerous remedies are prescribed for migraine, including many from folk medicine.

Mental disorders are covered in chapter 11. Preuss discusses in detail the mental illness of King Saul of Israel. After considerable deliberation, Preuss concludes that Saul was a "melancholic in the psychiatric sense"; today we would say that he suffered from a paranoid psychopathia. His raving and ranting, his affliction with evil spirits, and the stripping off of his clothes, are interpreted by Preuss to represent epilepsy or an epileptic equivalent. Visual and auditory hallucinations, insanity, "possession by demons or spirits," and exorcism in the Bible and Talmud are described by Preuss. An imbecile is considered to be mentally deficient and is equated with a minor and a deaf-mute in Jewish law: he cannot testify in court, his contracting of marriage is invalid, etc. The Talmud defines someone who is mentally ill: "He who goes out at night alone, and he who spends the night in a graveyard, and he who tears his garments, and destroys everything that is given to him" (*Ḥagigah* 3b).

In the chapter on skin diseases, Preuss points out that an enormous number of books and treatises have been written about the thirteenth chapter of the Book of Leviticus, which deals with an illness called *zara'at,* probably leprosy. As a result, says Preuss, "one might think that every detail would have been clarified and every linguistic and archaelogical problem solved. However, just the opposite is the case."

Preuss discusses the fundamental law of *zara'at,* and describes the various skin lesions, scabs, boils, scars, eczema, burn wounds, and the like mentioned in the Bible and Talmud. The diagnosis, treatment, and cure of leprosy are discussed. Leprosy was thought to represent punishment for the sin of slander. The illness *shehin* and its various forms, the *shehin* of Egypt, and the sicknesses of Job and King Hezekiah (possibly leprosy, elephantiasis, syphilis, diphtheria, variola, or some other malady) are also discussed. Preuss concludes that *shehin* is a collective name comprising many types of skin diseases, including inflammatory and traumatic lesions.

There are two appendices to this chapter. The first deals with gonorrhea, its causes and mode of transmission, and the Jewish ritual laws pertaining to someone afflicted with it. In the second appendix, which concerns cosmetics in the Bible and Talmud, Preuss describes haircutting instruments, haircuts and hair styles for both men and women, hair hygiene, depilatories, and wigs. Also discussed are embrocations, oils, perfumes, cosmetics, soaps, and facial makeup.

A brief chapter on gynecology deals primarily with menstruation and its ritual implications, vaginal bleeding and its causes and treatment, and castration in the female. Most remedies are from folk medicine; for example, "give the woman with vaginal bleeding Persian onions boiled in wine or cumin, safflower and fenugreek boiled in wine, and exclaim to her: cease your discharge!"

Chapter 14 is devoted to obstetrics. The first half of the chapter deals with normal physiological events surrounding pregnancy including the recognition and duration of pregnancy, the fetus and fetal development, sex determination, multiple births, premature births, parturition, the birthstool, the placenta, postpartum ritual purification, the newborn infant, washing, salting, and swaddling of the newborn, lactation and suckling, wet-nurses and nursing from an animal or bottle. Of particular interest is the recognition by Mar Samuel in the Talmud that a fetus begins to assume form and shape at forty days after conception. Prior to that time, it is "mere fluid." Also of interest is the "preserving stone," which women carried with them to insure normal pregnancies. Furthermore, the concept of superfecundity, that is, one woman becoming pregnant from two men, was accepted in the Talmud.

The second half of the chapter on obstetrics deals with pathological occurrences. Among the subjects discussed are sterility, oral contraception by means of a "potion of herbs," abortion and the abortus, moles, monster births and the "sandal" fetus, false pregnancy, difficult labor and embryotomy, sorcery in obstetrics, Caesarean sections, and puerperal illnesses. Numerous methods of contraception are discussed in the Talmud, but perhaps the most interesting is the "potion of herbs," also known as the "cup of roots." This remedy is prepared from Alexandrian gum, liquid alum, and garden crocus, powdered and mixed with beer or wine (*Shabbat* 110a).

In chapter 15, which is entitled "Materia Medica," Preuss first discusses the plant remedies which the Talmud recommends as abortifacients, emetics, purgatives, digestives, etc., as well as various types of plasters, compresses, poultices, bandages, and the like, and their various medicinal ingredients. Also discussed are animal remedies, such as honey, goat's milk, crushed pearl, animal dung and urine, and the great theriac. Nonmedicinal remedies can be exemplified by the talmudic suggestion that for abdominal pain, one should place warm clothes on the abdomen or a hot cup or bottle on the navel. Sunbathing is said to heal a variety of ailments. Certain foods should be avoided for certain illnesses. The final part of the chapter is devoted to a discussion of Jewish hospitals in antiquity (or lack thereof) and the visiting of the sick. The traditional Jewish concept of visiting the sick is that it is not a social call but a visit in which to help the patient by cooking or cleaning for him, or by assisting him in any other manner.

Chapter 16 is very lengthy and deals with sex ethics in the Bible and Talmud. The subjects discussed by Preuss in this chapter are: chastity, marriage, procreation, genealogy in marriage, conjugal duties, cohabitation, impotence, unnatural coitus, *coitus interruptus,* abstention from procreation, times when cohabitation is prohibited, cohabitation and sexual desire, aphrodisiacs, the *duda'im* or mandrakes, conception *sine concubito,* proscribed marriages, punishment for incest, rarity of punishment infliction, the incest of Lot and his daughters, Amnon and Tamar, Levirate marriage, adultery, lustful thoughts, the *sotah* or suspected adulteress, rape, seduction, virginity, prostitution, the street of harlots, harlots in biblical times, their skills, attire, hire, the *jus primum noctis,* Hegemonian coitus, masturbation, pederasty and homosexuality, transvestism, sodomy and bestiality, tribady and lesbianism.

In chapter 17, Preuss discusses the Jewish dietary laws, ritual slaughtering, and the biblical prohibitions of blood and certain fat. He then describes the laws of ritual purity and impurity known as *tumah* and *taharah* of the human body, utensils, and clothing, and the rules of defilement relating to the Temple, priests, cadavers, people afflicted with leprosy and/or gonorrhea, and the purification process, including the ritual immersion. Even though these rules may serve a hygienic purpose, they are not meant to be "hygienic laws" but are divine commands. The importance of washing and bathing in ancient times is emphasized by Preuss.

Preuss also discusses death and dying in this chapter. In Jewish law, a dying person may not be touched or moved lest his death be hastened. The recognition of death requires the cessation of respiration and the absence of a heartbeat. Furthermore, one must be certain that the person has not just fainted or fallen in a swoon. The perfuming and embalming of the dead are then described. The five biblical cases of suicide are mentioned, including those of Saul, Ahithophel, and Omri. Remarkable are the biblical and talmudic descriptions of marble and wooden coffins. Graves were either in the ground or in natural or man-made caves. Biblical and talmudic discussions of the sepulchers of the Patriarchs and of burial, cremation, and the decomposition of bodies, conclude the section on death and dying.

The final chapter, entitled "Dietetics," deals with the rules which a healthy person should follow in order not to become ill. Preuss asserts that dietetics refers not only to nutrition, as the modern usage of the word connotes, but also includes the entire mode of life of an individual, since residence, clothing, sports, work, and many other things have certain influences on health, and hence belong in the word "diet."

The general rules of health and nutrition, among others, are: eat moderately, eat simply, eat slowly, and eat regularly. Chronic alcoholism, a rare disorder among Jews, is mentioned because of the juridical difference in Jewish law between a *shattuy* (tipsy or fuddled) and a *shikkor* (drunk or intoxicated). Regarding exercise, R. Yoḥanan said: "Do not sit too much, for sitting provokes hemorrhoids; do not stand too much, for standing is harmful to the heart (or stomach); do not walk too much, for (excessive) walking is harmful to the eyes" (*Ketubot* 111a).

With regard to domicile, it is said that it is healthy to live in an open city, and harmful to live in a fortified or closed city. In the latter, houses are built close together, but in the former there are gardens and parks and the air is good.

How does one find words to emphasize the enormity of the contribution to medicine and Judaica of Preuss's book? I believe that the editorial written by J. O. Leibowitz in the May 1961 issue of the Hebrew periodical *Korot,* devoted to the memory of Julius Preuss, expresses it best:

> Preuss was one of the greatest Jewish historians of medicine; endowed with intimate insight in the field of early Hebrew medicine; outstanding in his critical approach, wide knowledge and unbiased honesty. Dear to our heart, his memory may serve as a shining and stimulating example for present and future historians.

REFERENCES

1. S. Muntner, *Introduction to the Book of Asaph the Physician* [Hebr.] (Jerusalem: Geniza, 1957).
2. H. Friedenwald, *The Jews and Medicine* (Baltimore: Johns Hopkins University Press, 1944), 1:99–145.
3. D. I. Macht, "In Memoriam: Dr. Julius Preuss," *Johns Hopkins Hospital Bulletin* 25 (March 1914): 277.
4. S. Muntner, "Julius Preuss: Father of Hebrew Medical Research," in *Biblisch-Talmudische Medizin* by J. Preuss, reprint ed. (New York: Ktav, 1971), pp. vii–xii.
5. H. L. Gordon, "The Centenary of the Birth of Dr. Julius Preuss [Hebr.], *Harofe Haivri* 1–2 (1961): 196–204.
6. S. Muntner, "Julius Preuss as a Founder of Research in the Field of the Ancient Hebrew History of Medicine" [Hebr.], *Korot* (Jerusalem–Tel Aviv), 2, nos. 9–10 (May 1961): 410–13.
7. J. O. Leibowitz, "Julius Preuss and the Medico-Historical Research in Bible and Talmud," ibid., pp. 414–25 [Hebr.], and pp. i–iii [Eng.]
8. J. Moeller, "My Memories of Julius Preuss" [Hebr.], ibid., pp. 404–6.
9. K. Sudhoff, "Julius Preuss" [Hebr.], ibid., pp. 407–9.
10. D. Margalith, "Obituary: Dr. Yizḥak (Julius) Preuss. Sept. 5, 1861 to Sept. 23, 1913" [Hebr.], ibid., pp. 479–80.
11. S. Muntner, "Bibliographie der Schriften von Julius Preuss," ibid., pp. xii–xv.
12. S. R. Kagan, *Jewish Medicine* (Boston: Medico Historical Press, 1952), p. 562.
13. D. Margalith, *Physician Forerunners of Modern Israel* (Tel Aviv: Jerusalem Academy of Medicine, 1973), pp. 163–64.
14. D. Maraglith, *The Way of Israel in Medicine* [Hebr.] (Jerusalem: Jerusalem Academy of Medicine, 1970), pp. 348–49.
15. K. Sudhoff, *Essays in the History of Medicine* (New York: Medical Life Press, 1926), pp. 351–53.
16. J. L. Pagel, *Biographisches Lexicon Hervorragender Aerzte des Neunzehnten Jahrhunderts* (Berlin and Vienna: Urban & Schwarzenberg, 1900–1901).
17. Jacob Preuss, personal communication, August 31, 1974.
18. R. Rosenthal, "The Care of the Sick in the Bible and the Talmud," translated from "Julius Preuss (1861–1913)," in *Victor Robinson Memorial Volume*, ed. S. R. Kagan (New York: Froben Press, 1948), pp. 353–58.
19. J. Snowman, *A Short History of Talmudic Medicine* (London: John Ball, Sons & Danielsson, 1935), p. 94.

BIBLIOGRAPHY OF JULIUS PREUSS

1. "Ueber die Syphilis als Aetiologie der Tabes Dorsalis und der Dementia Paralytica." Inaugural Dissertation welche zur Erlangung der Doctorwuerde in der Medicin und Chirurgie, mit Zustimmung der Medicinischen Facultaet der Freiedrich-Wilhelms Universitaet zu Berlin am 6 Februar 1886 nebst den angefuegten Thesen oeffentlich verteidigen wird der Verfasser *JULIUS PREUSS* aus Gross-Schoenebeck (Mark). Opponenten: Herr Dd. med. M. Birnbaum, Herr Dd. med. J. Lazarus, Herr Cand. med. M. Caro, Cursist. A. Itzkowski 1886. 30 p. 1. 2.8°.

2. "Vom Versehen der Schwangeren; eine historisch kritische Studie." *Berl. Klinik*, vols. 4–5 (heft 51): 1–50, 1892–93.

2a. Ibid, *Deutsche Medizinal Zeitung* #79:924–26 (Oct. 3) 1892.

3. "Zur Pathologie der Zunge." *Centralblatt fur Chirurgie 20* (9): 203–5 (Mar. 4) 1893.

4. "Der Arzt in Bibel und Talmud; Eine Historische Studie." *Virchow's Archiv. fur Patholog. Anat. und Physiol. und fur Klin. Med. 138:* 261–83, 1894. Hebrew trans. by Kahan published in vol. 1 of *Ha-Me'assef,* ed. Rabbinowitz, pp. 79–91.

5. "Die Askara Krankheit im Talmud. Ein Beitrag zur Geschichte der Diphterie." *Jahrbuch fur Kinderheilkunde,* new series *40:* 251–57, 1895.

6. "Zur Geschichte der Aderlasses." *Wien. Klin. Wochenschrift 8*(34): 608–11 (Aug. 22) 1895 and *8* (35): 625–29 (Aug. 29) 1895.

7. "Neuere Arbeiten uber Biblisch-Talmudische Medizin." *Israelitische Monatsschrift.* Berlin. Nov. 26, 1896.

8. "Schriften uber Medicin in Bibel und Talmud. Ein Nachtrag nebst einigen Berichtungen zu Steinschneider's Artikel." *Brody's Ztschr. fur Hebr. Bibliographie,* vol. 2, pt. 1, p. 22, 1897.

9. "Das Auge und Seine Krankheiten nach Bibel und Talmud. Eine Historische Studie." *Wiener Medizinische Wochenschrift 46* (49): 2151–56, 1896; *46* (50): 2201–3, 1896; *46* (51): 2245–49, 1896; *46* (52): 2295–98, 1896; *46* (53): 2341–43, 1896; *47* (1): 38–40, 1897; *47* (2): 79–82, 1897; *47* (3): 121–24, 1897.

10. "Die Beschneidung nach Bibel und Talmud." *Wiener Klin. Rundschau 11* (43): 708–9 (Oct. 24) 1897, and *11* (44): 724–27 (Oct. 31) 1897.

11. "Die Mundhöhle und ihre Organe nach Bibel und Talmud." *Deutsche Medizinal Zeitung 18* (16): 143–44 (Feb. 25) 1897; *18* (17): 151–52 (Mar. 1) 1897, and *18* (18): 169–70 (Mar. 4) 1897.

12. "Die Männlichen Genitalien und ihre Krankheiten nach Bibel und Talmud." *Wiener Mediz. Wochenschrift 48* (12): 569–72, 1898; *48* (13): 617–19, 1898; *48* (14): 661–63, 1898; *48* (15): 709–12, 1898; *48* (24): 1193–95, 1898; *48* (25): 1239–40, 1898; *48* (26): 1285–89, 1898.

13. "Materialien zur Geschichte der Alten Medicin. Die Organe der Bauchhohle nach Bibel und Talmud." *Allg. Med. Central Ztg.* (Berlin) *67* (39): 489–90 (May 14) 1898; *67* (40): 502 (May 18) 1898: *67* (41): 514–15 (May 21) 1898; *67* (42): 526–27 (May 25) 1898; *67* (43): 538–39

(May 28) 1898; *67* (44): 551 (June 1) 1898; 67 (45): 564 (June 4) 1898; *67* (46): 575 (June 8) 1898.

14. "Materialien zur Geschichte der Talmudische Medizin. Das Nervensystem." *Deutsche Medizinal Zeitung. 20* (37): 416–18 (May 8) 1899, and *20* (38): 428–30 (May 11) 1899.

15. "Nerven und Geisteskrankheiten nach Bibel und Talmud." *Ztschr. fur Psychiatrie*, etc. #56: 107–37, 1899.

16. "Materialien zur Geschichte der "Talmudischen Medicin. Die Organe der Brusthohle." *Allg. Med. Central Ztg.* (Berlin) *68* (61): 740–41 (Aug. 2) 1899; *68* (62): 752–53 (Aug. 5) 1899; *68* (63): 764–65 (Aug. 9) 1899; *68* (64): 777–78 (Aug. 12) 1899.

17. "Materialien Zur Geschichte der Talmudischen Medicin. Nase und Ohr." *Allg. Med. Central Ztg.* (Berlin) *68* (76)): 921–22 (Sept. 23) 1899; *68* (80): 970–71 (Oct. 7) 1899; *68* (81): 981–983 (Oct. 11) 1899.

18. "Chirurgisches in Bibel und Talmud." *Deutsche Zeitschrift fur Chirurgie* (Leipzig) *59* (5–6): 507–34 (May) 1901.

19. "Materialien zur Geschichte der Talmudische Medicin. Der Tote und seine Bestattung." *Allg. Med. Central Ztg.* (Berlin) *71* (25): 294–95 (Mar. 26) 1902; *71* (26): 306–7 (Mar. 29) 1902; *71* (27): 320–21 (Apr. 2) 1902.

20. "Biblisch-Talmudischen Pathologie und Therapie." *Ztschr. fur Klin. Medicin* (Berlin) *45* (5–6): 457–89, 1902.

21. "Die Strafrechtliche Verantwortlichkeit des Arztes im Altertum." *Müncher Medizin. Wochenschrift. 49* (12): 489–90 (Mar. 25) 1902.

22. "Die Medizin der Juden" in *Handbuch der Geschichte der Medizin,* ed. M. Neuburger and J. Pagel, vol. 1, pp. 110–18. Jena: Gustav Fisher Verlag, 1902.

23. Malum Malannum. *Medicinische Blätter.* (Vienna) *26* (24): 404–5 (June 11) 1903. Reprinted in *Jubilee Volume Honoring the 70th Birthday of A. Berliner.* Berlin, 1910.

24. "Materialien Zur Geschichte der Biblisch-Talmudischen Medicin. Die Erkrankungen der Haut." *Allg. Med. Central Ztg.* (Berlin) *72* (21): 431–34 (May 23) 1903; *72* (22): 455–57 (May 30) 1903; *72* (23) 474–77 (June 6) 1903.

25. "Angina Lacunaris and Kali Chloricum (Vergiftungsfalle)." *Deutsche. Med. Ztg.* (Berlin) *24* (1): 447–48 (May 21) 1903.

26. "Waschungen und Bäder nach Bibel und Talmud." *Wiener Mediz. Wochenschrift 54* (2): 83–86, 1904; *54* (3): 137–40, 1904; *54* (4): 185–88, 1904; *54* (7): 327–29, 1904; *54* (9): 397–400, 1904; *54* (10): 439–42, 1904.

27. "Schwangerschaft, Geburt und Wochenbett nach Bibel und Talmud." *Zeitschrift fur Geburtshulfe und Gynäkologie* (Stuttgart) *53* (3): 528–73, 1904.

28. "Materialien zur Geschichte der Biblische-Talmudische Medicin. XVI. Die Weiblichen Genitalien." *Allg. Med. Central Ztg.* (Berlin) *74* (5): 96–98 (Feb. 4) 1905; *74* (6): 115–18 (Feb. 11) 1905; *74* (7): 135–37 (Feb. 18) 1905.

29. "Die Pathologie der Geburt nach Bibel und Talmud." *Zeitschrift fur Geburtshulfe und Gynäkologie.* (Stuttgart) *54* (3): 448-81, 1905.
30. "Sexuelles in Bibel und Talmud." *Allg. Med. Central Ztg.* (Berlin) *75* (30): 571–73 (July 28) 1906; *75* (31): 589–92 (Aug. 4) 1906; *75* (32): 608–10 (Aug. 11) 1906; *75* (33): 625–27 (Aug. 18) 1906; *75* (34): 642–43 (Aug. 25) 1906; *75* (35): 659–61 (Sept. 1) 1906.
31. "Prostitution und Sexuelle Perversitäten nach Bibel und Talmud." *Monatshefte fur Praktische Dermatol.* (Hamburg). *43* (6): 271–79 (Sept. 15) 1906; *43* (7): 342–45 (Oct. 1) 1906; *43* (8): 376–81 (Oct. 15) 1906; *43* (9): 470–77 (Nov. 1) 1906; *43* (10): 549–55 (Nov. 15) 1906.
32. "Biblische und Talmudische Bezeichnungen der Gesichtsfarbe." *Festschrift zum Vierzigjährigen Amtsjubiläum des Herrn Rabbiners Dr. Salomon Carlebach in Lubeck.* July 16, 1910. Gewidmet von Freunden und Verwandten. Published by Von Moritz Stern. Berlin, 1910. Printed by H. Itzkowski, Auguststrasse 69.
33. *Biblisch-Talmudische Medizin. Beiträge Zur Geschichte der Heilkunde und der Kultur Uberhaupt.* Berlin: S. Karger, 1911, pp. 735 & 8° Reprinted unchanged by S. Karger in 1921 and again in 1923. Reprinted unchanged by Gregg International Publishing Co., Westmead Farnborough, England, in 1969. Reprinted unchanged by Ktav Publishers (New York) in 1971 but with an Introduction by Suessman Muntner and a Register of Hebrew and Aramaic Terms by Adolph Löwinger, translated and edited by Samuel Paley.

Unpublished Articles
34. "Ueber Untersuchung des Blutes zur Diagnostischen Zwecken," 1885.
35. "Kurpfuscherei und 'Geheimmittel' 1893" (lecture delivered to the Handwerker-Verein, Berlin, 1893).
36. "Frauenlob" (undated).
37. "Eine Aufgabe fuer Juedische Aerzte" (undated).
38. "Wohnungshygiene" (undated).

Fig. 1. Julius Preuss
(Courtesy of Mr. Jacob Preuss, Herzliya, Israel.)

בס״ד יום ד׳ ל׳ מקץ בׁשׁוׁשׁן לׁפׁ

Hochwürdiger Herr!

Fig. 2. Letter written by Julius Preuss in 1898 to Immanuel Löw, expressing his fear that he would not be able to complete his work because of ill health. The letter is signed: Dr. Preuss, *Rofe velo lo* ("physician, but not for himself").

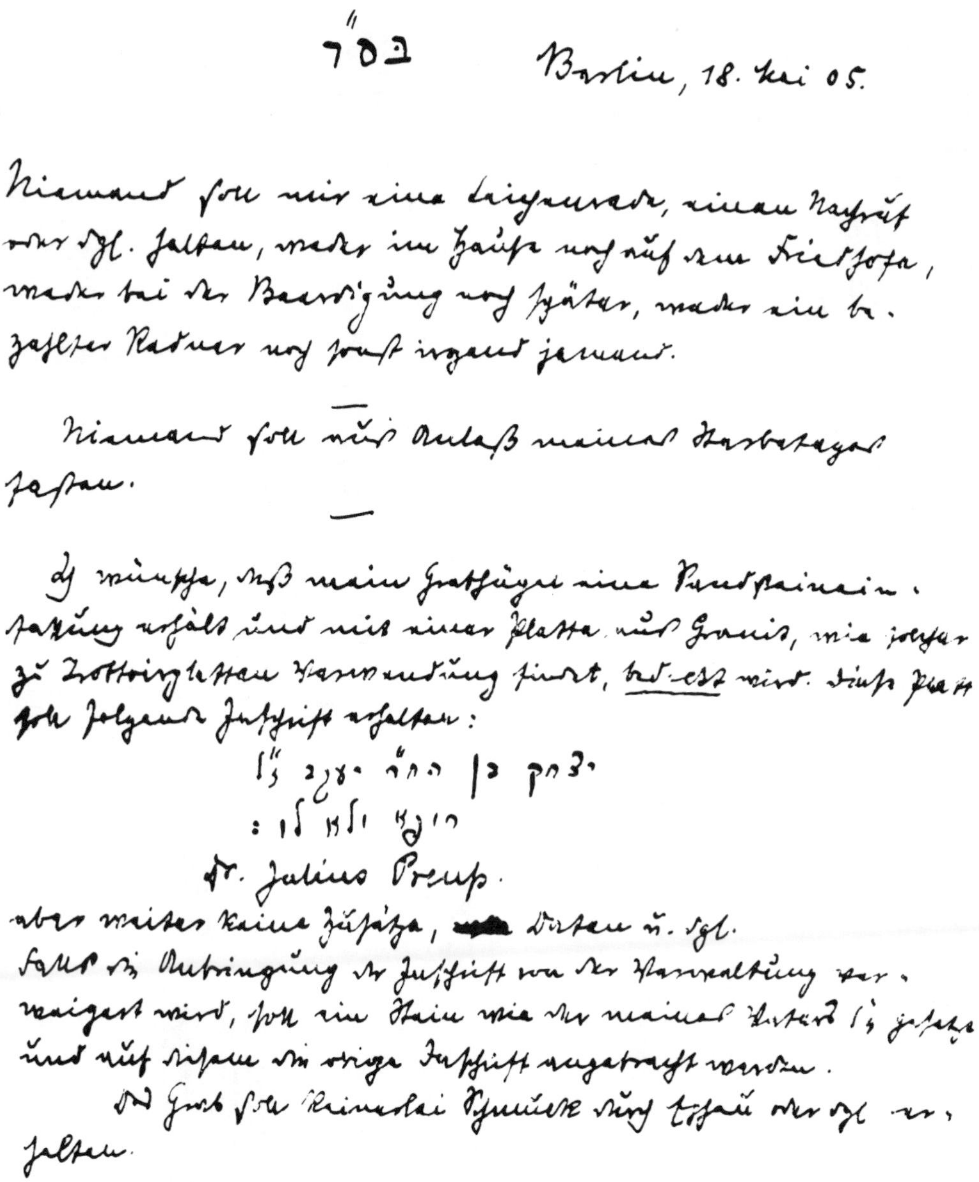

בס״ד Berlin, 18. Mai 05.

Niemand soll mir eine Leichenrede, einen Nachruf
oder dgl. halten, weder im Hause noch an der Friedhofe,
weder bei der Beerdigung noch später, weder ein be-
zahlter Redner noch sonst irgend jemand.

Niemand soll mir aus Anlaß meines Sterbetages
halten.

Ich wünsche, daß mein Grabstein eine Bruchsteinein-
fassung erhält und mit einer Platte aus Granit, wie solche
zu Trottoirplatten Verwendung findet, bd. es wird. Auch sie
soll folgende Inschrift erhalten:

יצחק בן מהר״ר יואל צבי
מורה צדק נ׳׳ו :

Dr. Julius Preuss.

aber weiter keine Zusätze, ~~—~~ Daten u. dgl.
Falls die Anbringung der Inschrift von der Verwaltung ver-
weigert wird, soll ein Stein wie der meines Vaters I; gesetzt
und auf diesen die obige Inschrift angebracht werden.

Das Grab soll keinerlei Schmuck und haben oder dgl. erhalten.

Fig. 3. Last Will and Testament of Julius Preuss, dated May 18, 1905.
(Courtesy of Mr. Jacob Preuss, Herzliya, Israel.)

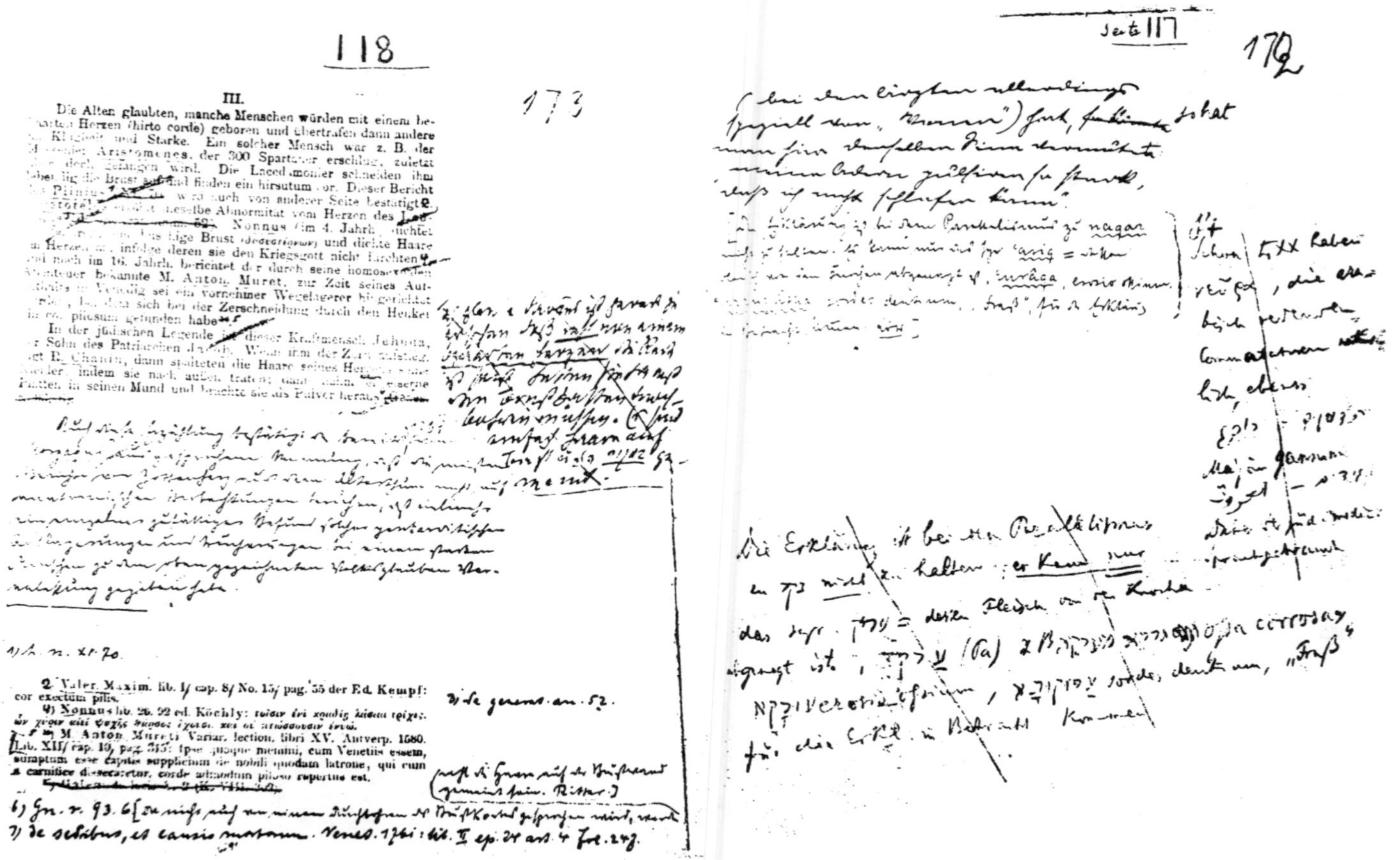

Fig. 4. Photograph of pages 117 and 118 of the original manuscript of Preuss's *Biblisch-Talmudische Medizin*, showing notes and comments by Oberrabbiner Dov Ritter (p. 118 middle right), Oberrabbiner Dr. Immanuel Löw (p. 117 middle right and bottom), Julius Preuss himself (p. 118 bottom and middle), and Preuss's wife, Martha (p. 117 top 5 lines).

Part II
Specific Diseases

Hemophilia in the Talmud

Classic hemophilia is a hemorrhagic disease due to a deficiency of anti-hemophilic globulin (factor VIII). It occurs almost exclusively in males and is transmitted as a sex-linked recessive gene by the female. An essentially identical disorder develops as a result of deficiency of a different factor, plasma thromboplastin component (factor IX). In addition, there are other coagulation disorders that resemble classic hemophilia.[1-4]

John Conrad Otto (1774–1844), an American physician who succeeded Benjamin Rush at the Philadelphia Dispensary in 1813, provided the first accurate account of hemophilia in the modern medical literature.[5-6] His investigation of "bleeders" was published in a New York journal (*Medical Repository* 6[1803]: 1) under the title, "An Account of an Hemorrhagic Disposition Existing in Certain Families." Otto pointed out that hemophilia is a familial disorder affecting males but not females, although the latter transmit the ailment. Otto's classic description of hemophilia has since been reprinted.[7] Nasse in 1820 formulated the law of transmission of this disease [8] and the name "hemophilia" was given by Schönlein in 1839.[5-6]

Medieval and ancient references to hemophilia are practically non-existent. Major states that the famous Islamic surgeon of the tenth century, Albucasis, wrote about hemophilia in his encyclopedic work on medicine and surgery entitled *Al Tasrif*.[9]

The present paper points out the recognition and description of hemophilia and its genetic transmission as found in the fifth-century Talmud and in rabbinic writings thereafter.

The Babylonian Talmud, in the tractate *Yebamot* 64b, states:

> For it was taught: "If she circumcised her first child and he died [as a result of bleeding from the operation], and a second one also died [similarly], she must not circumcise her third child." These are the words of Rebbe [R. Judah the Patriarch, redactor of the Mishnah, the second-century compilation of Jewish law]. Rabban Simeon ben

Gamliel, however, said: "She may circumcise the third child but must not circumcise the fourth child."

R. Judah and R. Simeon do not differ on the question of the maternal transmission of the disease but on the number of repetitive events required to establish a pattern and to remove a subsequent similar event from the category of chance. This is a technical point of talmudic law. Although, in general, three repetitive events are necessary to establish a pattern, in matters of life and death, the view of R. Judah is upheld that two suffice. No other form of diagnosis was then available.

R. Isaac Alfasi quotes the above passage from the Talmud and then states that the final ruling is according to the opinion of R. Judah.[10]

Moses Maimonides, the physician and talmudist,[11] in his massive fourteen book codification of biblical and talmudic law, the *Mishneh Torah,* carries the discussion on hemophilia somewhat further. He states:

If a woman had her first son circumcised and he died as a result of the circumcision, which enfeebled his strength, and she similarly had her second [son] circumcised and he died as a result of the circumcision—whether [the latter child was] from her first husband or from her second husband—the third son may not be circumcised at the proper time [on the eighth day of life]. Rather one postpones the operation for him until he grows up and his strength is established. One may only circumcise a child that is totally free of disease because danger to life overrides every other consideration. It is possible to circumcise later than the proper time but it is impossible to restore a single [departed] soul of Israel forever.[12]

Maimonides may be alluding to the mode of death when he states "enfeebled his strength," that is, exsanguination. This conclusion may be unwarranted, however, as Maimonides may have lumped together circumcision mortality from numerous causes, such as prematurity and anemia, in addition to bleeding disorders. As a physician, his desire was to delay circumcision until health was established.

R. Joseph Karo, in his commentary on the above passage from Maimonides, states that the prohibition against further circumcision in an afflicted family is "because there are families in which the blood is weak [lit. loose]." Furthermore, whereas the Talmud does not state when circumcision can be performed in an afflicted child (perhaps never, as discussed below),

Maimonides specifically set a time limit—that is, circumcision may be performed at such time that the child is declared medically fit. Maimonides thus seems to feel that spontaneous remission or perhaps medical therapy can control or even cure hemophilia. Maimonides also recognizes that a single woman transmits the disease to all her male offspring even if the latter were conceived from different fathers. The *Tur,* by R. Jacob ben Asher, cites Maimonides nearly verbatim.[13]

The most important code of Jewish law, the *Shulḥan Arukh,* compiled by R. Joseph Karo, states:

> If a woman had her first son circumcised and he died as a result of the circumcision, which enfeebled his strength, and she also had her second [son] circumcised and he died as a result of the circumcision, then it is established that her children die as a result of circumcision irrespective of whether she had one husband or two. The third [child] should not be circumcised. Rather one postpones [the operation] for him until his strength is established. The same applies if a man circumcised his first son and then his second and they [both] died as a result of the circumcision, he should not circumcise his third [son], whether he had them from one woman or two. And the same rule applies if a woman had her son circumcised and he died as a result of the circumcision and her sister also had her son circumcised and he died as a result of the circumcision, then the other sisters should not have their sons circumcised but wait until they are grown and their strength established.[14]

Karo thus introduces the possibility of hemophilia being transmitted through the male. He prohibits circumcision of the third son of a man whose earlier sons, born of different mothers, died as a result of the circumcision. This view is subscribed to by R. Hayim Joseph David Azulay, who, in his commentary entitled *Birkei Yoseph,*[15] on the above passage from Karo, states that if two sons of a man and woman died as a result of circumcision and they were divorced and both remarried to others, then the man's sons from his new wife and the woman's sons from her new husband may not be circumcised until they grow up and their health is established. R. Azulay also quotes another rabbinic authority, R. Jacob Reischer, to support this viewpoint. R. Reischer, in his work entitled *Shevut Yaakov,* [16] states that if in one family there are three women whose firstborns died as a result of circumcision, then these women should not circumcise their sons until they grow up and become healthy. The same applies to brothers and a father and son or grandson whose children died as a result of circumcision.

Contrary to the opinions of Rabbis Karo, Azulay, and Reischer that males can occasionally transmit the disease, is the viewpoint of the foremost commentator on Karo, R. Moses Isserles (1510–1572), known as the *Ramah*. Isserles agrees with the Talmud, Maimonides, and Jacob ben Asher that only females transmit hemophilia although males are afflicted with it. Isserles specifically states: "There are some who disagree with Karo and consider this [rule] not to apply to a man [with more than one wife] but only to a woman [with two or more husbands]." [14]

R. David ben Samuel Halevi, known as the *Turei Zahav* and R. Elijah of Vilna, known as the Vilna Gaon, both explain Isserles when they mention "because the blood comes from the woman." [14]

The rabbinic responsa literature represents formal replies to legal queries addressed to scholars of all generations. The writing of R. Ezekiel Landau exemplifies this literature. He was asked about a three-year-old boy whose three brothers died as a result of circumcision. In his responsum Rabbi Landau answered that even the third brother should not have been circumcised.[17] He further states that if it were not for Maimonides, Jacob ben Asher, Karo, and others who say that circumcision should only be postponed, he would recommend that circumcision never be performed on the child under consideration. He quotes the Talmud, Alfasi, and R. Asher ben Yeḥiel, another codifier of Jewish law—all of whom simply state, "the third [son] should not be circumcised"; the implication is forever. The fact that adult uncircumcised Israelites exist is supported by several talmudic references.[18] Additional responsa literature dealing with this subject is cited by R. Abraham Zvi Hirsch Eisenstadt.[19]

Another pertinent ruling is found identically in two places in the Talmud where the following story is related:

> R. Nathan said: "I once visited the coastal towns and a woman came before me who had her first son circumcised and he died and her second son and he died. The third [son] she brought before me. I saw that he was red [Rashi explains that all the blood is below the skin and circumcision will lead to exsanguination], so I told her to wait until his blood was absorbed. She waited until his blood was absorbed and had him circumcised, and he lived and he was called Nathan the Babylonian after my name. On another occasion, I went

to the land of Kaputkia, and a woman came before me who had her first son circumcised and he died and her second son and he died. The third [son] she brought before me. I saw that he was green [Rashi explains that he was anemic and weak from lack of blood production as yet], and I examined him and saw no covenant blood in him. I told her to wait until he becomes fullblooded. She waited and then had him circumcised, and he lived and he was called by the name Nathan the Babylonian after my name."[20]

Although the "red" and "green" probably refer to erythema neonatorum and icterus neonatorum or anemia, respectively,[21] the above story is very similar to the rules cited in the Talmud regarding hemophilic boys, and therefore is presented here.

R. Shlomo Eger, in his commentary entitled *Gilyon Maharsha* on Karo's code,[14] tries to differentiate a bleeding disorder from other causes of neonatal death after circumcision by observing whether the blood actually clotted at circumcision and deciding if the death could be attributed to other than recognized causes of neonatal mortality. The question is raised whether only true lack of coagulation at circumcision would preclude the circumcision of subsequent siblings if they appear healthy at birth. Indeed, in the talmudic story R. Nathan seems to have attempted to differentiate bleeding disorders from other causes of neonatal mortality by carefully examining the newborn, and not to have accepted the blanket dictum that all subsequent children not be circumcised. Further discussion on talmudic and rabbinic laws regarding hemophilia is available in English,[22] German,[23] and Hebrew.[12,13,21,24]

The conclusion to be drawn from the above discussion is that the sages of the Talmud in the second century and subsequent rabbinic authorities had a remarkable knowledge of the genetic transmission of a familial bleeding disorder, probably hemophilia. All recognized that females transmit the disease, but some thought that males can also do so. It is unclear, however, whether the rabbis were dealing only with hemophiliacs. Vitamin K deficiency, possibly determined by diet in certain families, or other bleeding disorders, such as congenital hypofibrinogenemia, may have been involved in some cases. Certainly, a recognized bleeder who continued to bleed throughout his life would not be circumcised. Some of the rabbis felt that if an individual proves to be healthy, he should be circumcised. The rabbis who postulate that the male sibling of bleeders who died as a result of circumcision should never be circumcised may fear the possibility of causing bleeding in a hitherto undiscovered hemophiliac. They had no way of diagnosing the presence of a covert bleeding tendency except by the sibling history. No rabbi states that a known hemophiliac should be circumcised. Since many of the rabbis did not understand the true nature of hemophilia and do not discuss the natural course of the disease, they probably lumped hemophilia together with other causes of neonatal mortality precipitated by circumcision.

The observations recorded in the Talmud and by the codifiers of Jewish law are incomplete, however. Although families with "loose blood"—that is, bleeding disorders—were recognized, the question of the circumcision of the child whose maternal uncles died of bleeding after circumcision is not considered. A woman whose brothers bled to death after circumcision could well be a carrier. Only the direct maternal transmission of the disease was recognized, whether demonstrated in siblings or maternal cousins.

For practical purposes in this day of hematological sophistication, where antihemophiliac globulin (factor VIII) assays can establish the diagnosis of hemophilia at or shortly after birth, one is not permitted to circumcise any child so diagnosed even if he did not have older siblings who exsanguinated after this operation. A positive diagnosis established by the finding of low to absent antihemophilic globulin levels in the plasma of a newborn infant is equivalent by Jewish law to a history of two siblings having died after circumcision.[25] A woman whose brothers bled to death after circumcision cannot have her child circumcised until the coagulation profile of her son is shown to be normal.

With the advent of fresh frozen plasma and cryoprecipitate for the treatment of hemophilia,[26,27] one might consider performing elective circumcision. However, in spite of these therapeutic aids, the risks of bleeding after the operation are still substantially greater in a hemophiliac child than a normal infant. Thus, by Jewish law one must withhold this operation and abide by the rule enunciated by Maimonides: "one may only circumcise a child that is totally free of disease because danger to life overrides every other consideration. It is possible to circumcise later than the proper time [i.e., when cure is achieved], but it is impossible to restore a single [departed] soul of Israel forever." [12]

REFERENCES

1. R. Biggs and R. G. MacFarlane, *Human Blood Coagulation and Its Disorders,* 3d ed. (Philadelphia: F. A. Davis, 1962), p. 474.
2. M. M. Wintrobe, *Clinical Hematology,* 6th ed. (Philadelphia: Lea & Febiger, 1967), p. 1287.
3. R. G. Biggs and R. G. MacFarlane, *Treatment of Haemophilia and Other Coagulation Disorders* (Philadelphia: F. A. Davis, 1966), p. 391.
4. M. Stefanini and W. Dameshek, *The Hemorrhagic Disorders,* 2d ed. (New York and London: Grune & Stratton, 1962), p. 614.
5. A. Castiglioni, *A History of Medicine* (New York: Alfred A. Knopf, 1941). p. 707.
6. F. H. Garrison, *An Introduction to the History of Medicine,* 3d ed. (Philadelphia: W. B. Saunders, 1924), pp. 451, 461.
7. R. H. Major, *Classic Descriptions of Disease,* 3d ed. (Springfield, Ill.: Charles C. Thomas, 1945), pp. 522–24.
8. C. F. Nasse, "Von einer erblichen Neigung zu todtlichen Blutungen," *Arch. Med. Erfahr.* 1 (1820): 385.
9. R. H. Major, *A History of Medicine* (Springfield, Ill.: Charles C. Thomas, 1954), 1:252.
10. Alfasi on B. T. *Yebamot* 64b.
11. F. Rosner, "Moses Maimonides (1135–1204)," *Annals of Internal Medicine* 62 (1965): 372.
12. *Mishneh Torah, Hilkhot Milah* 1:18.
13. *Tur Shulḥan Arukh, Yoreh Deah* 263.
14. *Shulḥan Arukh, Yoreh Deah* 263:2, 3.
15. Ibid.
16. J. Reischer, *Shevut Yaakov* (Lemberg, 1860).
17. E. Landau, *Responsa Noda Biyehudah, Yoreh Deah* 165.
18. Mishnah *Yebamot* 8:1; B. T. *Ḥullin* 4b.
19. A. Z. H. Eisenstadt, Commentary *Pit'ḥei Teshuvah on Shulḥan Arukh, Yoreh Deah* 263:1–11.
20. B. T. *Ḥullin* 47b, *Shabbat* 134a.
21. I. L. Katzenelsohn, *Hatalmud Ve'ḥokhmat Harefuah* (Berlin: Chaim Publishers, 1928), pp. 226–33.
22. I. Jakobovits, *Jewish Medical Ethics* (New York: Bloch, 1959), pp. 198–99.
23. J. Preuss, *Biblisch-Talmudische Medizin* (Berlin: S. Karger, 1923), p. 285.
24. *Arukh Hashulḥan, Yoreh Deah* 263:6–11.
25. Moses Feinstein, dean of the Tifereth Jerusalem Rabbinical Seminary, New York City, personal communication, October 12, 1966.
26. J. G. Pool and A. E. Shannon, "Production of High Potency Concentrates of Antihemophilic Globulin in a Closed-Bag System: Assay in Vitro and in Vivo," *New England Journal of Medicine* 273 (1965): 1443.
27. P. D. Dallman and J. G. Pool, "Current Concepts: Treatment of Hemophilia with Factor VIII Concentrates," *New England Journal of Medicine* 278 (1968): 199.

81-51

Rabies In The Talmud

Rabies (hydrophobia) is a disease of great antiquity, having been described in the pre-Mosaic Eshunna Code of ancient Mesopotamia approximately four thousand years ago.[1,2] The disease was more specifically described by Democritus in the fifth century B.C.E. and later by Aristotle,[1,2] Galen,[1,2,3] and Celsus.[2,4] The disease was known to Rufus of Ephesus in the second century,[5] Oribasius in the fourth century,[6] and Aetius of Amida in the sixth century.[7]

Major progress in the understanding and treatment of rabies was made with Louis Pasteur's description of preventive vaccination in 1885, and the discovery in 1903 by Adelchi Negri of cell inclusions, staining deeply with methylene blue eosin, in the central nervous system of patients afflicted by hydrophobia.

The present essay is an examination of the talmudic statements dealing with the bite of a mad dog, the description of the symptomatology of such a rabid dog, and the recommended cures for one bitten by such a dog.

The Babylonian Talmud states as follows:

"If one was bitten by a mad dog, he may not be given the lobe of its liver to eat, but R. Matia ben Heresh permits it. . . ." (Mishnah *Yoma* 8:6). The therapeutic use of parts of the rabid animal, particularly the liver, for individuals bitten by such an animal, was recommended by many ancient physicians, including Dioscorides, Galen, and others.[8] In the Talmud, only R. Matia ben Heresh, who lived in Rome, advocates this type of therapy, since he believed in its curative values (perhaps a forerunner of modern homeopathics), and hence permitted the consumption of the liver of the rabid animal by the patient. The other sages of the Mishnah consider it useless, deny its curative value, and hence prohibit its use since it is derived from a non-kosher animal.

The Talmud continues with the following description of a rabid animal:

Our rabbis taught that five things were mentioned in connection with a mad dog: its mouth is open, its saliva is dripping, its ears

50

flap, its tail hangs between its thighs, and it walks on the edge of the road. Some say it also barks without its voice being heard. Where does it [the dog's madness] come from? Rab said, "Witches are having their fun with the dog," Samuel said, "An evil spirit rests on it. . ." [*Yoma* 83b]

The talmudic discussion then mentions that even if a person only rubs against the mad dog, there is danger and he should remove and destroy his clothes. Samuel further said that one should kill it by throwing something at it and avoid direct contact with the rabid animal. From these talmudic statements, it is obvious that the etiology of rabies was not at all understood, although the symptomatology was correctly recognized.

The treatment for someone bitten by a mad dog is detailed in the Talmud as follows:

What is the remedy [for the bite of a mad dog]? Abaye said: "Let him take the skin of a male hyena [or leopard] and write upon it: 'I, so and so, the son of that and that woman, write upon the skin of a male hyena *Kanti, kanti, kloros, God, God, Lord of Hosts, Amen, Amen, Selah.'* Then let him strip off his clothes and bury them in a grave at the crossroads for twelve months of a year. Then he should take them out and burn them in an oven, and scatter the ashes. During the twelve months, if he drinks water, he shall not drink it but out of a copper tube, lest he see the shadow of the demon and be endangered. Thus the mother of Abba ben Martha, who is Abba ben Minyumi, made for him a tube of gold [for drinking purposes]." [*Yoma* 84a]

The reason for the copper tube is explained by Preuss[8] and Ebstein[9]: otherwise the patient would see the reflection of the mad dog in the water and would be further endangered by cramps in the throat and inability to drink, i.e., hydrophobia.

The Jerusalem Talmud (*Yoma* 8:5) relates that Rebbe (R. Judah the Patriarch) gave "liver" to his Germanic servant, who had been bitten by a mad dog, but in vain. The effort was futile and the patient died, from which the Talmud concludes: "let no man tell you that he was bitten by a mad dog and lived." This statement is also found elsewhere in the Jerusalem Talmud (*Berakhot* 8:5).

A final statement dealing with the bite of a mad dog is found in the Babylonian Talmud:

> R. Joshua ben Levi said: "All animals that cause injury [i.e., kill] may be killed [even] on the Sabbath." R. Joseph objected. "Five may be killed on the Sabbath, and these are they: the Egyptian fly, the hornet of Nineveh, the scorpion of Adiabene, the snake in Palestine, and a mad dog anywhere." [*Shabbat* 121b]

The above ruling is codified by Maimonides[10] and Karo.[11] Other animal bites are mentioned in the Talmud (*Yoma* 49a, *Ḥullin* 7b, *Baba Kamma* 84a), but the wound inflicted was probably not associated with rabies. Furthermore, snakebites are frequently discussed in the Talmud, but the poisons injected by venomous snakes do not produce the clinical picture of what is today known as rabies, or hydrophobia.

It seems appropriate to conclude with a quotation from Moses Maimonides' *Treatise on Poisons,*[12] written in the year 1198, wherein he not only depicts the signs and symptoms of rabies and the treatment therefore, but in which he recognized the long incubation period:

> On mad dogs. The early physicians already noted the varied character of a mad dog's symptoms. . . . The mad dog always wanders about by himself, in a roundabout way, leaning on walls and never barking. . . . Everything mentioned in the literature against the bite of a mad dog is useful, if at all, only when applied before rabies sets in. When such is the case I have as yet seen nobody who escaped with his life. A person bitten by a mad dog does not always experience greater pain than that following the bite of a normal dog. The dangerous symptoms indicating rabies appear as a rule only after eight days, sometimes even much later. It therefore follows that anybody bitten by a stray [insane] dog should adhere to the general rules, that is, bandaging, incision, sucking out, copious blood-letting from the affected spot by means of cupping glasses, vomiting, and treatment by theriac. Then he should follow the directions bearing on the eventual application of the remedies against the bite of mad dogs, which I am about to enumerate . . . *Rhamnus infectoria—Lycium hindi—*of which half a *siklus* should be taken daily in cold water. Another remedy: Gentiana lutea, crushed and sifted, 1 siklus daily in cold water. Best of all are river crab, roasted,

ground and sifted, the ashes mixed with water and taken daily 1 dram a day . . .[13]

The exciting conclusion of Maimonides' lengthy discussion on the therapeutics of rabies concerns the story of a weaver's boy who was bitten by a dog. There was no indication that it was a mad dog, and therefore the physicians closed the wound at the end of a month. The boy recovered from the bite, but "a long time afterwards" the boy developed the usual symptoms of rabies and died.

The remedy suggested by the Talmud (*Yoma* 84a) for the bite of a mad dog is derived from folk medicine and probably has no scientific validity. The contemporary reader should not adopt a superior attitude because of it, however. On the other hand, the treatment suggested by Maimonides—"bandaging, incision, sucking out, copious bloodletting from the affected spot"—is very modern in its approach. The bite of any animal, where poison is believed to have been injected into a human being, is today treated by the application of a tourniquet above the bite, incision of the skin between the tourniquet and the site of the bite, and the sucking out, or expression, of blood from the wound in an attempt to remove the poison before it spreads through the body. This subject is discussed in greater detail in the chapter on snakes and serpents.

REFERENCES

1. T. F. Sellers, "Rabies," in *Principles of Internal Medicine,* ed. T. R. Harrison et al., 2d ed. (New York: McGraw-Hill, 1954), p. 1106.
2. H. Koprowski, "Rabies," in *Textbook of Medicine,* ed. P. B. Beeson and W. McDermott, 12th ed. (Philadelphia: Saunders, 1967), p. 50.
3. A. Castiglioni, *A History of Medicine* (New York. Alfred A. Knopf, 1941), p. 223.
4. D. LeClerc, *Histoire de la Médecine* (The Hague: Van Der Kloot, 1792), p. 459.
5. R. H. Major, *A History of Medicine* (Springfield, Ill.: Charles C. Thomas, 1954), 1:183.
6. C. Singer and E. A. Underwood, *A Short History of Medicine* 2d ed. (New York: Oxford University Press, 1962) p. 240.
7. F. H. Garrison, *An Introduction to the History of Medicine,* 3d ed. (Philadelphia: W. A. Saunders, 1924), p. 112.
8. J. Preuss, *Biblisch-Talmudische Medizin* (Berlin: S. Karger, 1923), pp. 224–25.
9. W. Ebstein, *Medizin im Neuen Testament und im Talmud* (Munich: Werner Fritsch, 1965), p. 258.
10. *Mishneh Torah, Hilkhot Shabbat* 11:4.
11. *Shulḥan Arukh, Oraḥ Ḥayyim* 316:10.
12. F. Rosner, "Moses Maimonides' Treatise on Poisons," *Journal of the American Medical Association* 205 (1968): 914–16.
13. S. Muntner, *Moses Maimonides' Treatise on Poisons and Their Antidotes* (Philadelphia: Lippincott, 1966), pp. 39–44.

Scurvy In The Talmud

In the thirteenth century Jacques de Vitry described a disease, considered by some to be scurvy, in which "the gums and teeth are attacked by a sort of gangrene, and the patient can eat no more. Then the bones of the legs become horribly black." [1] Another early description of what might be scurvy is that of Jean, Sire de Joinville, who described a sickness in which "the leg shrivelled up and became covered with black spots, and . . . the gums became putrid with sores, and . . . the nose began to bleed. . . ." [1]

The understanding, treatment, and prevention of scurvy in the modern era is said to date from the two classic writings of James Lind (1716–1794), *Treatise on the Scurvy* (Edinburgh, 1753) and *An Essay on the Most Effectual Means of Preserving the Health of Seamen in the Royal Navy* (London, 1757).[2-4] Lind demonstrated how scurvy might be prevented by the use of fresh fruit or, if this was not available, the use of preserved lemon juice. His work led to the routine use of lemon juice in the rations of British sailors, with the result that scurvy all but disappeared as a medical problem. The whole question of what was called scurvy is a general problem beyond the scope of this report. This essay is restricted to a disease interpreted by many to be scurvy, as described in early Jewish writings.

The fifth-century Babylonian Talmud is a rich source not only of rabbinic but also of medical and other scientific knowledge. A disease called *zafdinah* is described in which gum bleeding is the major symptom. The evidence to be presented that *zafdinah* is scurvy is quite devious, and the reader is asked to keep this qualification in mind. Even so, *zafdinah* in most Jewish sources, is translated as scurvy. Therefore, the talmudic description of this malady, if in fact it represents scurvy, antedates Lind by twelve centuries. Goldstein and Schechter claim that *zafdinah* was

55

already known in the time of Hippocrates, although they give no sources to support this possibility.[5]

The Talmud relates that R. Yoḥanan suffered from scurvy (*zafdinah*) and went to a matron seeking a remedy (*Yoma* 84a). According to Preuss, quoting the Jerusalem Talmud (*Shabbath*, 14:14, 30), the matron was a Roman woman, daughter of a certain Domitian.[6] She prepared a remedy for R. Yoḥanan on a Thursday and Friday.

> He said to her: "How shall I do it on the Sabbath?" She answered him: "You will not need it any more" . . . [she swore him to secrecy not to reveal the remedy]. . . . What did she give to him? R. Aḥa, son of R. Ammi, said: "the water of leaven, olive oil, and salt." R. Yemar said: "leaven itself, olive oil, and salt." R. Ashi said: "geese fat smeared with a goose feather." Abaye said: "I tried every-thing, without achieving a cure for myself, until an Arab recom-mended: 'take the stones of olives which have not become ripe one-third, burn them in fire upon a new rake, and stick them into the inside of the gums' [lit. inside the row of teeth]. I did so and was cured." Whence does [scurvy] come? From eating very hot wheat foods and remnants of fish hash and flour. What is its symp-tom? If he puts anything between his teeth, his gums will bleed.

The word *zafdinah* is interpreted by Rashi to refer to a "sickness of the teeth and gums which begins in the mouth and ends in the intestines, and is dangerous to life." *Zafdinah,* in both the classic German and English versions of the Talmud, as well as in modern Hebrew dictionaries, is translated as scurvy.[7-9] Bible-Talmud scholars also accept scurvy as the translation of *zafdinah*. Ebstein reluctantly subscribes to this view, al-though he states there is insufficient evidence in the Talmud to arrive at such a conclusion and suggests "gum bleeding" as an alternate transla-tion.[10] Preuss, in his classic book, states that *zafdinah* undoubtedly refers to stomatitis, perhaps scorbutic.[6] He also states that no conclusion can be drawn concerning the exact identification of this disorder from the etiologic and therapeutic descriptions in the Talmud.

The story of R. Yoḥanan's scurvy and the remedy provided by the Roman matron is found elsewhere in the Talmud (*Abodah Zarah* 28a) but with two variations from the earlier version. The symptoms are de-scribed before the treatment, and the cause for scurvy is given as eating "very cold wheat foods and very hot barley foods and remnants of a pie of fish-hash and flour." Another talmudic tractate states the following:

> R. Matia ben Ḥeresh said: "If one has pain in his throat, he may pour medicine into his mouth on the Sabbath because there is a possibility of danger to human life, and every danger to human life suspends the laws of the Sabbath." [Mishnah *Yoma* 8:6].

Some talmudic commentators, notably Alfasi and Asheri, interpret this passage literally. Others, however, notably the *Tur,* Bertinoro, and *Tosafot Yom Tov,* change the phrase "pain in the throat" to "pain in the teeth so that the gums begin to rot and the palate and throat become secondarily involved." Also supporting the latter viewpoint is Maimonides, who states, in his commentary on the previously mentioned talmudic passage, that "pain in the mouth means the gums, which are rotting, and if nothing is done, the palate will also rot." Whether R. Matia ben Ḥeresh described scurvy or another malady of the mouth, teeth, gums, and throat cannot be answered with certainty.

Another sage who suffered from presumed scurvy is R. Judah the Patriarch (*Baba Meẓia* 85a). He observed that R. Eleazar, son of R. Simeon, had submitted to much suffering for which he was divinely rewarded in that his body remained intact, defying decomposition and decay, for many years. Thereupon R. Judah the Patriarch undertook to suffer likewise for thirteen years, six through stones in the kidneys or bladder, and seven through scurvy. The talmudic word for scurvy here is *ẓipparna,* which Preuss claims is a variation of *ẓafdinah.* R. Nathan ben Yeḥiel states that the manuscript versions of the Talmud in fact have the word *ẓafdinah.*[11] He translates it as *mundfäule,* or thrush. The English translation of the Babylonian Talmud also renders *ẓipparna* as scurvy. In several places in the Midrash, we are told of a thirteen-year toothache of R. Judah the Patriarch (*Gen. Rabbah* 33:3 fol. 68d, 96:4 fol. 178c; *Kohelet Rabbah* 11:1 fol. 29a). Whether this ailment is identical to the presumed scurvy from which R. Judah suffered is unknown.

That *ẓafdinah* is an affliction of the teeth which is a potential hazard to life because it begins in the mouth but spreads to the intestines is also evident from the Jerusalem Talmud (*Abodah Zarah* 2:2 fol. 10b). Whether *ẓafdinah* represents true scurvy, as appears to be the opinion of most talmudic commentators and translators, or whether it is another ailment, such as pyorrhea, thrush, tooth abscess, or the like, as the medical description in the Talmud would appear to indicate, is a problem which may never be resolved.

REFERENCES

1. R. H. Major, *Classic Descriptions of Disease,* 3d ed. (Springfield, Ill.: Charles C. Thomas, 1945), p. 585.
2. A. Castiglioni, *A History of Medicine* (New York: Alfred A. Knopf, 1941), pp. 469, 772.
3. C. Singer, and E. A. Underwood, *A Short History of Medicine* (New York: Oxford University Press, 1962), p. 186.
4. F. H. Garrison, *An Introduction to the History of Medicine,* 3d ed., (Philadelphia: W. B. Saunders, 1924), p. 375.
5. A. Goldstein and M. Schechter, *Otzar Harefuah Vehabriyuth* [Medical and health Thesaurus] (Tel Aviv: Dvir, 1955), 2:1000.
6. J. Preuss, *Biblisch-Talmudische Medizin* (Berlin: S. Karger, 1923), p. 196.
7. L. Goldschmidt, ed., *Der Babylonische Talmud mit Einschluss der vollstandigen Mishnah,* (Berlin: Menorah, 1897–1902), 2:1012.
8. I. Epstein, ed., *The Babylonian Talmud: Tractate Yama and Tractate Abodah Zara* (London: Soncino Press, 1935) pp. 413, 138.
9. R. Alcalay, *The Complete Hebrew-English Dictionary* (Hartford, Conn.: Prayer Book Press, 1965), p. 2202.
10. W. Ebstein, *Die Medizin im neuen Testament und im Talmud* (Stuttgart: Ferd. Enke Verlag, 1903), p. 269.
11. A. Kohut, ed., *Nathan ben Yeḥiel's Sefer Arukh Hashalem* (Lexicon of Targum, Talmud & Midrash). (New York: Pardes, 1955), 7:35.

Gout in the Bible and Talmud

The first modern description of gout is attributed to Thomas Sydenham (1624–1689) in his classic work entitled *Tractatus de Podagra et Hydrope*. This disease may have already been known, however, in biblical and talmudic times.

King Asa of Judah (915–875 B.C.) reigned happily and peacefully for over forty years. In his old age, he suffered from a disease in his feet considered to be gout. The key passage is found in 1 Kings 15:23, where it is stated:

> Now the rest of all the acts of Asa and all that he did and the cities which he built, are they not written in the book of chronicles of the Kings of Judah? But in the time of his old age, he was diseased in his feet.

The Babylonian Talmud, in two separate discussions (*Sanhedrin* 48b, *Sotah* 10a), comments on King Asa's illness as follows:

> But in the time of his old age, he was diseased in his feet. Concerning this Rab Judah said in Rab's name: "He was afflicted with *podagra*." Mar Zutra, the son of R. Naḥman, asked R. Naḥman: "What is [this complaint] like?" He answered: "Like a needle in the raw flesh." But how did he [R. Naḥman] know that? Either because he himself suffered with it, or alternatively, he had a tradition from his teacher . . . or he knew it [by divine revelation].

The expression "like a needle in the raw flesh" is used elsewhere in the Talmud (*Berakhoth* 18b, *Shabbat* 13b and 152a). Rashi (*Sanhedrin* 48b) states that the name of this illness, *podagra*, "is the same even in our language," i.e., French, Rashi's native tongue.

Further mention of the illness of King Asa is found in 2 Chronicles 16:12, where it is written: "And in the thirty-ninth year of his reign, Asa became diseased in his feet; his disease was exceedingly great." Recent historians, such as Sprengel, Corradi, and Delpeuch, are also of the opinion that King Asa's illness was, in fact, gout.

Another pertinent citation on gout is found in the Mishnah, which states: "One may go out [on the Sabbath] with a *sela* upon a *zinit*" (*Shabbat* 6:6).

A *sela* is a silver coin, used as a cure for foot ailments such as bunions. The word *zinit* is interpreted by the Jerusalem Talmud to mean *podagra* (*Shabbat* 6:8:22). The Babylonian Talmud, however, considers *zinit* to refer to a corn or a bunion (*Shabbat* 65a).

An excellent recent article, entitled "King Asa's Presumed Gout," published by two prominent Israeli physicians in the *New York State Journal of Medicine* (February 1975, p. 452), raises doubts as to whether King Asa's illness was really gout. The authors assert that the evidence for its having been gout appears rather scanty, and they conclude that the diagnosis of peripheral obstructive vascular disease with ensuing gangrene seems a more probable assumption. They base this conclusion primarily on the advanced age at which King Asa became ill and the severity of his disease, leading to his death within two years from the onset. However, as the authors themselves point out, clinical gout first occurring at an advanced age is compatible with a diagnosis of gout. It is also not stated in the biblical text that King Asa died from the same disease which afflicted him two years earlier. Hence, I would remain with the classic interpretation of King Asa's illness as gout.

Gout is an illness that continues to interest physicians nearly three hundred years after Sydenham's classic description and two thousand years after its mention in the Talmud.

Kordiakos in the Talmud

The term *kordiakos* appears several times in the Talmud (vide infra) and its meaning has been the subject of recent controversy.[1-2] The present essay examines the original sources dealing with *kordiakos* and the various interpretations and explanations thereof given by the major talmudic commentaries.

In the Mishnah we find the following:

> If a man is seized with *kordiakos* and says, "Write a bill of divorce for my wife," he has said nothing. If he says, "Write a bill of divorce for my wife," and is then seized with *kordiakos* and retracted and said, "Do not write it," his last words count for nothing . . . [*Gittin* 7:1]

The above ruling is codified by both Maimonides[3] and Karo.[4] The Talmud itself explains what *kordiakos* represents when it asks and answers:

> What is *kordiakos?* Samuel said: "Being overcome [lit. bitten] by new wine from the vat." Then why does it not say if one is overcome by new wine? The mode of expression teaches us that this spirit (or demon which causes the dizziness) is called *kordiakos.* Of what use is this [knowledge]? For a charm. What is the remedy for it? Red [i.e., without fat] meat broiled on the coals, and highly diluted wine. [*Gittin* 67b]

Based upon the above passage, most of the commentaries on the Talmud state that *kordiakos* is an alcohol-induced confusion of the mind. Thus, Rashi states that *kordiakos* is the name of the demon which rules in a person who drinks much wine from the vat. Maimonides, himself a physician, says that *kordiakos* is "an illness which occurs as a result of

61

filling of the chambers of the brain, and the mind becomes confused therefrom; it is one of the varieties of falling sickness [i.e., epilepsy]."

Bertinoro affirms that the individual afflicted with *kordiakos* is one whose mind is confused because of the demon which reigns in someone who drinks new wine. *Tosafot Yom Tov* states that the demon is called *kordiakos*. The latter interpretation of *kordiakos* is identical to that enunciated by *Ran* (R. Nissim Gerondi, 1320–80). *Tiferet Yisrael* (R. Israel Lipschuetz, 1782–1860) considers *kordiakos* to be an illness in which the intellect of the person is confused. The same occurs in someone who is "drunk like Lot" (see Gen. 19:31–38).

Other commentaries on the aforementioned talmudic passage, including *Tosafot Rid* (R. Isaiah da Trani, 13th cent.) and *Shiltei Gibborim* (R. Joshua Boaz Baruch, 16th cent.) also state that *kordiakos* is a bad spirit which prevails over a person who drinks wine from the vat. Such a person is confused, his mind is not clear, and he does not have an intact intellect.

Elsewhere in the Talmud (*Gittin* 70b), Resh Lakish compares a man with *kordiakos* to one who is asleep, whereas R. Yoḥanan compares him to a madman. Resh Lakish does not put a man with *kordiakos* on the same footing as a madman because for the latter there is no cure, whereas an individual with *kordiakos* can be treated with red flesh broiled on the coals and diluted wine (ibid. 67b). R. Yoḥanan does not compare him to one who is asleep because a sleeper needs no therapy, whereas a person with *kordiakos* does.

The Jerusalem Talmud, in two separate places (*Gittin* 7:1, *Terumot* 1:1) begins, as does the Babylonian Talmud (vide supra), with the following passage:

> If a man is seized with *kordiakos* and says, "Write a bill of divorce for my wife," he has said nothing. If he says, "Write a bill of divorce for my wife," and is then seized with *kordiakos* and retracted and said, "Do not write it," his last words count for nothing . . .

However, the Jerusalem Talmud adds:

> The signs of a fool [*shoteh*] are as follows: he goes out at night [alone], he sleeps in the cemetery, he tears his clothes, and he loses what he is given. . . . *Kordiakos* has none of the above symptoms. What is *kordiakos*? R. Jose answers, *ḥamim*. A case came before R. Jose concerning a weaver who was given red in black [diluted red wine or red thread while working with black thread?] and he

babbled [Heb.: *velu'a*, i.e., he talked nonsense]. Then he was given black in red and he babbled. This is the *kordiakos* of which the sages spoke; sometimes he is mad and sometimes sane. At a time when he is mad he is considered like a madman in all respects, and when he is sane, he is sane in all respects [i.e., a bill of divorce should be written for his wife as per his instructions]. . . .

The Hebrew word *velu'a* occurs in the Bible (Obad. 16). Most biblical commentators state that *velu'a* means "confused." The notable exception is R. Abraham Ibn Ezra (1092–1167), who asserts that *velu'a* means "swallowed."

The two major commentaries on the Jerusalem Talmud, *Penei Mosheh* (R. Moses Margolis, 18th cent.) and *Korban Ha'Edah* (R. David Fraenkel, 18th cent.), both state that *kordiakos* refers to one whose mind is confused because of a demon which prevails over someone who drinks new wine. The name of the demon is *kordiakos*, and hence the name of the affliction. The Jerusalem Talmud clearly distinguishes an idiot or a fool from someone afflicted with *kordiakos*. The latter is thought to be a person suffering from temporary and reversible insanity or madness caused by imbibing fresh wine from a vat.

Penei Mosheh also states that *ḥamim* is the name of an illness where the patient is confused. He supports this contention by citing the Babylonian Talmud (*Baba Meẓia* 80a), where confusion (*sha'amumit*, from the Hebrew noun *ḥamim*) is considered equivalent to madness or epilepsy (i.e., temporary derangement of mental faculties). The same word *sha'amumit* occurs twice more in the Talmud (*Ketubot* 59b, *Nedarim* 81a) and in both places means confusion or madness or stupefaction.

The renowned scholar of biblical and talmudical medicine, Julius Preuss, suggests that the word *ḥamim* may be derived from the Hebrew term *ḥomom*, meaning hot, i.e., febrile.[5] There is, however, no evidence for this assertion. Preuss further states that *kordiakos* is undoubtedly an acute illness and refers to the *morbus cardiacus* of the heathen physicians. Unfortunately, continues Preuss, the meaning and cause of this illness in the writings of these ancient physicians are questionable, and the exact nature is not at all clear from their descriptions. The copious sweating and the insomnia (neither symptom mentioned in the Talmud) seem to indicate a state of delirium tremens with precordial anxiety. However, says Preuss, Celsus specifically states that in *kordiakos*, in contrast to phrenesy, the state of consciousness is not disturbed, and he feels the condition represents imbecilic behavior. Galen, according to Preuss, contradicts himself, whereas Puschmann quotes authors who aver that *kordiakos* represents anemia and chlorosis (Landsberg) or exudative hemorrhagic pericarditis associated with scurvy (Ziegler). Preuss thus raises the possibility, based on non-talmudic sources, that *kordiakos* refers to cardiac or intestinal (i.e., stomach) illness.

Turning to more recent translations, the Soncino English version of the Babylonian Talmud states that *kordiakos* is "a kind of delirium in which the patient does not know exactly what he is saying." [6] The Jastrow dictionary of talmudic terms translates *kordiakos* as "delirious, delirium and delirium tremens." [7] The modern Hebrew term for delirium tremens is *tezazit marida*.[8]

Hankoff suggests that the origin of the word *kordiakos* lies in a corruption of the term *crocydismus,* which appears in the Greek writings of Galen and Aretaeus.[2] Gordon points out that *kordiakos* must refer to mental illness, since the Talmud discusses it together with the symptoms of the foolish behavior of an idiot or imbecile.[1] Gordon further points out that someone who sleeps in the cemetery alone at night may be frightened into thinking he is a wolf or a dog (Greek *liknatropos* and *kinatropos,* respectively). Confusion in the interpretation of the Greek word *kordiakos* is further compounded by the possibility of its derivation from *kordex,* meaning an Athenian dance, or *kardia,* meaning heart, or *chordee,* meaning cord, or *chondros,* meaning cartilage, or *hypochondrios,* meaning hypochondrium or hypochondriac.

What, then, is the real meaning of the word *kordiakos?* The Jerusalem Talmud is clear in categorically stating that *kordiakos* does not mean folly or idiocy. Both the Jerusalem and Babylonian Talmuds are equally clear in their descriptions of *kordiakos* as a syndrome characterized by confusion, dizziness, and mental incompetence following imbibition of wine from a new vat of wine. The syndrome is temporary and reversible with specific therapy of red meat and dilute wine.

Whether one identifies *kordiakos* as chronic alcoholism,[1] delirium tremens,[2] or a form of epilepsy (Maimonides, vide supra) is not of great consequence, since all three can be reconciled as a single entity. That is, following indulgence in alcoholic beverages by a chronic alcoholic, the patient may develop epileptic seizures in the course of delirium tremens.

The suggestion in Preuss and in Gordon that ancient physicians considered *kordiakos* a disease of the heart or of the stomach is probably erroneous.[1,5]

REFERENCES

1. H. L. Gordon, " 'Mi She'aḥazo Kordiakos' Be'talmud Uve'mada Harefu'i" [He who is seized with *Kordiakos*" in the Talmud and in medical science], *Perakim* (New York), 3 (January 1963): 117–30.
2. L. D. Hankoff, "Ancient Descriptions of Organic Brain Syndrome: The *Kordiakos* of the Talmud," *American Journal of Psychiatry* 129 (August 1972): 233–36.
3. *Mishneh Torah, Hilkhot Gerushin* 2:14–15.
4. *Shulḥan Arukh, Even Ha'ezer* 121:1–2.
5. J. Preuss, *Biblisch-Talmudische Medizin* (Berlin: S. Karger, 1923), pp. 368–69.
6. I Epstein, ed., *The Babylonian Talmud: Seder Nashim*, vol. 4, *Tractate Gittin* (London: Soncino Press, 1936), p. 320.
7. M. Jastrow, *A Dictionary of the Targumim, the Talmud Babli and Yerushalmi, and the Midrashic Literature* (New York: Pardes, 1950), 2:1341.
8. J. Even-Odem and Y. Rotem, *Milon Refu'i Ḥadash* [New medical dictionary] (Jerusalem: Rubin Mass, 1967), p. 233.

Sunstroke in the Bible and Talmud

Perhaps the earliest account of heatstroke or sunstroke is the one related in the Bible. In chapter 4 of 2 Kings are described some of the miraculous deeds of Elisha the prophet. One of these acts was to promise the birth of a son to a barren woman from the town of Shunam who gave hospitality to Elisha. The prophecy of Elisha was fulfilled but was followed by the tragic death of the boy. Verses 17–20 read:

> And the woman conceived and bore a son at that season, when the time came round, as Elisha had said to her. And when the child was grown, it happened on a day, that he went out to his father to the reapers. And he said unto his father: "My head, my head." And he said to a servant: "Carry him to his mother." And when he had taken him, and brought him to his mother, he sat on her knees till noon, and then died.

Most biblical commentators interpret the child's illness as sunstroke, since this was the boy's first exposure to the fiercely hot sun of the Middle East. The child's revival by Elisha is described later in the same chapter:

> And he went up and lay upon the child, and put his mouth upon his mouth, and his eyes upon his eyes, and his hands upon his hands; . . . and he crouched over him; and the child sneezed seven times, and the child opened his eyes. [vv. 34–35]

Some interpret this incident as of purely miraculous connotation. *Radak* (R. David Kimḥi, 1160–1235), however, states that Elisha attempted to breathe on the child in order to provide warmth from the natural body heat which emanated from his mouth and eyes. *Radak* further states that most miracles are performed with direction and guidance from worldly and natural actions. *Meẓudat David* (R. David Altschul, 17th cent.) states that Elisha tried to pour some of the life of his own body into the limbs of the child. *Ralbag* (R. Levi ben Gerson, 1288–1344) gives an identical interpretation but adds that "he [Elisha] did this after he prayed." *Ralbag* and *Radak* thus seem to consider a combination of natural and miraculous events as having contributed to the child's revival.

There are many puzzling aspects to this story. Why did the Shunammite woman not search out a physician rather than, or in addition to, calling for Elisha? Was the boy revived by artificial respiration? [1] Some mesmerists believe that Elisha performed witchcraft or sorcery.[2] Perhaps the boy was not really dead? This possibility seems to be considered in the Babylonian Talmud, where R. Joshua ben Hananiah was asked, "Does the son of the Shunammite woman convey [ritual] uncleanness?" and replied, "A corpse conveys uncleanness but no live person conveys uncleanness" (*Niddah* 70b). In other words, the boy was not dead.

On the other hand, Rashi states that the boy was unquestionably dead and the talmudic question is whether he is considered a corpse after he was resurrected.

Be that as it may, the type of illness that afflicted the child is clearly enunciated in the Jerusalem Talmud: "R. Manna stated that at harvest time accidents happen, because the sun only blazes on a person's head at harvest time, as it is written: 'And when the child was grown, it happened on a day, that he went out to his father to the reapers' " (*Yebamot* 15:2).

The talmudic commentary *Korban Ha'Edah* explains that at harvest time a person may faint from the scorching sun, and die thereof. Another talmudic commentary, *Penei Moshe,* states that sickness or even death occurs at harvest time, because of the torrid sun, as in the case of the Shunammite boy. The same two commentaries interpret the phrase "who hast protected my head in the day of battle" (Ps. 140:8) to refer to sunstroke. The "day of battle" is thought to be the "day when winter kisses the summer"; that is, when summer ends and winter begins, one should cover one's head to avoid sunstroke in accordance with the aphorism: "The end of the summer is worse than the summer."

One dissenting viewpoint considers the Shunammite boy's death to have been due to a snakebite.

Another incident, nearly identical to that of Elisha and the Shunammite woman's child, is described in chapter 17 of 1 Kings. Here prophet Elijah, the predecessor of Elisha, warns King Ahab of Israel (reigned ca. 875–

853 B.C.E.) of a drought which would last for several years. To escape the
drought, Elijah traveled to Zarephath, where he received hospitality from
a sinful widow who had an only son. The Bible then relates:

> And it came to pass after these things that the son of the woman,
> the mistress of the house, fell sick; and his sickness was so sore,
> that there was no breath left in him. And she said unto Elijah:
> "What have I to do with thee, O thou man of God? Art thou come
> unto me to bring my sin to remembrance and to slay my son?" And
> he said unto her: "Give me thy son." And he took him out of her
> bosom, and carried him up into the upper chamber, where he abode,
> and laid him upon his own bed. And he cried unto the Lord, and
> said: "O Lord my God, hast thou also brought evil upon the widow
> with whom I sojourn, by slaying her son?" And he stretched himself
> upon the child three times, and cried unto the Lord and said: "O
> Lord my God, I pray thee, let this child's soul come back unto him."
> And the Lord hearkened unto the voice of Elijah, and the soul of
> the child came back into him, and he revived. [vv. 17–22]

The phrase "there was no breath left in him" is interpreted by Josephus
to mean that he appeared to be dead (*Antiquities* 8, 13, 3). Most biblical
commentators, however, including Rashi, *Ralbag, Mezudat David,* and
Radak, believe that the boy actually died. *Mezudat David* remarks that
the verse "And he stretched himself upon the child" means that Elijah
placed his mouth on the child's mouth and his eyes on the child's eyes,
just as Elisha did to the son of the Shunammite woman. *Radak* again
states that this was done to breathe onto the boy and warm him with
Elijah's natural body warmth. *Ralbag* also supports this viewpoint, and
further remarks that it was as if the prophet wished to transfer the breath
of his limbs to the limbs of the child.

In this incident the boy was definitely dead, as stated in the Babylonian
Talmud: "And it is written: 'And it came to pass after these things that
the son of the woman, the mistress of the house, fell sick.' Elijah prayed
to God that He give him the key to the resurrection of the dead." (*Sanhedrin* 113a).

Whether this boy also died of sunstroke or not is impossible to state,
nor do the commentaries shed any light on the question.

Another case of sunstroke is described in the Apocrypha, where we
are told that as Judith's husband, Manesseh, "was overseeing the men who

were binding sheaves on the plain, the heat affected his head, and he threw himself upon his bed and died" (Jth. 8:3).

Finally, a legal pronouncement concerning a hypothetical case of sunstroke is made in the Talmud: "Raba said: 'If one bound his neighbor in the sun, and he died [of heatstroke], he is liable [i.e., he is considered a murderer]' " (*Sanhedrin* 77a).

Although the precise clinical picture of heatstroke is not described in the Bible and Talmud, there seems little doubt that this medical entity was recognized at that time and was the cause of death in the case of the Shunammite boy.

Electrocution, a phenomenon related to sunstroke, occurs once in the Torah in the story of the death of Aaron's sons Nadab and Abihu (Lev. 10:2). The "fire that devoured them" is considered by the Talmud to have effected burning of their souls, but their bodies were unharmed (*Sanhedrin* 52a). The late British Chief Rabbi Hertz, in his Bible commentary, states that it is probable that the fire took the form of a lightning flash, killing them without destroying their garments or their bodies. Other interpretations of the mode of death of Nadab and Abihu, such as suffocation, are also possible.

REFERENCES

1. F. Rosner, "Artificial Respiration in Biblical Times," *New York State Journal of Medicine* 69 (1969): 1104–5.
2. Julius Preuss, *Biblisch-Talmudische Medizin,* 2d ed. (Berlin: S. Karger, 1921), p. 192.

Yerakon in the Bible and Talmud

The modern Hebrew word for jaundice is *zahevet,* derived from the word *zahav,* meaning gold. The biblical term *yerakon* (derived from the word *yerek,* meaning green or green plant), is variously translated as jaundice, chlorosis, and mildew. Chlorosis is an iron-deficiency anemia found in adolescent girls just past puberty, and is characterized by a greenish color of the skin, weakness, and menstrual disturbances. It is also called green-sickness.

The term *yerakon* is found six times in the Bible (Deut. 28:22; 1 Kings 8:37; Jer. 30:6; Amos 4:9; Ḥag. 2:17; 2 Chron. 6:28). With one exception (Jer. 30:6), this word always appears in association with the word *shidaphon,* and most English translations render these two words "blasting and mildew."

Rashi and others consider *yerakon* to represent diseases that afflict grain in the field, the symptoms of which are that the surface of the grain becomes pale and ultimately turns yellowish-green. Other Bible commentators, including Samson Raphael Hirsch (1808–88), interpret *yerakon* either as jaundice or as chlorosis, illnesses afflicting human beings. The reference in Jeremiah seems to refer to chlorosis or jaundice and not mildew. Whether the name *yerakon* in the six biblical citations actually represents human or plant afflictions remains controversial, although most commentators espouse the latter interpretation.

Identification of Yerakon

That the biblical *yerakon* refers to some type of epidemic is clear from talmudic discussions, such as the "alarm is sounded." (*Ta'anit* 19a) and prayers are recited (*Ketubot* 8b) on account of *shidaphon* and *yerakon.* The dual explanation of the word *yerakon* is provided by Bertinoro, when he states: *"Yerakon* is grain whose appearance became pale. And there are some who interpret *yerakon* to be an illness where the facial appearance of a person turns green like the grass of the field" (*Ta'anit* 3:5).

As no symptoms of this disease are described anywhere in the Bible or Talmud, we are dependent upon the derivation of the word *yerakon* for its proper understanding. There is little doubt that *yerakon* is derived from the word *yerek* or *yarok,* meaning "green." The word *yerek* itself is found many times in the Bible (Gen. 1:30, 9:3; Exod. 10:15; Num. 22:4; Deut. 11:10; 1 Kings 21:2; 2 Kings 19:26; Isa. 15:6, 37:27; Ps. 37:2; Prov. 15:17; Job 39:8) and always refers to a green herb or grass. Also in the Talmud the word *yarok* signifies the color green (*Sukkah* 34b, *Shabbat* 20b, and others). One commentary on the Talmud (*Tosafot Niddah* 19b) states that *yarok* is yellow, but ordinarily *yarok* or *yerek* means green. The biblical term *yerakrak* (Lev. 13:49, 14:37; Ps. 68:14) is considered to signify dark green by some commentators (e.g., Rashi) and light green by others (*Tosefta Nega'im* 1:5). In the Midrash dark green vegetables in a vegetable garden (*ginat yerek*) into which a spring flows are said to turn black (*Lev. Rabbah* 15:3).

A bluish (venous) tinge to the green is implied in the case of a suspected adulteress whose "face turns green, whose eyes protrude and whose veins stand out" (Mishnah, *Sotah* 3:4). In addition, one of the talmudic commentaries (*Tosafot Hullin* 47b) specifically states that *yarok* is indigo or sky-blue. A final interpretation of the word *yerek* or *yerakon* is pallor that may occur due to extreme fear (Jer. 30:6). In the Talmud, *yarok* also refers to pallor (as opposed to a healthy ruddy countenance), whether it is due to illness, as in the case of a suspected adulteress (*Num. Rabbah* 9:21), or whether it is caused by hunger (*Ruth Rabbah* 3:6). If a man is frightened to death, his face may also become greenish, i.e., pale (*Ketubot* 103b, *Abodah Zarah* 20b). If a man is shamed in public, his face blanches (Mishnah *Abot* 3:11) because the blood is drained from the victim's face (*Baba Mezia* 58b).

The following story concerning R. Nathan, which is related three times in the Talmud (*Shabbat* 134a, *Hullin* 47b, *Tosefta Shabbat* 16,5), illustrates the difficulty in the interpretation of the word *yarok:*

> . . . if an infant is too red, so that the blood is not yet absorbed in him, we must wait until he is full-blooded and then circumcise him. For it was taught, R. Nathan said: "I once visited the coastal towns and a woman came before me who had her first son circumcised and he died and her second son and he died. The third [son] she brought before me. I saw that he was red [Rashi explains that all the blood is below the skin and circumcision will lead to exsan-

guination], so I told her to wait until his blood was absorbed. She waited until his blood was absorbed and had him circumcised, and he lived and was called Nathan the Babylonian after my name. On another occasion, I went to the land of Kaputkia and a woman came before me who had her first son circumcised and he died, and her second son and he died. The third [son] she brought before me. I saw that he was green [yarok]; [Rashi explains that he was anemic and weak from lack of blood production as yet], and I examined him and saw no covenant blood in him. I told her to wait until he becomes full-blooded. She waited and then had him circumcised, and he lived and he was called by the name Nathan the Babylonian after my name."

The "red" probably refers to erythema neonatorum but modern Bible scholars offer differing explanations for "green" (yarok).[1-3] They state that yarok may represent either severe pallor from anemia, or jaundice secondary to icterus neonatorum. Furthermore, the talmudic discussion in Ḥullin indicates that yarok can also mean various shades of yellow (including egg-yolk color) or "green resembling the leek" (ibid.). There is also a postmenstrual flow that is colored yarok (Mishnah Niddah 2:6) that may or may not represent blood or a blood breakdown product that would render the woman niddah (ritually unclean). Finally, the milk of a clean (i.e., kosher) animal is said to be white, whereas the milk of an unclean animal is said to be greenish in color (Abodah Zarah 35b).

Preuss offers the following thought to reconcile the two different interpretations of yarok, i.e., anemia (pallor) and jaundice.[1] He cites R. Ishmael, who compares the skin color of Israelites (i.e., Semites) to boxwood (Mishnah Nega'im 2:1) and states that the skin color of Semites is in between the dark skin color of Ethiopians and the light skin color of Germanic people. Preuss proposes that pallor in Semitic people thus resembles jaundice.

The human malady of jaundice (yerakon) is said by the sages of the Talmud to result as divine punishment for causeless hatred (Shabbat 33a). It is said to be produced by the withholding of urination (Berakhot 62b, Tamid 27b, Bekhorot 44b). Perhaps a disease of the gallbladder is the affliction that was erroneously thought to be caused by urinary retention. Perhaps the uremic coloration in a patient with advanced kidney disease is meant.

Treatment for Yerakon

Numerous therapeutic regimens are recommended in the Talmud for jaundice. Urine from an ass, if imbibed, is good for jaundice (*Bekhorot* 7b). According to R. Matia ben Ḥeresh, the flesh of a donkey should be eaten by someone suffering from jaundice (*Yoma* 84a). Water of palm trees and a potion of roots are said to be efficacious for jaundice (*Shabbat* 109b). Water of palm trees was thought to "pierce the gall" (ibid. 110a). A useful potion of roots is explained by R. Yoḥanan as follows:

> The weight of a *zuz* of Alexandrian gum is brought, a *zuz* weight of liquid alum, and a *zuz* weight of garden crocus, and they are powdered together. . . . For jaundice two-thirds thereof are mixed with beets and drunk, and the patient (although cured of his jaundice) becomes impotent.

Other remedies for jaundice are also mentioned in the Talmud (ibid. 110b):

> . . . let him take the head of a salted *shibuta* [name of a fish, probably mullet], boil it in beer, and drink it. If not, let him take brine of locusts. If brine of locusts is not available, let him take brine of small birds [alternate translation: clear fish brine], carry it into the baths, and rub himself therewith. If there are no baths, he should be placed between the stove and the wall [to make him perspire].
>
> R. Yoḥanan said: "If one wishes to make the patient with jaundice warm he should wrap him well [or rub him] in his sheet. R. Aḥa ben Jacob suffered therewith, so R. Kahana treated him thus and he recovered. But, if not, let him take 3 *kapiza* of Persian dates, 3 *kapiza* of dripping wax [dripping from an overflowing honeycomb], and 3 *kapiza* of purple aloes, boil them in beer, and drink it. If not, let him take a young ass; then the patient shaves half his head, draws blood from its forehead, and applies it to his own head, but he must take care of his eyes, lest the blood blind him. If not, let him take a buck's head which has lain in preserves [vinegar], boil it in beer, and drink it. If not let him take a speckled swine, tear it open, and apply it to his heart. If not, let him take porret [leeks] from the wastes of the valley [Rashi: from the middle of the furrow, where the leeks are sharp] . . ."

The biblical term *yerakon* probably refers to an affliction of grains in the field as divine retribution for sin. The single exception is the passage in Jeremiah (30:6) where *yerakon* represents a human affliction, either pallor or anemia (chlorosis) or jaundice. The talmudic reference to *yerakon* can, in the final analysis, refer either to jaundice or anemia (chlorosis). Preuss and Krauss lean toward anemia as the proper interpretation of *yerakon;* [1,4] Katzenelsohn considers it to represent jaundice,[2] whereas Ebstein cannot decide whether the reference is to jaundice or anemia.[3]

As *yerakon* is said to be due to causeless hatred, and hatred and anger were thought to be related to yellow bile or gall, it would seem logical to conclude that *yerakon* is, in fact, jaundice. However, the care of the newborn baby who is green (either pale or yellow or both), and for whom circumcision must be postponed, does not provide convincing evidence for either interpretation. The question thus remains unresolved.

REFERENCES

1. J. Preuss, *Biblisch-Talmudische Medizin* (Berlin: S. Karger, 1923), p. 189, 285.
2. I. L. Katzenelsohn, *Hatalmud Ve'hokhmat Harefuah* (Berlin: Chaim, 1928), p. 226-33.
3. W. Ebstein, *Medizin im Neuen Testament und im Talmud* (Stuttgart, 1903; reprint ed., Munich: Werner Fritsch, 1965), p. 264-67.
4. S. Krauss, *Talmudische Archaeologie* (Leipzig, 1910–12), 1:255.

Part III
Specific Organs

The Heart in the Bible and Talmud

Heart in the Bible

The Hebrew word for heart is *lev*. This word occurs 190 times in the Bible.[1] Variations of the word, such as "the heart," "and the heart," "in the heart," "like the heart," "from the heart," "my heart," "in my heart," "from my heart," "our heart," "your heart," etc., are found an additional 388 times. Another Hebrew word for heart is *levav*. This word is present 26 times in the Bible, and variants of this word as above occur an additional 223 times. Hence, the word *lev* and its variations are found a total of 827 times in Scripture.

Most often the term for heart is used in a figurative sense. For example, the Bible speaks of "circumcising the foreskin of the heart" (i.e., open the heart) (Deut. 10:16; Jer. 4:4), the "heart of the ocean" (Exod. 15:8; Ezek. 27:25–27; Prov. 23:34, 30:19; Ps. 46:3), the "heart of heaven" (Deut. 4:11), and the "heart of Jerusalem" (Isa. 40:2).

The heart can reflect the emotions of anguish (Jer. 23:9), wisdom (Exod. 31:6), evil (Gen. 8:21) and good (Ezek. 13:22) inclinations, delight (1 Kings 8:66), pleasure (Ps. 16:9), praise (Ps. 9:2), warmth (Ps. 39:4), shame (Ps. 69:21), singing (Ps. 84:3), and charity (Exod. 35:22).

Statements are made regarding the heart of a villain (1 Sam. 25:36), the heart of a king (Prov. 25:3), the heart of a prince (Jer. 4:9), the heart of a fool (Prov. 12:23), the heart of a widow (Job 29:13), the heart of a man (Prov. 19:21), and the heart of an understanding person (Prov. 14:33).

Various adjectives are used to describe the heart, including haughty (Ezek. 31:10), frightened (Deut. 28:67), pure (Ps. 24:4), happy (Prov. 15:13), fleshy (Ezek. 11:19), melting (Naḥ. 2:11), perfect (1 Chron. 28:9), intelligent (Prov. 11:29), broken (Ps. 51:19), upright (Ps. 97:11), stout (Ps. 76:6), trembling (Deut. 28:65), listening (1 Kings 3:9), fat

(Isa. 6:10), oppressed (Isa. 57:15), pained (Isa. 65:14) and uncircumcised (Jer. 9:25).

In the *Midrash Rabbah* (Lev. 4:4), the heart is described as the decision-making organ as follows:

> Ten things serve the soul: the gullet for food, the windpipe for the voice, the liver for anger, the lungs for drinking, the first stomach to grind the food, the spleen for laughter, the maw for sleep, the gall for jealousy, the reins think out, and the heart decides; and the soul is above them all.

Perhaps the most complete exposition of the heart's functions and activities is found in the *Midrash Rabbah* commentary on the phrase "I spoke with my own heart" (Eccles. 1:16). It is presented here in its entirety.*

> The heart sees, as it is said, "My heart hath seen much." It hears, as it is said, "Give Thy servant therefore a heart that hears" (I Kings 3:9). It speaks, as it is said, I SPOKE WITH MY OWN HEART. It walks, as it is said, "Went not my heart?" (II Kings 5:26). It falls, as it is said, "Let no man's heart fall within him" (I Sam. 17:32). It stands, as it is said, "Can thy heart stand?" (Ezek. 22:14). It rejoices, as it is said, "Therefore my heart is glad and my glory rejoiceth" (Ps. 16:9). It cries, as it is said, "Their heart cried unto the Lord" (Lam. 2:18). It is comforted, as it is said, "Bid Jerusalem take heart" (Isa. 40:2). It is troubled, as it is said, "Thy heart shall not be grieved" (Deut. 15:10). It becomes hard, as it is said, "The Lord hardened the heart of Pharaoh" (Ex. 9:12). It grows faint, as it is said, "Let not your heart faint" (Deut. 20:3). It grieves, as it is said, "It grieved Him at His heart" (Gen. 6:6). It fears, as it is said, "For the fear of thy heart" (Deut. 28:67). It can be broken, as it is said, "A broken and contrite heart" (Ps. 51:19). It becomes proud, as it is said, "Thy heart can be lifted up" (Deut. 8:14). It rebels, as it is said, "This people hath a revolting and rebellious heart" (Jer. 5:23). It invents, as it is said, "Even in the month which he had devised of his own heart" (I Kings 12:33). It cavils, as it is said, "Though I walk in the stubbornness of my heart" (Deut. 29:18). It overflows, as it is said, "My heart overfloweth with a goodly matter" (Ps. 45:2). It devises, as it is said,

---

* Reprinted from the English translation of the Midrash with kind permission from the Soncino Press, Ltd., London.

"There are many devices in a man's heart" (Prov. 14:21). It desires, as it is said, "Thou hast given him his heart's desire" (Ps. 21:3). It goes astray, as it is said, "Let not thy heart decline to her ways" (Prov. 7:25). It lusts, as it is said, "That ye go not about after your own heart" (Num. 15:39). It is refreshed, as it is said, "Stay ye your heart" (Gen. 18:5). It can be stolen, as it is said, "And Jacob stole Laban's heart" (ib. 31:20). It is humbled, as it is said, "Then perchance their uncircumcised heart be humbled" (Lev. 26:41). It is enticed, as it is said, "He spoke enticingly unto the damsel" (Gen. 34:3). It errs, as it is said, "My heart is bewildered" (Isa. 21:4). It trembles, as it is said, "His heart trembled" (I Sam. 4:13). It is awakened, as it is said, "I sleep, but my heart waketh" (Song of Songs 5:2). It loves, as it is said, "Thou shalt love the Lord thy God with all thy heart" (Deut. 6:5). It hates, as it is said, "Thou shalt not hate thy brother with thy heart" (Lev. 19:17). It envies, as it is said, "Let not thy heart envy sinners" (Prov. 23:17). It is searched, as it is said, "I the Lord search the heart" (Jer. 17:10). It is rent, as it is said, "Rend your heart, and not your garments" (Joel 2:13). It meditates, as it is said, "The meditation of my heart shall be understanding" (Ps. 49:4). It is like a fire, as it is said, "There is in my heart as it were a burning fire" (Jer. 20:9). It is like a stone, as it is said, "I will take away the stony heart out of thy flesh" (Ezek. 36:26). It turns in repentance, as it is said, "That turned to the Lord with all his heart" (II Kings 23:25). It becomes hot, as it is said, "While his heart is hot" (Deut. 19:6). It dies, as it is said, "His heart died within him" (I Sam. 25:37). It melts, as it is said, "The hearts of the people melted" (Josh. 7:5). It takes in words, as it is said, "And these words, which I command thee this day, shall be upon thy heart" (Deut. 6:6). It is susceptible to fear, as it is said, "I will put My fear into their hearts" (Jer. 32:40). It gives thanks, as it is said, "I will give thanks unto the Lord with my whole heart" (Ps. 111:1). It covets, as it is said, "Lust not after her beauty in thy heart" (Prov. 6:25). It becomes hard, as it is said, "He that hardeneth his heart shall fall into evil" (ib. 28:14). It makes merry, as it is said, "It came to pass when their hearts were merry" (Judg. 16:25). It acts deceitfully, as it is said, "Deceit is in the heart of them that devise evil" (Prov. 12:20). It speaks from out of itself, as it is said, "Now, Ḥannah, she spoke in her heart" (I Sam. 1:13). It loves bribes, as it is said,

"But thine eyes and thy heart are not but for thy covetousness" (Jer. 22:17). It writes words, as it is said, "Write them upon the table of thy heart" (Prov. 3:3). It plans, as it is said, "A heart that deviseth wicked thoughts" (ib. 6:18). It receives commandments, as it is said, "The wise heart will receive commandments" (ib. 10:8). It acts with pride, as it is said, "The pride of thy heart hath beguiled thee" (Obad. 3). It makes arrangements, as it is said, "The preparations of the heart are man's" (Prov. 16:1). It aggrandises itself, as it is said, "Will thy heart therefore lift thee up?" (II Chron. 25:19). Hence, I SPOKE WITH MY OWN HEART, SAYING: LO, I HAVE GOTTEN GREAT WISDOM.

The word "heart," in the classic verse "Thou shalt love the Lord thy God with all thy heart" (Deut. 6:5), is interpreted by the rabbis to refer to one's desires and passions, i.e., emotions, rather than one's intellect.

Heart in the Talmud

In the Talmud the Hebrew word *lev* (or its Aramaic equivalent, *libba*) has meanings other than heart, e.g., stomach, chest, breast, or mind. The word *lev* is used to denote the stomach, as exemplified by the phrase "all medicines are to be imbibed on an empty stomach [lit. empty heart]" (*Gittin* 70a). Another illustration is the statement of R. Judah that "he who eats asafetida on an empty stomach [lit. empty heart] will shed his skin" (*Hullin* 59a). Finally, R. Joseph said that "he who eats sixteen eggs, forty nuts, and seven caperberries, and drinks one quarter of a *log* of honey in one meal on an empty stomach [lit. empty heart], in the summer months, snaps his heart strings asunder" (*Hullin* 59a). R. Joseph seems to indicate that such gross overeating puts a strain on his heart. Even the Bible occasionally uses the word "heart" to mean stomach. For example, "and wine maketh glad the heart of man . . . and bread sustains man's heart [i.e., his stomach]" (Ps. 104:15).

The word *lev* is also used by the Talmud to refer to the chest or the breast. Mourning for one's father or mother in Jewish law includes the tearing of one's garment (*Moed Katan* 22b) to expose the chest or breast. The expression in the Talmud is that one "rends one's garments up to the heart" (*Semahot* 9:5, *Sanhedrin* 68a), meaning that one bares the chest. R. Akiba is said to have kept beating his heart (i.e., chest) until the blood flowed, as a sign of mourning for his deceased colleague R. Eliezer.

The Pentateuchal passage dealing with a suspected adulteress (Num. 5:11–31) is commented upon in the Mishnah as follows: "a priest seizes her garments [at the neck]—if they are torn they are torn, and if they become unstitched, they are unstitched—until he uncovers her bosom [lit. heart] . . ." (*Sotah* 1:5).

Elsewhere (*Kelim* 26:5), the Talmud describes a covering for the heart (i.e., chest) of a child which served either to protect the clothes from becoming soiled (commentary of Moses Maimonides) or to protect the child from being scratched by a rabid cat (commentary of Bertinoro).

The placing of phylacteries (*Tefillin*) "on your hearts" (Deut. 11:18, 6:6–9) is interpreted by the Talmud to mean on the left biceps, in apposition to the left chest or breast (*Menahot* 37a). Also of interest is the quotation "set me as a seal upon thy heart" (Song of Songs 8:6). Seals were suspended from the neck with a cord worn by a woman over her heart (i.e., chest or breast).

Finally, the Hebrew word *lev* connotes the mind. The Talmud states (*Baba Batra* 12b) that before a man eats and drinks he has two hearts (i.e., he can't make up his mind), but after he eats and drinks he has only one heart, as it says, "A hollow man is two-hearted" (Job. 11:12).

Anatomy of the Heart and Great Vessels

The Mishnah recognized (*Hullin* 3:1) that "if the heart [of an animal] was pierced as far as the cavity thereof," the animal cannot survive and is declared *terefah* (unfit for ritual slaughtering and consumption). R. Zera raised the question: "Does it mean as far as the small cavity or as far as the large cavity?" (*Hullin* 45b). Apparently, "small cavity" seems to mean the right and "large cavity" the left part of the heart, not a differentiation of atrium and ventricle as we now know it. Moses Maimonides, in his *Mishneh Torah,* reiterates the fatal outcome of a pierced heart, but also describes left and right chambers of the heart as follows:

> If the heart is pierced as far as the chambers thereof, whether as far as the large chamber on the left or the small one on the right, the animal is *terefah*. If only the flesh of the heart is pierced, but the perforation does not penetrate inside the chamber, it is permitted. The aorta, that is, the large artery which leads from the

heart to the lung, is like the heart: if it is perforated to the smallest
extent into its cavity, it is *terefah*. [*Ḥilḥot Sheḥitah* 6:5]

The code of Jewish law of Joseph Karo states that "the heart has three
chambers" (*Shulḥan Arukh, Yoreh Deah* 40:1). It remained for more
recent anatomists to correctly describe the four chambers of the mam-
malian heart. There is also no mention of heart valves in the Talmud
and the major commentaries thereon.

The piercing of an animal's heart, and the possible use to which such
a "nonviable" animal may be put, is discussed in other parts of the Talmud (*Abodah Zarah* 29b, *Sefer Torah* 1:2, *Soferim* 1:2).

The aorta is also described in the Talmud as follows:

> As to the aorta [lit. the artery of the heart], Rab says the slightest
> perforation therein [will render the animal *terefah*] and Samuel says
> [it is *terefah* only if] the greater portion [of its circumference was
> severed]. . . . Amemar said in the name of R. Naḥman: "There are
> three main vessels, one leads to the heart [aorta], one leads to the
> lungs [pulmonary artery], and one leads to the liver [inferior vena
> cava?]" [*Ḥullin* 45b]

The two carotid arteries are described by Maimonides in his *Commentary on the Mishnah* (*Ḥullin* 1:1), where he calls them "the pulsating
vessels on the side of the neck."

Symptoms Related to
Diseases of the Heart

Disorders of the heart are described in the Talmud under several categories, including pain of the heart (*ke'ev lev*), weakness of the heart
(*ḥulsha de'libba*), heaviness of the heart (*yukra de'libba*), palipitations
of the heart (*pirḥa de'libba*), and pressure on the heart (*kirḥa de'libba*).
These will be discussed individually.

Pain of the Heart (*Ke'ev lev*)

The following statement is quoted from the Talmud: "rather any complaint, but not a complaint of the bowels; any pain, but not heart pain;
any ache, but not headache; any evil, but not an evil wife . . ." (*Shabbat*
11a). Although the above heart pain may, in fact, refer to organic heart
disease, the following citation obviously describes psychological "heart

pain": "if one draws out his prayer and expects therefore its fulfillment, he will in the end suffer heart pain, as it says 'hope deferred maketh the heart sick' [Prov 13:12]"—(*Berakhot* 55a). The expression "heart pain" in Isaiah 65:14 also refers to vexation of spirit, and not organic disease.

Therapy for heart pain (perhaps heartburn?) consists of the ingestion (but not inhalation) of black cumin: "one who regularly takes black cumin will not suffer from heart pain. . . . The mother of R. Jeremiah used to take bread for him and stick black cumin on it [so that it should absorb the taste] and then scrape it off [to remove the smell] . . ." (*Berakhot* 40a). Apparently smelling the aroma of black cumin was thought to be harmful, but eating black cumin was considered to be specific therapy for heart pain.

Weakness of the Heart (*Ḥulsha de'libba*)

R. Ḥisda and R. Huna sat all day engaged in judgments and their "hearts grew weak" (*Shabbat* 10a). Perhaps hunger pangs or hypoglycemia is meant here. R. Zera was unable to teach because his "heart felt faint" or weak (*Ta'anit* 7a). R. Awia had "weakness of the heart" and did not go to hear the lecture of R. Joseph (*Berakhot* 28b). Therapeutically, the Talmud advises that if someone takes mustard regularly once in thirty days, he keeps sickness away from his house. He should not, however, take it every day because it "weakens the heart" (*Berakhot* 40a). A final talmudic citation dealing with weakness of the heart is the following:

> Abaye's nurse said: "If a man suffers from weakness of the heart, let him fetch the flesh of the right flank of a male beast, and excrements of cattle cast in the month of Nissan; and if excrements of cattle are not available, let him fetch some willow twigs, and let him roast the flesh on the fire of the twigs, eat it and after that drink some diluted wine." [*Erubin* 24b]

Preuss, in his classic book, states that the above remedy is evidently an emetic.[2]

Heaviness of the Heart (*Yukra de'libba*)

Heaviness of the heart is not described in the Talmud but two remedies therefore are enunciated. If *ḥiltit* (probably *asafetida,* an umbelliferous plant used for medicinal purposes) is dissolved in cold or warm water and three gold dinar weights thereof imbibed on three consecutive days, it is therapeutically effective for "heaviness of the heart" (*Shabbat* 140a). Omitting the last dose may be detrimental to the patient's health (ibid.). The Soncinco English version of the Talmud translates *yukra de libba* in the previous citation as "asthma,"[3] whereas Preuss suggests it refers to melancholy or depression.[2]

The other remedy for "heaviness of the heart" is to eat three barley cakes streaked with *hamak* (a Persian sauce of milk) and to wash them down with well-diluted wine (*Gittin* 69b).

Palpitations of the Heart (Pirha de'libba)

The remedy suggested in the Talmud for "palpitations of the heart" is to take three cakes of wheat, streak them with honey, eat them, and wash them down with strong wine (*Gittin* 69b).

Pressure of the Heart (Kirha de'libba)

The remedy for this ailment is to consume the size of three eggs of mint, and an egg of camon and an egg of sesame (*Gittin* 69b). Some commentators suggest that *kirha de'libba* refers to inflammation of the heart rather than pressure of the heart.[2]

Preuss points out that the last three conditions discussed above (*yukra de'libba, pirha de'libba,* and *kirha de'libba*) are described in the Talmud among the remedies for stomach ailments.[2] Hence the word *libba* may refer to stomach or abdomen rather than heart.

A final talmudic citation dealing with disorders of the heart concerns a certain pious man who groaned or cried out from "pain in his heart" (*goneiah milibbo*). When the doctors were consulted, they said that there was no remedy for this man unless he sucked hot milk from a goat every morning (*Temurah* 15b).

It cannot be determined with certainty whether or not any of these "heart" ailments in fact refer to organic heart disease in the modern sense. Hence, it is impossible to state whether or not any of the proposed remedies has scientific validity or justification.

Heart as a Food

The consumption of heart as a food substance is said to be contra-indicated in at least one circumstance:

Five things make one forget one's studies: eating something from which a mouse or a cat has eaten, eating the heart of a beast, frequent consumption of olives, drinking the remains of water that was used for washing, and washing one's feet one above the other. Others say: he also who puts his clothes under his head . . . [*Horayot* 13b]

Concluding Note

The Hebrew Bible contains the word "heart" or a variant thereof 827 times, mostly in the figurative sense. The Talmud serves as a prime source of preoccupation with the anatomy of the heart (recognition of chambers but not valves) and great vessels, symptoms related to diseases of the heart (pain, weakness, heaviness, palpitations, pressure) and remedies for these disorders, and the contraindication of using heart as a food. Some doubt exists as to whether the Hebrew word *lev* in the Bible and the Aramaic word *libba* in the Talmud always refer to the heart, since the context of some of the citations suggest alternate meanings, such as stomach, chest, or breast.

REFERENCES

1. S. Mandelkorn, *Concordanzia Letanakh*. Tel Aviv: (Shocken Publishers, 1959), 1:627–31.
2. J. Preuss, *Biblisch-Talmudische Medizin* (Berlin: S. Karger, 1923), p. 205.
3. I. Epstein, *The Babylonian Talmud: Tractate Shabbat* (London: Soncino Press, 1938), p. 708.

The Spleen in the Talmud

There is no mention of the spleen in the Bible, but the anatomy, functions, and illnesses of this organ are discussed at some length in the Talmud and post-talmudic literature.

Anatomy of the Spleen

The spleen is called *tehol,* and its convex side is named the splenic breast or *dad;* the capsule is referred to as the skin or *kerum,* and the vessels of the hilum are called strings or *huttim* (*Hullin* 93a). The eating of hilar vessels and splenic capsule is said to be forbidden since they are included in the prohibition of eating fat and blood (Lev. 3:15). Although some blood exudes from the splenic hilum (*Keritot* 21b) and is subject to the aforementioned prohibition, the substance of the spleen, or *shumna,* is considered to be primarily composed of a fatty juice (*Hullin* 11a). Whereas meat cannot be rid of its blood unless it is thoroughly salted and rinsed and thus rendered fit for consumption (i.e., kosher), the substance of the spleen requires no such elaborate preparations before being eaten. This rule is enunciated by Maimonides in his *Mishneh Torah:* "It is permitted to cook the spleen, even together with meat, since it does not consist of blood but is merely flesh which resembles blood" (*Hil. Ma'akhalot Asurot* 6:9). The Midrash states that every prohibited food is counterbalanced by a permitted food (*Lev. Rabbah* 22:10). Thus, the prohibition of blood is balanced by the permissibility of eating spleen.

Functions of the Spleen

The spleen is believed to produce laughter, as is clearly enunciated in the Talmud:

> . . . the kidneys prompt, the heart discerns, the tongue shapes [words], the mouth articulates, the gullet takes in and lets out all kinds of food, the windpipe produces the voice, the lung absorbs

86

all kinds of liquids, the liver is the seat of anger, the gall lets a drop fall into it and allays it, the spleen produces laughter, the large intestine grinds [the food], the maw brings sleep, and the nose awakens. [*Berakhot* 61b]

A similar but not identical pronouncement is found in the Midrash:

. . . the ten organs that minister to the soul are: the gullet for the passage of food, the windpipe for voice, the liver for anger, the gall for jealousy, the lungs to absorb liquids, the stomach to grind food, the spleen for laughter, the kidneys to advise, the heart to give understanding, and the tongue to decide. [*Eccles. Rabbah* 7:19]

The famous *Zohar,* book of Jewish mysticism ascribed to the talmudic sage R. Simeon ben Yoḥai, appeared in the thirteenth century through Moses DeLeon. This work, too, considers the spleen to be the seat of laughter: "the spleen produces laughter in young children" (*Zohar* 3:234). A century earlier, Judah Halevy (1086–1145), in his celebrated *Book of Kuzari* (pt. 4, sec 25), related that "the spleen is called laughing because it is its nature to cleanse both blood and spirit from unclean and obscuring matter. If they are pure, cheerfulness and laughter arise." Moses Maimonides, in his major medical work, *The Aphorisms of Moses,*[1] also mentions the blood-purifying properties of the spleen but fails to mention that laughter is produced in the spleen (chap. 2, aphorism 9). Preuss mentions that Serenus Samonicus, in the third century, wrote that individuals with swollen spleens had a silly laughter, and if one extirpated the splenic tumor, the laughter would cease, and these individuals would develop serious looks on their faces.[2]

Another or alternate function of the spleen cited in the Talmud is the crushing action of this organ (*Abot DeRabbi Nathan* 31:3). The stomach is compared to grinding mills, the spleen to crushing mills, the belly to refuse bins, urine to running waters, bones to trees, and hips to hills.

Spleen as a Remedy

The Talmud relates that spleen is good for the teeth but bad for the bowels (*Berakhot* 44b). How can one take advantage of this apparent paradox? The answer given is to chew it well and then spit it out. It is also considered beneficial to drink spleen broth on the day one is phlebotomized (*Ḥullin* 111a) or to eat a dish of pieces of spleen (*Shabbat* 129a).

Diseases of the Spleen

The following talmudic quotation gives a vivid description of various ways to make the spleen shrivel up into nothing:

> For swelling of the spleen, let him take seven leeches and dry them in the shade and every day drink two or three in wine. Alternatively he may take the spleen of a she goat which has not yet had young, and stick it inside the oven and stand by it and say, "As this spleen dries, so let the spleen of so and so, son of so and so, dry up." Or again, he may dry it between the rows of bricks in a house and repeat these words. Or again, he may look out for the corpse of a man who had died on the Sabbath and take his hand and put it on the spleen and say, "As this hand is withered so let the spleen of so and so, son of so and so, wither." Or again, he can take a fish and fry it in a smithy and eat it in the water of the smithy and wash it down with the water of the smithy. A certain goat which drank from the water of a smithy was found on being killed to have no spleen. Another remedy is to open a barrel of wine expressly for him [i.e., he should drink plenty of wine]. [*Gittin* 69b]

Another prescription for "medical splenectomy" seems to be provided by Maimonides when he states that "a cattle hoof, if burned and drunk with oxymel, will shrink an enlarged spleen and stimulate the desire for coitus." [3]

Elsewhere, the Talmud teaches that asparagus brewed in wine is good for the spleen, whereas asparagus brewed in beer is bad for it (*Berakhot* 51a). The type of splenic malady being treated is not mentioned.

Surgical Splenectomy

Although splenectomy is said to have been performed first by Zaccarrelli in 1549 and Zambeccari in 1680,[4] this operation was already referred to in the time of the Talmud. After the death of King David of Israel, Adonijah attempted to usurp the throne of Solomon, as related in 1 Kings 1:5: "and he [Adonijah] prepared him chariots and horses and fifty men to run before him." The Talmud asks what was so remarkable about those fifty men (*Sanhedrin* 21b). The answer given is that "they all had their spleens removed," concerning which Rashi states that the spleen causes a sensation of heaviness. Its removal would thus facilitate fast running. Recent writers suggest that this operation was for the relief of the splenomegaly of chronic malaria, endemic in the Middle East in the time of the Talmud.[5]

The Talmud also states that if an animal's spleen was pierced, the animal would die, whereas if the spleen was completely removed, the animal would live normally (*Ḥullin* 55a).

Post-Talmudic Jewish Writers

The earliest Jewish medical writing is that of Asaph the physician, who lived in Egypt in the seventh century.[6,7] The first European Jewish medical author is Shabtai Donnolo (913–985) of Italy.[8] Numerous references to the spleen, its anatomy, functions, and disorders, are found in the medical works of both these Jewish physicians. Other medieval, Renaissance, and more recent Hebrew medical writers are described by Friedenwald in his classic magnum opus.[9]

The most illustrious of all Jewish physicians, Moses Maimonides, in his *Aphorisms of Moses,*[10] makes numerous statements concerning the spleen in health and disease. For example, he states that "the spleen touches the left side of the liver" (chap. 1:54); that "the spleen is nourished by thin black blood whereas the liver is nourished by thick red blood" (chap. 3:35); that "he whose liver is swollen appears pale and green [icteric?], but he whose spleen is swollen appears green and dark [plethoric?]" (chap. 6:47). Concerning therapy for a diseased spleen, Maimonides recommends that "the best type of treatment for a hardened spleen consists of compresses from roots of caper, wormwood, vinegar, and honey" (chap. 9:77); and that "inflammations of . . . the spleen or liver or stomach are all clearly benefited by bloodletting from the basilic vein" (chap. 12:29); and that "one should apply a cataplasm over the spleen in patients with illnesses of the spleen" (chap. 19:17). Non-inflammatory disease of the spleen is described as follows: "Physicians have the custom of calling 'spleen patients' those in whom hardness or calcification of the spleen without inflammation is found" (chap. 23:89).

Concluding Note

A twentieth-century physician cannot help but be impressed by the precise anatomical description of the spleen in the Talmud, including its shape, capsule, and vascular supply. The laughing function of the spleen, as described by the Talmud, Midrash, *Zohar, Kuzari,* and others, makes no sense today. However, the blood-purifying properties of the spleen is one of the recognized functions of this organ. Somewhat like a sieve, the spleen filters out senescent, damaged, or altered blood cells, including red and white blood cells and platelets. It is hard to imagine that ancient and medieval Jewish rabbis properly understood this recently discovered function of the spleen, although they use the expression "the spleen cleanses both blood and spirit."

One must remember that the medieval concept of the four body humors, viz., black bile (melancholy), red bile (blood), white bile (phlegma), and yellow bile, was that health consisted of a normal mixing of these four liquids within the body. If any one was present in excessive amounts or was deficient, illness resulted. Hence, the modern concept of the classic function of the spleen as a reticuloendothelial organ cannot possibly be equated with the "blood-cleansing properties" ascribed to the spleen by the sages of old.

The remedies for swelling of the spleen are obviously folk-remedies and have no scientific merit, as far as can be determined. The talmudic mention of surgical splenectomy with survival of the patients is indeed remarkable. One wonders how these operations were performed.

Ancient and medieval Jewish writings continue to be a rich source of medical material awaiting modern scholarship for understanding and interpretation.

REFERENCES

1. S. Muntner, ed., *Pirké Moshe Birefuah* (Jerusalem: Mossad Harav Kook, 1959), p. 34.
2. J. Preuss, *Biblisch-Talmudische Medizin* (Berlin: S. Karger, 1923), p. 122.
3. Op. cit. (n. 1 above), p. 269.
4. B. Moynihan, *The Spleen and Some of Its Diseases.* (Philadelphia: W. B. Saunders, 1921), p. 5.
5. R. Isaacs, "Hematology in the Bible and Talmud," *Medical Leaves* 1 (1937): 76–80.
6. I. Simon, *Asaph Ha Jehoudi, medecin et astrologue du moyen âge* (Paris: Librairie Lipschutz, 1933).
7. S. Muntner: "The Antiquity of Asaph the Physician and His Editorship of the Earliest Hebrew Book of Medicine," *Bulletin of The History of Medicine* 25 (1951): 101–31.
8. S. Muntner, ed., *R. Shabtai Donnolo: Medical Works and Contributions to the History of Jewish Medicine* (Jerusalem: Mossad Harav Kook, 1949).
9. H. Friedenwald, *The Jews and Medicine,* 2 vols. (Baltimore: Johns Hopkins Press, 1944).
10. F. Rosner & S. Muntner, *The Medical Aphorisms of Moses Maimonides* (New York: Bloch, 1973).

The Gallbladder

Introduction

The Hebrew word for bile or gall is *marah,* and the gallbladder is known as the *mererah, kis-hamarah,* or *shalphuḥit hamarah.* Preuss points out that the Mishnaic term *marah,* which literally means "bitter," is used to denote both bile and the gallbladder.[1] The biblical terms *merorah* and *mererah* only refer to the liquid bile. Scripture, as well as popular usage even today, considers bitterness, poison, and gall to be derived from the above term.

Maror means "bitter herbs," and the precise identification of these herbs is discussed at length in the Talmud (*Pesaḥim* 39a). One sage compares *maror* to the gall of the *kufia* fish (ibid.). The Hebrew word for "embittered" is derived from the same root as *maror* (Exod. 1:14).

In the Book of Job, Zophar's second speech asserts that man's ill-gotten gains soon turn to gall and his prosperity does not endure: "it is the gall of wasps within him" (Job 20:14). Zophar compares sin to a morsel which is delicious when savored, but when swallowed, soon turns to bitter and deadly poison. The Mishnah also uses the term *marah* to denote snake poison (*Terumot* 8:5). In antiquity, Pliny said: "it is the gall which constitutes the poison of asps."

The term *mar,* meaning "bitter," is found about twenty-five times in the Bible.[2] Additional meanings of "gall," both in English and in Hebrew, include anger and temerity. The expression "and cast bile among the students" is used as a figure of speech meaning: introduce a firm discipline among the students (*Ketubot* 103b).

In two separate discussions (*Abodah Zarah* 20b, *Kallah Rabbati,* chap. 3, fol. 52b), the Talmud describes the angel of death: from the sole of his feet to the top of his head, he is covered all over with eyes, his clothing is of fire, his feet are of fire, and on the fiery sword in his hand hangs a drop of gall. As the sick person beholds it, he trembles and opens his mouth in fright. The angel of death then drops the gall into the patient's

91

mouth and it is from this that he dies and from this that the corpse decomposes and from this that his face becomes sallow.

Diseases of the Gallbladder

R. Eleazar said that the text "And the Lord shall take away from thee all sickness [*mahalah*]" (Deut. 7:15) refers to diseases of the gall (*Baba Mezia* 107b). It was also taught that the word *mahalah,* meaning "sickness" (Exod. 23:25), refers to illness caused by the gall. Why is it called *mahalah?* Because it sickens the whole human body. Alternatively, it is so called because eighty-three illnesses are dependent upon the gall and the numerical value of *mahalah* amounts exactly to this. All of these illnesses can be counteracted by partaking in the morning of bread dipped in salt followed by a jugful of water (*Baba Mezia* 107b). A similar talmudic passage is found elsewhere (*Baba Kamma* 92b).

Water of palm trees is also recommended for dysfunction of the gall because such water is sharp and pierces the gall (*Shabbat* 110a, *J.T. Shabbat* 14:3).

R. Yohanan once fell ill and R. Hanina went to visit him. He said to him: "Are your sufferings welcome to you?" He replied: "Neither they nor their reward" (*Berakhot* 5b). The Talmud does not specify the type of illness or the symptoms of R. Yohanan. However, the Midrash states that the illness was gallstones:

> R. Yohanan had the misfortune to suffer from gallstones for three and a half years. Once R. Hanina went to visit him saying: "How do you feel?" He replied: "My sufferings are worse than I can bear. . . ." When the pain was greater than he could bear, R. Hanina used to go to him and utter an incantation which gave him relief. [*Song of Songs Rabbah* 2:16:2]

Function of the Gallbladder

The Midrash states that the gallbladder is the organ of jealousy.

> Ten things serve the soul: the gullet for food, the windpipe for the voice, the liver for anger, the lungs to absorb liquids, the first stomach to grind the food, the spleen for laughter, the maw for sleep, the gall for jealousy, the kidneys to discern, and the heart to decide; and the soul is above them all. [*Lev. Rabbah* 4:4]

Yeḥiel Michael Epstein, a nineteenth-century codifier of Jewish law, in his famous work entitled *Arukh Hashulḥan* (*Yoreh Deah* 42:1), explains that the function of the gallbladder is to assuage the heat of the liver and its anger. Without this, it would be impossible for a living being to survive because of the extreme heat of the liver. Therefore, if the gallbladder is pierced and all the bile is lost, the heat of the liver cannot be tolerated. For this reason, the Talmud and post-talmudic Hebrew writings (vide infra) consider a man or animal in whom the gallbladder is missing or was removed to be a *terefah*. There are some species of animals (Karo's code cites pigeons and turtle doves as examples—*Yoreh Deah* 42:8) which have no gallbladder at all. It was assumed that these species do not have much heat in the liver.

Terefah is the term applied throughout classic Hebrew sources to denote an animal afflicted with a fatal organic disease or fatal physical defect, thus rendering it unfit for human consumption. The Talmud states that a pierced gallbladder is one of eighteen things which render an animal *terefah* (Mishnah *Ḥullin* 3:1 and Gemara 42b). The list is much longer in the *Code* of Maimonides (*Hil. Shehitah* 10:9), amounting to seventy items, including perforation, absence, or duplication of the gallbladder (vide infra).

Perforation of the Gallbladder

Job speaks of a sword or arrow piercing the gallbladder (Job 20:25). Job further states that God "poureth out my gall upon the ground" (Job 16:13). The Talmud assumes that Job's gallbladder was perforated and this would constitute a fatal condition (*Ḥullin* 43a). Yet Job continued to live! The answer given in the Talmud is that the cure of Job was by divine intervention.

Another biblical account of a pierced gallbladder (2 Sam. 2:23) is related in the Talmud (*Sanhedrin* 49a), where the death of Asahel at the hands of Abner is described: "Abner, with the hinder end of the spear smote him at the waist" (Heb. *ḥomesh*, loins, waist; also means fifth), concerning which R. Yoḥanan said: "It was at the fifth rib, where the gallbladder and the liver are suspended."

In his legal code, Maimonides states that there are eleven organs of the body which, if perforated to their cavity to the slightest extent, render the animal *terefah*, to wit: the wide part of the gullet, the membrane of the brain, the heart with its aorta, the gallbladder, the tube of the liver, the stomach, the maw, the omasum, the second stomach, the small bowels, and the lung with its tube (*Hil. Shehitah* 6:1). Furthermore, based on a talmudic discussion (*Hullin* 43a), Maimonides rules that if the gallbladder is pierced, but the perforation is completely closed by the liver, the animal is permitted; if the perforation is not so closed, even if it lies quite close to the liver, it is *terefah* (*Hil. Shehitah* 6:6). An identical statement is found in Karo's code, *Shulhan Arukh* (*Yoreh Deah* 42:1).

Ectopic Location of the Gallbladder

Karo states that the gallbladder of a deer is located near its tail and not adjacent to the liver (*Shulhan Arukh, Yoreh Deah* 42:8). Epstein asserts that in birds the gallbladder is usually found among the intestines (*Arukh Hashulhan, Yoreh Deah* 42:3). He further describes an animal in which the gallbladder protruded between the ribs; the gallbladder was intact and fully expanded. This animal was not considered *terefah* (ibid. 42:5).

Absence of the Gallbladder

Most post-talmudic Hebrew writings consider an animal in which the gallbladder is congenitally missing or was surgically removed to· be *terefah*. Thus, Maimonides states:

> In the case of every organ (except the spleen) concerning which the sages have declared that when it is perforated to the smallest extent it renders the animal *terefah,* if that organ is missing in its entirety the animal is also *terefah*. It is immaterial whether the organ has been removed as a result of disease, or by hand, or whether the animal was born without that organ. Similarly, if it was born with two such organs it is likewise *terefah,* since duplication of an organ is in this respect considered equivalent to the complete removal of that organ.
>
> Therefore, absence of the gallbladder or the presence of two gallbladders renders the animal *terefah*. [*Hil. Shehitah* 6:20]

A similar rule is found in the codes of Karo, Epstein, R. Solomon ben Abraham Adret (known as *Rashbah*), Asheri, and *Tur,* among many others. Beginning in the fourteenth century, Jewish sources state that one should taste the area of the liver where the gallbladder is missing to ascertain the presence or absence of a bitter taste. A bitter taste would indicate that bile is being produced by the liver, which assuages its heat and hence the animal is not *terefah*. Some authorities require vertical and horizontal incisions into the liver prior to the tasting for the presence of bile.

Duplication of the Gallbladder

Maimonides (loc. cit.), Karo (loc. cit.), and Epstein (loc. cit.), among others, affirm that the presence of two gallbladders renders an animal *terefah* just as if the gallbladder is missing. The reason is that the second gallbladder may, in fact, be an abscess that resembles a gallbladder. Such an abscess is considered fatal. A variety of cases regarding duplication of the gallbladder are also discussed. For example, if there are two gallbladders, one on each side of the liver, and one duct brings bile to both, the animal is not *terefah*. If one of the two gallbladders swells with water or air when the other is filled with water or air, it is considered like one gallbladder. If there were originally two gallbladders and they became fused into a single sac, the animal is not *terefah*.

Foreign Objects in the Gallbladder

The following rule enunciated by Maimonides is reiterated by numerous subsequent writers:

> In case a kernel is found in the gallbladder, the rule is as follows: if it is shaped like a date stone which has no sharp point, the animal is permitted; if it has a sharp point like the kernel of an olive, it is forbidden since the stone must have pierced the gallbladder when it entered, and the reason that the perforation is no longer visible is that the top of the wound has become covered with a crust. [*Hil. Shehitah* 6:7]

The gloss by Moses Isserles in Karo's code quotes a variety of authorities, including Maimonides, R. Nissim Gerondi (known as *Ran*), R. Joel Sirkes (*Bah*), and R. Solomon Luria (*Maharshal*), all of whom agree that if a needle or thorn is found in the gallbladder of an animal, the animal is *terefah*. The reason, according to Epstein (*Arukh Hashulhan Yoreh Deah* 42:46), is because the needle may have entered the gallbladder through the trachea and thence severed the liver or an important vessel. Another reason is that it may have perforated the gallbladder itself thus rendering the animal *terefah*.

Concluding Note

The anatomy, functions, and a variety of abnormalities of the gallbladder are described in the Bible, Talmud, and Jewish codes. One must be cognizant of the fact that Jewish religious writings are not primarily textbooks of medicine. Most discussions concerning perforation, absence, duplication of, and foreign bodies in the gallbladder pertain to animals. Such discussions are primarily of Jewish legal importance to determine whether an animal with such a defect is capable of living or whether a fatal outcome can be expected. In the latter case, the animal is *terefah* and unfit for human consumption.

In man, absence or duplication of the gallbladder is compatible with normal life. One or more foreign bodies, such as gallstones, in this organ may produce symptoms of pain, chills, fever, nausea, vomiting, and even jaundice, if the common bile duct becomes obstructed; death is rarely a consequence of such a sequence of events, unless the gallbladder becomes gangrenous or perforates. Perforation of the gallbladder in man, from whatever cause, may produce peritonitis and death, if untreated. However, if correctly diagnosed and treated, this complication can be reversed, and the patient's health can be restored.

As far as can be determined, there is no scientific validity for the "partaking of bread dipped in salt followed by a jugful of water in the morning" (*Baba Meẓia* 107b) or the drinking of "water of palm trees" (*Shabbat* 110a) for human gallbladder dysfunction. Perhaps the talmudic sages are recommending a bland diet, which is certainly an appropriate approach by modern standards. By implication, the avoidance of foods which are harmful for gallbladder disease (e.g., fatty, fried, and spicy foods), seems to be the corollary of the sages' dietary recommendations.

That the gallbladder is the organ of jealousy is probably based on the ancient concept of gall meaning anger or bitterness. It seems inconceivable that eighty-three illnesses are dependent upon the gall (*Baba Meẓia* 107b). This talmudic statement is directly derived from the method of biblical interpretation called *Gematria,* which is the calculation of the numerical value of the Hebrew letters (i.e., *maḥalah* has the numerical value of eighty-three). Acrostics or abbreviated notations and anagrams are no doubt closely akin to *Gematria* and serve to complete that family of systematic Torah interpretation based upon the fathomless sanctity of the Hebrew alphabet.

REFERENCES

1. J. Preuss, *Biblisch-Talmudische Medizin* (Berlin: S. Karger, 1911), p. 111.
2. S. Mandelkorn, *Concordanzia Le'tanakh* (Tel Aviv: Shocken, 1959), pp. 702–3.

Part IV
Ethics and Prayers
for the Jewish Physician

Physician and Patient in Jewish Law

Introduction

Does man have a part in shaping his future? Is man's lifespan on this earth predetermined or can he alter the course of events during his stay in this world. The predetermination of a person's lifespan, or lack thereof, has been discussed at length by philosophers and theologians, including Jewish savants such as Rav Hai Gaon,[1] Rav Saadia Gaon,[2] and Moses Maimonides,[3] with most scholars concluding that the duration of life is not predetermined. What can man do, then, to lengthen his life? One way is to behave in the manner prescribed by God and receive as a reward "added years." Another way is to improve one's health so as to live longer. These alternatives pose the following questions: Does a sick person have the right to secure healing of his body, or should the illness run its course without interference? Should a person rely solely on Divine Providence for his physical as well as spiritual healing? These questions pertain to the patient. From the physician's standpoint, a similar series of questions can be raised. Is a mortal allowed by Jewish law to become a physician and practice medicine, or does such an act constitute "interference with the deliberate designs of Providence"?[4] Does a physician play God when he practices medicine? Part I of this chapter deals with the duties of the physician; Part II discusses the role of the patient.

In a midrashic story, R. Ishmael and R. Akiba were walking through the streets of Jerusalem and met a sick man.[5] The ill person said: "Masters, tell me how I can be cured." They answered: "Do thus and thus until you are cured." He said to them: "And who afflicted me?" "The Holy One, blessed be He," they replied. He said: "And you interfered in a matter which is not your concern. God afflicted me and you wish to heal?" The rabbis asked: "What is your vocation?" He responded: "I am a tiller of the soil. Here is the vine-cutter in my hand." They queried: "But who created the vineyard?" "The Holy One, blessed be He," he answered. "You interfered in the vineyard which is not yours? He created it and you

101

cut away its fruits?" they asked. "Do you not see the vine-cutter in my hands? Were I not to go out and plow and till and fertilize and weed, the vineyard would not produce any fruit," he explained. They said: "Fool, from your own work you have not learned what is written: 'As for man his days are as grass' (Ps. 103:15). Just as the tree, if not weeded, fertilized, and ploughed will not grow and bring forth its fruits . . . so it is with the human body. The fertilizer is the medicine and the healing means, and the tiller of the earth is the physician."

PART I

"For I Am the Lord That Healeth Thee"

The extreme viewpoint, namely, total rejection of the permissiblity of human healing, was espoused by the Karaites,* who vehemently objected to medicine and physicians.[4] They relied entirely on prayer for their healing, as "Man must ever pray not to become ill for if he becomes so, it is demanded of him to show merit in order to be healed" (*Shabbat* 32a). The Karaites must further have adhered to the literal interpretation of the following biblical phrase: "And he said: if thou wilt diligently hearken to the voice of the Lord, thy God and wilt do that which is right in His eyes, and wilt give ear to His commandments and keep all His statutes, I will put none of the diseases upon thee, which I have put upon the Egyptians, for I am the Lord that healeth thee" (Exod. 16:26).

The last phrase, "for I am the Lord that healeth thee," literally translated from the original Hebrew means "for I am the Lord thy physician." In fact, R. Abraham Ibn Ezra, in his commentary, states that just as God "healed" the undrinkable waters at Marah for the Israelites, so too, God will remove or heal all plagues on the earth and there will be no need for physicians. This, perhaps, is the basis for the Karaitic objection to human healing and medicine.

Alternate interpretations of the above scriptural verse are possible. The Talmud asks, If we are told that God "will put none of the diseases upon thee," what need is there for a cure (*Sanhedrin* 101a)? R. Yoḥanan answers that the verse means as follows: "If thou wilt harken [to the voice of the Lord], I will not bring disease upon thee, but if thou wilt not, I will; yet even so, 'I am the Lord that healeth thee'." R. Barukh

---

*An eighth-century sect that opposed the rabbinic interpretation of Scripture.

Halevi Epstein, in his *Torah Temimah,* explains that the intent of this biblical phrase is to show that the illness of the Egyptians was incurable, as it is written: "the boil of Egypt . . . wherefrom one cannot be healed" (Deut. 28:27). However, afflictions of the Israelites can be healed by God.

Rashi explains "for I am the Lord that healeth thee" to mean that God teaches the laws of the Torah in order to save man from these diseases. Rashi uses the analogy of a physician who says to his patient not to eat such and such a food lest it bring him into danger from disease. So too, it is stated, continues Rashi, obedience to God "will be health to thy body and marrow to thy bones" (Prov. 3:8). In a similar vein, the extra-talmudic collection of biblical interpretation known as the *Mekhilta* asserts that the words of Torah are life as well as health, as it is written: "For they are life unto those that find them and health to all their flesh" (Prov. 4:22). Other commentators (*Siftei Ḥakhamim,* and R. Samson Raphael Hirsch among others) extend this thought by propounding that the Divine Law restores health, and certainly prevents illness from occurring, thus serving as preventive medicine against all physical and social evil.

R. Jacob ben Asher, known as the *Ba'al Haturim,* states that heavenly cure comes easily whereas earthly or man-made cures come with difficulty. Finally, R. Meir Leib ben Yeḥiel Michael, known as *Malbim,* in his commentary on the phrase "for I am the Lord that healeth thee," speaks of mental illness. He asserts that the laws of the Torah were given by God to Israel not like a master ordering his slave but like a physician ordering his patient. In the former case, the master benefits, not the slave. In the latter case, the patient and not the physician is healed from illness. Similarly, God's statutes are for our benefit, not His.

The multitude of interpretations of the scriptural phrase "for I am the Lord that healeth thee" indicates that this verse is not to be understood literally. There is no prohibition inherent in this verse against a mortal becoming a physician and healing the sick. In fact, specific permissibility and sanction for the physician to practice medicine is given in the Torah as described below. The physician, however, must always recognize that God is the true healer of the sick and that a doctor is only an instrument of God in the ministrations to the sick.

"And Heal He Shall Heal"

Compensation for personal injuries is described in the Bible in the following verses: "And if men quarrel and one smiteth the other with a stone or with his fist and he die not, but has to keep in bed. . . . he must pay the loss entailed by absence from work and cause him to be thoroughly healed" (Exod. 21:14–20).

The last phrase translated literally reads, "and heal he shall heal." The Talmud interprets this duplicate mention of healing as intended to teach us that authorization was granted by God to the physician to heal (*Baba Kamma* 85a). Rashi extends the words of the Talmud when he asserts, "lest it be said that God smites and man heals." Thus he implies that a need exists for specific biblical sanctioning of human healing.

Many Bible commentators, including Hirsch and Epstein (*Torah Temimah*) echo the above talmudic teaching. That is, by the insistence or emphasis expressed in the double wording, the Torah uses the opportunity to oppose the erroneous idea that having recourse to medical aid shows lack of trust and confidence in divine assistance. The Torah takes it for granted that medical therapy is used and actually demands it.

Other commentaries on the scriptural phrase "and heal he shall heal," including those of the *Mekhilta* and R. Meir Leib ben Yehiel Michael (*Malbim*), explain that the repetition of the word "heal" means that the patient must be repeatedly healed if the illness or injury recurred or became aggravated. In discussing the above case concerning personal injury, the Talmud also requires that where ulcers have grown on account of the wound and the wound breaks open again, the offender would still be liable to heal it (i.e., pay the medical expenses) even repeatedly (*Baba Kamma* 85a).

The most popular interpretation of "and heal he shall heal" (Rashi, *Targum Onkelos,* Talmud *Baba Kamma* 85a, and others) is that compensation for the injury must be paid by the offender. Such compensation consists of five items: the physician's fees and medical bills, payment for loss of time from work, the shame incurred by disfigurement, the pain suffered, and the physical damage produced. All agree, however, that human healing is sanctioned by this phrase of the Bible, if not explicitly, at least implicitly.

R. Abraham Ibn Ezra seems to place a restriction on the permissibility for a physician to heal when he states that only external wounds can be healed by man. Internal wounds or ailments should be left to God. However, there is nearly universal acceptance that the sanctioning to the physician to heal is all-inclusive, encompassing all internal and external physical and mental illness. In fact, a commentary on the Talmud by *Tosafot* specifically states that not only is it permitted to heal man-induced wounds but even heavenly-induced sicknesses and afflictions, *i.e.,* all ill-nesses (*Baba Kamma* 85a).

"And Thou Shalt Restore It to Him"

The above scriptural phrase refers to the restoration of lost property. Moses Maimonides says that this law also includes the restoration of the health of one's fellowman, if he has lost it. Thus, Maimonides derives the biblical sanction for human healing from a different phrase in the Scriptures than most other Jewish savants. Epstein (*Torah Temimah*), in two separate places (Deut. 22:2, Exod. 21:19), asks why Maimonides totally omits the phrase "and heal he shall heal" as a warrant for the physician to heal. Epstein offers an answer to his own question when he states that the verse in Exodus only grants permission for a physician to heal, whereas "and thou shalt restore it to him" makes it obligatory.

Maimonides' reasoning is probably based upon a key passage in the Talmud (*Sanhedrin* 73a) where it states: "whence do we know that one must save his neighbor from the loss of himself? From the verse 'and thou shalt restore it to him.' " Thus, not only if one is sick is a physician required but also if someone is attempting suicide, one must provide psychiatric or other competent assistance to save the person's life and health. Maimonides' major pronouncement on this matter is found in his *Commentary on the Mishnah* (*Nedarim* 4:4). He states: "It is obligatory from the Torah for the physician to heal the sick and this is included in the explanation of the scriptural phrase 'and thou shalt restore it to him,' meaning to heal his body."

"Neither Shalt Thou Stand Idly by the Blood of Thy Neighbor"

Duties toward our fellowmen are described in Leviticus 19:11–16. According to Hertz, these precepts restate the fundamental rules of life in human society that are contained in the Second Tablet of the Decalogue.[6] These moral principles were expounded by the sages and applied to every phase of civil and criminal law. One example cited in the Talmud is:

> Whence do we know that if a man sees his neighbor drowning or mauled by beasts or attacked by robbers, that he is bound to save him? From the verse "thou shalt not stand idly by the blood of thy neighbor." [*Sanhedrin* 73a]

Maimonides codifies the above Talmudic passage in his *Mishneh Torah* where he states:

> Whoever is able to save another and does not save him transgresses the commandment "neither shalt thou stand idly by the blood of thy neighbor" [Lev. 19:16]. Similarly, if one sees another drowning in the sea, or being attacked by bandits or being attacked by a wild animal and is able to rescue him . . . and does not rescue him . . . he transgresses the injunction "neither shalt thou stand idly by the blood of thy neighbor." [*Hil. Rozeiah* 1:14]

Such a case of drowning in the sea is considered as loss of one's body, and therefore, if one is obligated to save a whole body, one must certainly cure disease, which usually afflicts only one part of the body.

Code of Jewish Law and Medical Practice

From the discussion so far, it seems evident that permission for the physician to heal is granted in the Torah from the phrase "and heal he shall heal." Some scholars, notably Maimonides, claim that healing the sick is not only allowed but is actually obligatory. R. Joseph Karo, in his code of Jewish law (*Shulhan Arukh*) combines both thoughts: "The Torah gave permission to the physician to heal; moreover this is a religious precept and it is included in the category of saving life; and if he withholds his services, it is considered as shedding blood" (*Yoreh Deah* 336).

R. David ben Shmuel Halevi, known as *Taz,* asks: If it is a religious precept to heal, why did the Torah have to grant specific permission for the physician to do so? His answer is that true healing lies only with God, but God gives the physician the wherewithal to heal by earthly or natural means. Once permission has been granted, then it is a commandment on the physician to heal. A similar thought is expressed by R. Abraham Maskil Le'aytan, known as *Yad Abraham,* who states that permission is only granted if the physician heals with his heart toward heaven.

R. Shabtai ben Meir HaKohen, author of *Siftei Kohen,* offers an alternate reason for the Torah granting permission to heal—that is, in order to avoid the physician saying, "Who needs this anguish? If I err, I will be considered as having spilled blood unintentionally." In a similar vein, Karo, in his *Bet Yoseph* commentary on Jacob ben Asher's code of Jewish law, called the *Tur* (*Yoreh Deah* 336), quotes Nahmanides, himself a physician, who says that without the warrant to treat, physicians might hesitate to treat patients for fear of fatal consequences "in that there is an element of danger in every medical procedure; that which heals one may kill another."

The Jewish attitude toward the physician and his medical art, as well as the patient's responsibility to seek medical aid is beautifully depicted by Ben-Sira (Eccles. 38), who perceived in the physician an instrument of Providence:

> Honor a physician before need of him
> Him also hath God apportioned.
> From God a physician getteth wisdom
> And from a king he shall receive gifts.
> The skill of a phsyician shall lift up his head
> And he shall stand before nobles
> God bringeth out medicines from the earth
> And let a prudent man not refuse them.
> Was not water made sweet with wood
> For to acquaint every man with His power?
> And He gave man understanding
> To glory in His might.
> By them doth the physician assuage pain
> And likewise the apothecary maketh a confection,
> That His work may not fail
> Nor health from among the sons of men.
> My son, in sickness be not negligent
> Pray unto God, for He will heal.
> Flee from iniquity, and from respect of persons
> And from all transgressions cleanse thy heart.
> Offer a sweet savor as a memorial
> And fatness estimated according to thy substance.
> And to the physician also give a place
> And he shall not remove, for there is need of him likewise,
> For there is a time when in his hand is good success.
> For he too will supplicate unto God
> That He will prosper to him the treatment
> And the healing, for the sake of his living.
> He that sinneth against his Maker
> Will behave himself proudly against a physician.[7]

PART II

From the three biblical citations above and from Part I, it is perfectly clear that the Torah gave specific sanction to the physician to heal and, according to some authorities, made it obligatory upon him to provide his medical skills to cure disease. It is not evident from the above, however, that the patient is permitted by Jewish law to seek human healing. Is an individual who asks a physician to treat him denying Divine Providence? Is such an individual transgressing the biblical teaching "For I am the Lord that healeth thee" (Exod. 15:26)? Is a person's illness an affliction by God that serves as punishment for wrongdoing? And does such a person remove his atonement for sin by not accepting the suffering imposed by divine judgment? Should there be, or is there, a distinction between heavenly afflictions and man-induced sickness in regard to the patient seeking medical aid? How does one define heavenly illness? What is cancer—God-induced (i.e., genetic) or man-induced (i.e., drugs, viruses, irradiation), or both? The number of such questions is endless, and lengthy essays could be written attempting to analyze them.

The two sides of the question are illustrated in the Talmud, where it states that on going to be phlebotomized, a person should recite the following prayer:

> May it be Thy will, O Lord my God, that this operation may be a cure for me and mayest Thou heal me for Thou art a faithful healing God and Thy healing is sure since men have no power to heal but this is a habit with them. [*Berakhot* 60a]

From this passage it would appear that conflicting viewpoints could emerge. The fact that the Talmud describes a patient going to a physician for an operative procedure can be interpreted to mean that certainly this is permissible. The only requirement is for the patient to recognize that the physician is acting as an agent of the Divine Healer. In fact, Rashi explains the talmudic passage to mean that the afflicted person should have prayed for heavenly intervention rather than human healing and perhaps the bloodletting might not have been necessary.

And yet the talmudic statement continues with an assertion by Abaye to the effect that a patient should not utter such a prayer because, in fact, the Torah gave specific consent for human healing in the phrase "and heal he shall heal." Therefore, says Abaye, a patient should seek the help of a physician. A similar but not identical prayer is found in the codes of Jewish law of Maimonides (*Hil. Berakhot* 10:21) and Joseph Karo (*Shulḥan Arukh Oraḥ Ḥayyim,* 230:4).

A rather negative attitude to the question of the patient obtaining medical assistance is taken by Naḥmanides, who, in his commentary on the scriptural phrase "and My soul shall not abhor you" (Lev. 26:11), states that God will remove sickness from among the Israelites, as He promised "for I am the Lord that healeth thee" (Exod. 15:26). The righteous, continues Naḥmanides, during the epochs of prophecy, even if they sinned and became ill, did not seek out physicians, only prophets. What, therefore, is the need for physicians if God promised to remove all sickness from man? To advise which foods and beverages to avoid in order not to get sick, answers Naḥmanides, himself a physician. He explains the phrase "and heal he shall heal" to mean that the physician is allowed to practice medicine but the patient may not seek his healing, but must turn to Divine Providence. Only people who do not believe in the healing powers of God turn to physicians for their cure, and for such individuals the Torah sanctions the physician to heal. The latter should not withhold his healing skills for fear lest the patient die under his care nor should he say that God alone heals.

Other than the Karaites, who strongly objected to physicians and medicines, Naḥmanides seems to stand alone in his apparent prohibition for patients to seek medical aid. It is possible that he refers only to the righteous, who are free of illness because of their piety and who do not require human healing. Perhaps the general populace, however, even devout believers in God, are allowed to seek human healing. Such an interpretation of Naḥmanides' discussion is found in the commentary of R. David ben Shmuel Halevi, in his commentary *Turei Zahav* on Karo's code (*Yoreh Deah* 336:1). It may also be that Naḥmanides refers only to heavenly illnesses, but for man-induced wounds and sicknesses healing may be sought.

Karo does not seem to make such a distinction when he states that "He who fasts and is able to tolerate the fast is called holy; but if not, such as if he is not healthy and strong, he is called a sinner" (*Oraḥ Ḥayyim* 571). It appears evident from this quotation that it is an obligation upon man to take all possible action to insure a healthy body, and this includes the services of a physician. A less likely interpretation of Karo's statement is that if a person is able to tolerate sickness or pain, just as in the case of the fast, he should do so and not seek medical aid.

Another source that can be interpreted either in support of or against the permissibility for a patient to obtain human healing is the following story related in the Talmud (*Berakhot* 5b): R. Yoḥanan once fell ill and R. Ḥanina went to visit him, saying: "Are your sufferings welcome to you?" R. Yoḥanan replied: "Neither they nor their reward," implying that one who lovingly accepts sufferings in this world will be greatly compensated in the world to come. R. Ḥanina then said: "Give me your hand," which R. Yoḥanan did, and he cured him. Why could not R. Yoḥanan cure himself? asks the Talmud. The reply is, "Because the prisoner cannot free himself from jail," meaning the patient cannot cure himself. On the one hand, we see that R. Yoḥanan required healing from R. Ḥanina. On the other hand, R. Ḥanina did not use human healing, as he cured R. Yoḥanan by touching the latter's hand.

The strongest evidence from Jewish sources that gives the patient permission to seek treatment from a physician is found in Maimonides' *Mishneh Torah.* He states that a person should "set his heart that his body be healthy and strong in order that his soul be upright to know the Lord. For it is impossible for man to understand and comprehend the wisdoms [of the world] if he is hungry and ailing or if one of his limbs is aching" (*Hil. Deot* 3:3). He also recommends (ibid. 4:23), as does the Talmud (*Sanhedrin* 17b), that no wise person should reside in a city that does not possess a physician. Maimonides' position is further stated as follows: "Since when the body is healthy and sound [one treads in] the ways of the Lord, it being impossible to understand or know anything of the knowledge of the Creator when one is sick, it is obligatory upon man to avoid things which are detrimental to the body and acclimate himself to things which heal and fortify it" (ibid., 4:1). An English translation of this entire chapter in Maimonides' code, which deals with hygienic principles, is available for the interested reader (*Journal of the American Medical Association* 194 [Dec. 27, 1965]: 1352–54).

There are numerous talmudic citations which support the position that not only allows but requires the patient to seek medical aid when sick. We are told that he who is in pain should go to a physician (*Baba Kamma* 46b). Further, if one is bitten by a snake, one may call a physician even if it means desecrating the Sabbath, because all restrictions are set aside in the case of possible danger to human life (*Yoma* 83b). Similarly, if one's eye becomes afflicted on the Sabbath, one may prepare and apply medication thereto, even on the Sabbath (*Abodah Zorah* 28b). When R. Judah the Prince, compiler of the Mishnah, contracted an eye disease, his physician, Samuel Yarḥina'ah, cured it by placing a vial of chemicals under the rabbi's pillow so that the powerful vapors would penetrate the eye (*Baba Meẓia* 85b). The Talmud also speaks of another physician curing a patient (*Ketubot* 75a). Finally, in a case of bodily injury where the offender says to the victim that he will bring a physician who will heal for no fee, the victim can object and say "a physician who heals for nothing is worth nothing" (*Baba Kamma* 85a). If the offender offers to bring a physician from far away, the victim may say, "My eye will be blind before he arrives." If the injured person says to the offender, "Give me the money and I will cure myself," the latter can retort, "You might neglect yourself and remain a cripple." From these and other talmudic passages, it seems evident that an individual is undoubtedly permitted and probably required to seek medical attention when he is ill.

Further support for this contention is mentioned by the present Chief Rabbi of Great Britain, Immanuel Jakobovits, who cites the fifteenth-century philosopher Isaac Arama's work, *Akedat Yiẓhak*. Arama proves from biblical narratives, such as the Patriarchs' efforts to save themselves when in danger, and legislation, such as the duty to construct parapets around roofs for the prevention of accidents (Deut. 22:8), that man must not rely on miracles or Providence alone, but must himself do whatever he can to maintain his life and health.

R. Ḥayyim Azulai, a commentator on Karo's code of Jewish law, writing under the pen name of *Birkei Yoseph,* summarized Jewish thought and practice relating to our question. His views are cited in *Jewish Medical Ethics* as follows:

> Nowadays one must not rely on miracles, and the sick man is in duty bound to conduct himself in accordance with the natural order by calling on a physician to heal him. In fact, to depart from the general practice by claiming greater merit than the many saints [in previous] generations, who were cured by physicians, is almost sinful on account of both the implied arrogance and the reliance on miracles when there is danger to life. . . . Hence, one should adopt the ways of all men and be healed by physicians . . .[4]

One might arrive at the same conclusion if one were to literally interpret the Pentateuchal admonition "Take ye therefore good heed unto yourselves" (Deut. 4:15).

REFERENCES

1. D. Kaufmann, "Ein Responsum des Gaons R. Haya uber Gottes Vorher-
   wissen und die Dauer des Menschlichen Lebens," Leipzig. *Zeitschr. Deutsche
   Morgenlandische Gesellschaft,* 1895, ᴅ9:73–84.
2. G. Weil, *Maimonides Uber die Lebensdauer* (Basel: S. Karger, 1953).
3. F. Rosner, "Moses Maimonides' Responsum on Longevity," *Geriatrics* 23
   (1968): 170–78.
4. I. Jakobovits, *Jewish Medical Ethics* (New York: Bloch, 1959), pp. 2–6.
5. J. D. Eisenstein, *Oẓar Midrashim* (New York, 1915), 2:580–81.
6. J. H. Hertz, *The Pentateuch and Haftorahs,* 2d e. (London: Soncino Press,
   1962), pp. 499–501.
7. H. Friedenwald, *The Jews and Medicine* (Baltimore: Johns Hopkins Press,
   1944), 1:6–7.

Visiting the Sick

(*Bikkur Ḥolim*)

Introduction

Visiting the sick in Judaism is not just the paying of a social call. Historically, there were no hospitals in biblical and talmudic times, and hence a person who visited a sick friend or relative had to provide for the physical and emotional needs of the patient.

In addition to cheering the patient up and encouraging him to get better, the visitor would cook and clean and perform other tasks for the patient, as needed. Furthermore, Jewish law requires that the visitor pray for the recovery of the patient, either in the latter's presence or not. These three activities are all essential components of what is known as *bikkur ḥolim,* or visiting the sick, and are applicable to this very day.

History and Importance of Bikkur Ḥolim

It is a holy duty (*mizvah*) incumbent upon everyone to visit the sick. God visits the sick and we must emulate Him. How do we know this? Scriptures states: "Ye shall walk after the Lord your God" (Deut. 13:5). Is it possible to walk after God? The answer is that we should try to emulate His attributes. Just as He visited the sick, so, too, we should visit the sick (*Sotah* 14a). When did God visit the sick? He visited the Patriarch Abraham after the latter's circumcision, as it is written: "and the Lord appeared unto him" (Gen. 18:1). God blesses bridegrooms, adorns brides, visits the sick, buries the dead, and recites the blessing for mourners (*Gen. Rabbah* 8:13). It is also written: "and thou shalt show them the way they must walk" (Exod. 18:20), which the sages interpret to refer to the duty of visiting the sick (*Baba Kamma* 100a, *Baba Meẓia* 30b). There is a difference of opinion among the sages as to whether this *mizvah* is of biblical or rabbinic origin.

Another example in the Bible of visiting the sick is when the prophet Isaiah visited King Hezekiah when the latter was ill (Isa. 38:1). The

113

conversation between the two is vividly described in the Talmud (*Bera-khot* 10a) and concerns the fact that Hezekiah had never married and was admonished by Isaiah for not having fulfilled the commandment of procreation. The end of the story is a happy one in that Hezekiah did penitence and was cured of his illness and lived another fifteen years.

Numerous instances of sages visiting their sick colleagues are found in the Talmud. R. Yosei ben Kisma was ill and R. Ḥanina ben Teradion went to visit him (*Abodah Zarah* 18a). R. Yannai ben Ishmael was sick and R. Ishmael ben Zirud and others called to enquire about him (ibid. 30a). Comforting mourners, visiting the sick, and the practice of loving-kindness bring welfare into the world (*Abot de Rabbi Natan* 30:1).

The importance of visiting the sick is further underscored by the following talmudic passage:

> R. Ḥelbo once fell ill. Thereupon R. Kahana went and proclaimed: "R. Ḥelbo is sick." But none visited him. He rebuked them [i.e., the sages], saying: "Did it not once happen that one of R. Akiba's disciples fell sick and the sages did not visit him?" So R. Akiba himself entered [the disciple's house] to visit him and, because they swept and sprinkled the grounds before him [Asheri: R. Akiba, finding the room neglected, gave the necessary orders], he recovered. "My master," said the disciple, "you have revived me." Whereupon, R. Akiba propounded: He who does not visit the sick is like a shedder of blood. [*Nedarim* 40a]

Thus, helping to take care of the needs of a sick patient may save his life or certainly contribute to the restoration of his health. The concept of being guilty of shedding blood if one does not help one's ill fellowman is based on the biblical injunction: "neither shalt thou stand idly by the blood of thy neighbor" (Lev. 19:16). Maimonides codifies the talmudic passage (*Sanhedrin* 73a) which requires one to save one's fellowman if one can as follows:

> Whoever is able to save another, and does not save him, transgresses the commandment "neither shalt thou stand idly by thy neighbor." Similarly, if one sees another drowning in the sea, or being attacked by bandits or by a wild animal and is able to rescue him . . . and does not rescue him . . . transgresses the injunction "neither shalt thou stand idly by the blood of thy neighbor." [*Hil. Roẓeiaḥ* 1:14]

In addition to taking care of the physical and emotional needs of the patient, the second major purpose of visiting the sick is for the caller to pray in the patient's behalf. If one visits the sick on the Sabbath, one should say: "It is the Sabbath, when one must not cry out, and recovery will come soon" (*Shabbat* 12a). Others say: "May the Sabbath have compassion" (ibid.). Yet others say: "May God have compassion upon you and upon the sick of Israel" (ibid. 12b). Today, we recite special prayers for the sick in the synagogue and even give the patient an additional name as a supplication to God to heal him.

When not in the patient's presence, one should only pray in Hebrew since the ministering angels only understand Hebrew. In the patient's presence, one can pray in any language since God Himself ministers to the sick (Ps. 41:4), and the Divine Presence (*shekhinah*) rests upon the patient's bed (ibid.). For the same reason, one should not sit on the patient's bed.

Although the above may sound primitive and even mythical, we have here reflected the desire by the sages to emphasize the closeness of God to the patient, a point which is brought home by necessitating Hebrew in other situations while allowing any language in the presence of the patient.

Rab says: "He who visits the sick will be delivered from the punishments of Gehenna" (*Nedarim* 40a). Visits to the sick are considered among the most meritorious acts of true charity. The Talmud lists visiting the sick among those things the fruit of which man eats in this world while the principal remains for him for the world to come (*Shabbat* 127a). For other good deeds, the reward is only in the world to come. The importance of this obligation is recited daily in the morning prayers by observant Jews.

Procedures Regarding Bikkur Ḥolim

There is no limit to the visiting of the sick (*Nedarim* 39b). R. Joseph says this means that the reward is unlimited. Abaye says it means that even a prominent person must visit a simple person. Raba says it means that there is no limit to the frequency of such visits, even one hundred a day (ibid.). For the sake of good neighborly relations, one should also visit non-Jewish patients.

One talmudic sage asserts that he who visits the sick takes away one-sixtieth of his illness. If so, let sixty people visit and the patient will be cured? The answer is that each visitor removes one-sixtieth of the remaining illness (ibid.). R. Huna says, a visitor only reduces the patient's illness by one-sixtieth if he loves the patient like himself (*Lev. Rabbah* 34:1). Some sages allow even an enemy to visit his sick neighbor. Others feel it might cause anguish to the patient and hence should be avoided. Yet others state that an enemy may visit if he secures permission in advance from the sick patient.

One should not receive financial remuneration for visiting the sick (*Nedarim* 39a) either because he is demeaning the visit (*Asheri,* loc. cit.) or because one should not receive payment for fulfilling a divine commandment (*Tosafot,* loc. cit.).

One should not visit the sick during the first three hours or the last three hours of the day lest he misjudge the patient's status and not pray for him and not care for him. In the morning, the patient looks better and feels better than he really is, and in the evening the reverse is true (*Nedarim* 40a). The modern physician is well aware of the accuracy of this statement. Fever is usually lower in the morning and higher in the evening in a patient with a febrile illness.

One should not visit patients with illnesses of the bowel (diarrhea), eye diseases, or headaches; the first because of embarrassment and the latter two because speech is harmful to them (ibid. 41a). One can readily understand that a patient with diarrhea might be embarrassed in the presence of a visitor. There seems to be no rational medical reason, however, why speech is harmful to patients with eye diseases or headaches. Perhaps such patients would rather lie quietly without speaking because speech is uncomfortable for them, but there is no known medical detriment to their speaking, if they so desire. Mar Samuel said that one should not visit a patient until his fever has subsided (ibid.). Close relatives and friends usually visit first, and more distant relatives and acquaintances only visit after three days. If the illness occurred suddenly, all may visit simultaneously (J.T. *Peah* 3:17).

There is a difference of opinion among the codes of Jewish law and rabbinic responsa as to the obligation of visiting people ill with contagious diseases. The prevailing view is that no one is obligated to endanger his life to fulfill the precept of visiting the sick. Today, one can protect oneself from contracting a contagious disease by avoiding direct contact with the patient and by taking other precautionary steps as dictated by the medical circumstances.

R. Ḥanina once fell ill. R. Yoḥanan went to visit him. He said: "How do you feel?" He replied: "How grievous are my sufferings"! He said: "But surely the reward for them is also great!" He said: "I want neither them nor their reward!" (*Song of Songs Rabbah* 2:16:2).

R. Simeon ben Yoḥai used to visit the sick. He once met a man who was swollen and afflicted with intestinal disease uttering blasphemies against God. Said R. Simeon: "Worthless one! Pray rather for mercy for yourself." Said the patient: "May God remove these sufferings from me and place them on you . . ." (*Abot de Rabbi Natan* 4:1).

Recovery from Illness

R. Zera was once ill. R. Abbahu went to visit him and made a vow saying: "If R. Zera recovers I will make a feast for the rabbis." He recovered, so he made a feast (*Berakhot* 46a).

When a person recovers from a serious illness, he has to recite a special prayer of thanksgiving (*birkhat ha-gomel*). R. Judah was ill and recovered. R. Ḥanna of Baghdad and other sages went to visit him. They said: "Blessed is God, who gave you back to us." R. Judah answered "amen" and was absolved of reciting the *birkhat ha-gomel* (*Berakhot* 54b).

There may not be a precise non-Jewish equivalent of the *birkhat ha-gomel* but it seems logical that any God-fearing person, Jew or non-Jew, would offer some kind of thanks to the Lord upon recovering from a serious illness or operation. The format of the thanks, however, may vary from the recitation of a prayer of thanksgiving to the donation of money to charity.

Bikkur Ḥolim Societies

Already in the Bible, we find municipally regulated care of the poor whereby the provision for the needy is not left to the "good hearts" of the wealthy. This public care of the poor seems to have been built into a firm legal system in the Talmud. In many times, already during the Temple, there existed a town brotherhood, known as *hever ha'ir*, whose function was to collect and distribute funds to the poor. Brotherhoods (or societies) also concerned themselves with other charitable deeds, mainly the burial of the dead and the visiting of the sick. Such a *haberutha* is explicitly mentioned in the Talmud (*Moed Katan* 27b). It is also related that Abimi, a member of a sick-visiting society, used to visit the sick (*Gen. Rabbah* 13:16).

There are many *bikkur ḥolim* societies in existence today. Members of such societies visit not only sick relatives and friends but all the Jewish patients to offer comfort and encouragement. These societies perform an extremely useful and helpful function for the sick and thereby fulfill not only the Jewish legal obligation of visiting the sick, but also perform highly charitable and meritorious deeds. The history of these *bikkur ḥolim* societies has regretfully not yet been written.

REFERENCES

1. J. Preuss, *Biblisch-Talmudische Medizin*. (Berlin: S. Karger, 1911), pp. 515–19.
2. I. Jakobovits, *Jewish Medical Ethics* (New York: Bloch, 1959), pp. 106–9.
3. S. J. Zevin, *Talmudic Encyclopedia* [Hebr.] (Jerusalem, 1956) 4:158–62.

The Oath of Asaph

The oldest Hebrew medical manuscript is a work ascribed to Asaph Judaeus or Asaph ben Berakhiah, an ancient Jewish physician. Although Asaph is described under various names, including Asaph HaRofe (Asaph the physician), Asaph He Ḥakam (Asaph the wise man), Asaph HaYarḥoni (Asaph the Astronomer), and Asaph HaYehudi (Asaph the Jew), little is known about his life. In fact the major general medical historical texts, including Diepgen, Castiglioni, Haeser, Neuberger, Pagel, Puschmann Sprengel, and many others, make no mention of Asaph whatsoever. Historical dictionaries of medicine, such as Eloy's and Dezeimeri's four- and seven-volume works, respectively, omit any reference to Asaph or his medical writing.

In Garrison's *History of Medicine,* a single sentence concerning Asaph is recorded: "Perhaps the oldest Hebrew medical text written in Asia is a book of remedies by Asaf Judaeus, a Mesopotamian physician of the seventh century." [1]

The statement by George Sarton that Asaph "flourished in the ninth or tenth century" [2] is probably incorrect, since the *Book of Asaph* does not show the slightest influence of Arabic medicine that one would have expected had he lived during or after the conquest of the East by Islam in the seventh century. In addition, Asaph's book was already introduced into France early in the ninth century, as described below.

Although the exact period of the life of Asaph cannot be stated with certainty, it seems likely that he lived no earlier than the third century and not later than the seventh. This is based on the character of the teaching in the book, the purity of the Hebrew language, the description of the divisions of the hours of day and night and the blowing of the winds, the rendering of synonyms in the Persian language, the mention of certain medical authorities (such as Galen, Hippocrates, Rufus, and Dioscorides), the use of weights and measures peculiar to the period, the enumeration of the Hebrew months beginning with Tishri (approximately equivalent to October), not with Nissan (April), as usual later on, and many other similar instances more fully described elsewhere.[3]

In addition to the tradition of ancient Hebrew medicine, the book contains passages of Babylonian, Egyptian, Persian, and Indian medicine, as well as sections demonstrating the influence of the various schools of Greek medicine. In the *Book of Asaph* are the most ancient translations ever made from a Greek original into Hebrew, such as passages from the *Aphorisms* of Hippocrates, the *Prognosticon,* and the books of Rufus, Galen, and Dioscorides. No Arabic physician or remedy is mentioned anywhere in the book.

The book is also rich in tales of folklore. A rendition of the entire work from the available manuscripts remains a desideratum of the history of medicine since, with the exception of the introduction, the *Book of Asaph* has never been published in its entirety. Approximately fifteen more or less complete manuscripts scattered throughout the world comprise the total extant collection of this work. These include the manuscripts in Munich, Berlin, Oxford, Florence, British Museum, Paris, Leyden, Basel, Jerusalem (Friedenwald), and Leningrad. These have been studied and commented upon by Steinschneider, who used mainly the Munich Manuscript no. 231, which is the best and most complete of all.[4]

More recently Venetianer published an extensive monograph in German on the *Book of Asaph,* describing and translating relatively small sections of it.[5] To date it is the most definitive work available. In 1933, Isidore Simon published a thesis on Asaph in which he reiterated much of Venetianer's earlier work.[6] An introduction to the book of Asaph was published in 1957, with the hope of editing and publishing the entire work in the near future.[7]

There is an excellent brief description of Asaph and his book in Laignel-Lavastine's three-volume medical history text.[8] Translated from the French, it reads as follows:

> A clinician, Asaph the Jew is the author of the first book on medicine written in Hebrew [v. thesis of I. Simon, Paris 1933]. Originally from Palestine, Asaph taught medicine in one of the medical schools in Syria with his collaborators Yehuda and Yohanan HaYarhoni.
>
> He wrote a *Treatise on Drugs* inspired by Dioscorides in which he gives us a detailed description of more than one hundred plants. Guided by the works of Galen, he studied fevers, the pulse and

[therapeutic] regimens. His aphorisms, his practice of uroscopy and his prognostics were inspired by Hippocrates. Finding insufficient the terminology that he extracted from sources of the medical [parts of the] Talmud, he added neologisms taken from Greek and Latin. . . . Finally, after having studied Empedocles, he arrived at the conclusion that *the humor and illnesses are already on the sperm and are transmitted to the embryo.* His considerable work, justly admired by both Jewish and Christian sages, was introduced into France in the eighth century * by Rabbi Makhir, founder of the Rabbinic College of Narbonne, later in Egypt by Isaac Israeli in the tenth century and in Italy by the Jewish physician Shabtai Donnolo. The latter, from the inspiration of Asaph, composed a book of drugs in the tenth century [*Sefer HaMerkahot*].

This latter work has been published and extensively commented upon.[9] Perhaps the most concise description of the work of Asaph is given by Friedenwald:

It opens with a legendary account of the history of medicine. An account of the composition of the body, of the four elements, of anatomy, physiology and embryology follows; next there is a discussion of the four humors, of food and nutrition; of the special diseases pertaining to the several months and of the diseases of the different organs and their treatment; next 123 herbs are described with notes of their healing powers; a book of prescriptions and a list of antidotes, aphorisms and prognostics of Hippocrates in paraphrase, rules of uroscopy, symptoms of the pulse and fevers follow. The book closes with an oath similar to that of Hippocrates.[10]

The deontologic sermon that Asaph imposed on his pupils testifies to a high moral elevation. It is reproduced here, translated into English from the Oxford Hebrew Manuscript no. 2138:

And this is the covenant that Asaph, the son of Berakhyahu, and Yohanan, the son of Zabda, entered unto with their disciples and enjoined them saying:
"Take heed that you kill not any man with a root decoction; do

---

*Actually early in the ninth century.[7]

not prepare any potion that may cause a woman who has conceived in adultery to miscarry; and do not lust after beautiful women to commit adultery with them; and do not divulge a man's secret that he has confided unto you; and do not be bribed to do injury and harm and do not harden your heart against the poor and the needy; rather have compassion upon them and heal them. Do not speak of good as evil nor of evil as good. Do not follow in the ways of sorcerers to enchant by witchcraft and magic to part a man from his beloved or a woman from the husband of her youth. Do not covet any bribe or reward to assist in sexual misdemeanors. Do not make use of any manner of idol-worship to heal thereby nor trust in its healing powers but despise, detest and hate all its worshippers and those that trust in it and cause others to believe in it for it is all worthless and of no avail. They rely on demons and hosts which do not exist and inasmuch as they cannot help their lifeless bodies, how can they save the living? And now, trust in the Lord your God, the God of truth, the living God, for He puts to death and brings to life. He smites and heals, He bestows understanding to man and teaches him to serve. He wounds in righteousness and justice and heals in mercy and loving kindness: No guile is concealed from Him, and nothing is hidden from His sight. He causes healing plants to grow and puts skill to heal in the hearts of sages by His manifold mercies to declare His wonders to the multitudes and to understand all living things for He was their Creator and that apart from Him there is no Savior. The peoples trust in their idols that they may save them from their afflictions, but they cannot save them from their sorrows, for their trust and hope are in the lifeless.

"Therefore, it is fitting that you keep yourselves apart from them and hold yourselves aloof from the abomination of their idols and cleave unto the Lord of all flesh. Every living creature is in His hands to kill and to bring to life and none can be delivered from His hand.

"Be mindful of Him at all times and seek Him in truth and righteousness all the days of your life and in all that you do and He will help you in all your undertakings and you shall be happy in the eyes of all men. The peoples will neglect their gods and idols and will yearn to serve the Lord as you do, for they will perceive that they have put their trust in mockery and that they have labored in vain—when they turn to their god he will not help and will not save. And as for you, be strong and let not your hands slacken for you shall be rewarded for your labors.

"The Lord is with you when you are with Him and if you keep His covenant and walk in His statutes and cleave unto them you shall be as saints in the eyes of all flesh, for they will say 'Happy is the people that is in such a state; happy is the people whose God is the Lord.'

"And their disciples answered and declared: 'All that you have admonished us and commanded us we shall do for it is ordained in the Torah and we will carry it out with all our heart and soul and might; we will do and listen and not deviate nor turn to left or right.'

"Thereupon, their masters blessed them in the name of the Almighty God, the Lord of heaven and earth saying: 'Behold, the Lord your God, His prophets and His Torah are witnesses unto you; be you God-fearing, do not stray from His commandments; walk in His statutes; do not seek after unjust benefit and do not aid the evil-doer to shed innocent blood. Do not mix a poison for any man or woman to kill his fellow-man, nor disclose their constitution; do not give them to any man nor give any devious advice. Do not cause the shedding of blood by essaying any dangerous experiment in the exercise of medical skill; do not cause a sickness in any man; do not hasten to maim and do not cut the flesh of man by any iron instrument or by branding but first observe twice and thrice and then give your counsel. Guard against haughtiness and conceit. Do not bear a grudge against a sick man, and beware of revengeful acts. Do not set upon those that hate the Lord but keep His ordinances and commandments, walk in all His ways that you may find favor in His eyes, and that you may be pure, faithful and upright.'

"Thus did Asaph and Yoḥanan admonish and adjure their disciples."

The oath has much similarity to the oath of Hippocrates. Abstaining from the use of poisons and the administration of abortive remedies to pregnant women, the use of surgery only if qualified to do so, the avoidance of sexual contact in the homes of patients, and the confidentiality of medical information seem to be directly taken from the Hippocratic Oath. The opening statement of the latter oath, which begins with "I swear by Apollo, Physician and Asclepius and Hygieia and Panaceia and all the gods and goddesses," is, of course, omitted from the oath of Asaph. In its place is a lengthy statement of faith in the One God, the Lord of Israel and the whole world, the true Healer of the sick.

Thus, we see that the ethics of medicine and the high moral calling of physicians to their profession, preached throughout the ages, from Galen to Hippocrates, from Asaph to Maimonides, from Pasteur to Osler, remain and retain the high standards taught to today's student of medicine.

REFERENCES

1. F. H. Garrison, *An Introduction to the History of Medicine,* 4th ed. (Philadelphia: W. B. Saunders, 1929), p. 147.
2. G. Sarton, *Introduction to the History of Science* (Baltimore: Williams & Wilkins Co., 1927), 1:614.
3. S. Muntner, "The Antiquity of Assaph the Physician and His Editorship of the Earliest Hebrew Book of Medicine," *Bulletin of the History of Medicine* 25 (1951): 101.
4. M. Steinschneider, "Assaf Judaeus," *Hebr. Bibliogr.* 12 (1875): 85; 17 (1877): 114; 19 (1879): 35, 64, 85, 105.
5. L. Venetianer, *Asaf Judaeus, der Alteste Medizinische Schriftsteller in Hebraischer Sprache* (Strassburg: Trubner, 1916–17).
6. I. Simon, *Asaph-Ha-Jehoudi* (Paris: Lipschutz, 1933).
7. S. Muntner, *Introduction to the Book of Assaph the Physician* (Jerusalem: Geniza: 1957).
8. L. Lavastine, *Histoire Générale de la Médecine* (Paris: Albin-Michel, 1963), 2:119–20.
9. S. Muntner, *Shabtai Donnolo* (913–983): Medical Works (Jerusalem, 1949).
10. H. Friedenwald, *Jewish Luminaries in Medical History* (Baltimore, Johns Hopkins Press, 1946), pp. 3–4.

The Physician's Prayer
Attributed to Moses Maimonides

The Physician's Prayer attributed to Moses Maimonides (1135–1204) is a lofty and beautiful prayer which first appeared in print in a German periodical in 1783.[1] The editor of this journal, Heinrich Christian Boie, and his associate, Christian Wilhelm Dohm, provide no notes or commentaries nor any indication as to who the author is. The prayer bears only the title, "Daily Prayer of a Physician Before He Visits His Patients: From the Hebrew Manuscript of a Renowned Jewish Physician in Egypt from the Twelfth Century." A photostatic reproduction of this earliest version of the prayer appeared recently in a Hebrew medical journal.[2] Since the 1783 German edition, numerous versions, abbreviations, or excerpts thereof have been presented in English,[3-16] German,[17-23] Hebrew,[2,23-24] French,[25-27] Dutch,[28] and Spanish.[29]. There are undoubtedly others. Much heated debate exists among the various writers concerning the true authorship of the prayer. This controversy will be presented chronologically, and an attempt will be made to arrive at a reasonable conclusion as to whether or not Moses Maimonides actually wrote the "Prayer of Maimonides."

The first Hebrew version of the prayer was published by Isaac Euchel, editor of the Hebrew periodical *Ha-Me'assef,* in 1790.[24] The title indicates that Marcus Herz was its author and that it was translated at his request from German into Hebrew. Half a century later, in 1841, the London newspaper, *Voice of Jacob,* published the first English rendition from the Hebrew, under the title "Daily Prayer of a Physician."[3] The writer, using the pen name of "Medicus," states:

> The composition of this prayer has erroneously been attributed to Maimonides, but it is the production of the late Dr. Marcus Herz, a celebrated physician of Berlin. It was published by him in the

German language, and the Hebrew version, which is to be found in the (Ha) maasef, owes its existence to the prolific pen of Itzig Eichel.

We next find the prayer, again in German, in a German Jewish newspaper, the *Allgemeine Zeitung des Judenthums for* 1863.[17] The editor, Ludwig Philippson, makes no mention of authorship at all, but the title reads, "Daily Prayer of a Physician Before the Visits to His Patients: From the Hebrew Manuscript of a Celebrated Jewish Physician from the Twelfth Century." This title is nearly identical with that of the first German version which appeared eighty years earlier.[1] Philippson again reprinted the German version six years later (1869) in his voluminous book, *Weltbewegende Fragen in Politik und Religion aus den letzten dreissig Jahren.*[18] In 1892 yet another German version appeared in the *Allgemeine Zeitung des Judenthums*, this time by Julius Pagel, entitled "The Prayer of the Physician." [19]

In the last year of the nineteenth century, Rev. Madison C. Peters, pastor of the Bloomingdale Church in New York City, published a short English version of the prayer in his book, *Justice to the Jew.*[4] This English version, in which authorship is not mentioned at all, later initiated heated debates among Jewish scholars.

In the same year, Moïse Schwab, the celebrated bibliographer, published his *Répertoire,*[30] in which he states that Marcus Herz authored the prayer published over a century earlier in *Ha-Me'assef.*[24] At the turn of the century, Golden published excerpts of the prayer in English in an American medical journal.[5] His article, entitled "Maimonides' Prayer for Physicians," states that Maimonides composed the prayer. A later letter addressed to the *American Israelite* is evidence that he extracted the prayer from Peters' book.[4]

In 1902 the prayer appeared again in German under the title, "Prayer of a Jewish Physician in the Twelfth Century." [20] The writer, Dr. Theodor Distel, specifically states that the prayer was published originally in 1783 in the *Deutsches Museum,*[1] and that its importance prompted him to reprint it verbatim. Another quarter century was to pass before the 1783 version was again mentioned, in spite of the rather widespread interest in the prayer and its authorship, manifested by numerous articles on the subject during this period.

In 1902, the same year that Distel reprinted [20] the original German version of the prayer,[1] it was again copied in German in a Swiss newspaper, using Distel's title, "Prayer of a Jewish Physician in the Twelfth Century." [21] No commentary or discussion of authorship is to be found in this Swiss version. Rabbi Jules Wolff of La Chaux-de-Fonds, reading the prayer in the Swiss newspaper, was so impressed that he promptly translated it into French. In a letter, dated February 26, 1903, to the editor of the periodical *L'univers israélite,* which was published the following day, Wolff provides the first, and excellent, French version of the prayer.[25] He states that it is a "prayer composed by a famous Jewish physician from Egypt in the twelfth century (Maimonides?)." Thus Wolff seems to assume, perhaps with a little doubt, that Maimonides is the true author of the prayer; Moïse Schwab, however, is quick to reply three weeks later, in another letter to the editor of the same periodical, that the prayer could have been written by any Parisian physician.[31] He further states that the prayer is definitely the work of Marcus Herz, friend and physician of Moses Mendelssohn, that Herz wrote it in German in Berlin, and that a Hebrew translation was published by Isaac Euchel in *Ha-Me'assef* in 1790.[24]

Although later authors state that German versions of the prayer appeared in the February 4 and August 21, 1904, issues of the periodical *Israelitisches Familienblatt,* this writer has been unable to locate copies of these journals in numerous libraries in the United States. I cannot, therefore, verify this for myself and must leave it in doubt, since numerous errors in bibliography have crept into various subsequent papers published on this subject.

In 1908 Dr. Gotthard Deutsch, professor of Jewish history and literature at the Hebrew Union College of Cincinatti, wrote a letter to the editor of the *American Israelite,* vehemently denouncing those who believe Maimonides actually wrote the famous prayer.[32] The first part of his letter, tracing the prayer from 1790 [24] to 1903 [25,31] was reproduced in the miscellany section of the *Journal of the American Medical Association* in 1929.[33] The letter continues as follows:

> God only knows into how many medical journals, textbooks of medicine, etc., this prayer found its way. The first source of the error is evidently Philippson. How he could commit this blunder is inconceivable to me. He could not have quoted from memory, for he gives a fairly accurate translation and he could not have translated from the original without seeing in his text that the prayer was written by Marcus Herz in German and translated into Hebrew by

Euchel. Philippson, however, does not give Maimonides as the author, and I would like to know who was the author of this additional piece of historic information which I notice is stated by Wolff with a question mark. To me, this wandering hoax was a valuable piece of illustration of historic criticism.

Six years later, William W. Golden, superintendent of the Davis Memorial Hospital in Elkins, West Virginia, wrote a letter to the editor of The *American Israelite*. It was published in the June 25, 1914, issue as follows:

Sir: Reverend Madison C. Peters in one of the editions of his book "Justice to the Jew" quotes a prayer for physicians by Maimonides. Can you tell me where the original can be found, or at least in what authoritative work on history, literature or medicine can it be found, and oblige?

Yours very truly . . .

Golden, who in 1900 had published excerpts of the prayer,[5] and in no uncertain terms had attributed authorship to Maimonides, as described earlier in this paper, now seems to have had second thoughts on the matter. The reply to his letter came from Dr. Gotthard Deutsch in the same June 25, 1914, issue of The *American Israelite* and was subsequently reprinted in chapter 6 ("The Maimonides Prayer Myth") of Deutsch's *Scrolls*.[34]

Deutsch's reply begins as follows: "This so called prayer of Maimonides is an old hoax. It was actually written by Marcus Herz, a prominent physician of Berlin (1747–1803) who attended Moses Mendelssohn in his last illness." Deutsch thus reiterates all the arguments expounded in his earlier letter of 1908.[32] He further states that

Haeser embodied it in his "Geschichte der Medizin" 1, p. 837, Jena 1875. Having thus been recognized by a standard publication, it was accepted by Julius Pagel, professor of the history of medicine at the Berlin University (1851–1912), also a Jew, in his essay on Maimonides as physician, which forms part of the memorial volume "Moses Ben Maimon," edited by the Gesellschaft Zur Foerderung der Wissenschaft des Judentums, I, p. 244, Leipzic, 1908. Following all this, its authenticity could no more be doubted than the authenticity of the gospel of St. John. The Israelite (March 12, 1908) gave it its seal of approval, although I contested it in the subsequent issue, but repeatedly since it has been proclaimed as being written in distinctly Maimonidean spirit. Recently I wrote a letter to the editor of "Ost und West," who had published it as Maimonidean. He thanked me, but preferred not to publish it. As the very popular "Medizinische Wochenschrift" of Berlin published it in 1902, and any number of medical journals reprinted it, no amount of argument will rob Maimonides of the credit for having written this typically sweet-lemonade prayer, characteristic of the rationalistic tendencies of the era of "Aufklaerung," and I still have hopes that one hundred years hence, somebody will credit Herodotus or at least Rabbi Jose Ben Halafta, the genuine author of Seder Olam, with my "Foreign Notes."

It seems quite evident that Deutsch was unaware of the 1783 edition of the prayer,[1] and thus he attributes the authorship of the prayer to Marcus Herz, whose version did not appear until 1790.[24] This ignorance of the 1783 edition of the prayer must have been shared by Schwab [30,31] and numerous later writers who also ascribe the prayer to Marcus Herz in spite of the specific mention by Distel in 1902 of the existence of the 1783 edition antedating Herz by seven years.[20]

Thus, Deutsch's criticism of Philippson seems unfounded. Philippson was probably aware of the *Deutsches Museum* edition of 1783, and in his own 1863 and 1869 versions of the prayer,[17,18] he used the same title as in the 1783 original, namely "Daily Prayer of a Physician Before He Visits His Patients: From a Hebrew Manuscript of a Renowned Jewish Physician of the Twelfth Century." Deutsch further perpetuates the misconception,[32,34] later quoted by Friedenwald,[14] that the prayer was embodied in Haeser's textbook of the history of medicine.[35 p. 837] In actuality, only a brief footnote exists in Haeser's text, which, translated from the German, states: "Compare the beautiful morning prayer of a Jewish physician from the twelfth century in L. Philippson's Weltbewegende Fragen." In Haeser's discussion of Maimonides in the same work (pp. 595–97), no mention is made of the prayer. Nor is there any mention of the prayer in the two earlier editions of Haeser's textbook in 1845 and 1859 respectively. This indicates that Haeser, too, was unaware of the 1783 edition and first saw the prayer printed in Philippson's paper in 1863.[17]

Seeligmann in Holland writes in 1928 that, in response to an inquiry regarding a Hebrew version of Maimonides' prayer, he remembers that it was probably not composed by Maimonides.[28] He then states that Marcus Herz wrote it and traces its history from *Ha-Me'assef* in 1790 [24] through Philippson [17,18] and Haeser.[35] Seeligmann further writes that the first Dutch version is by Hektor Treub, which Dr. M. J. Premsela published in his brochure *Medische Fastoensleer* (Amsterdam 1903, pp. 52–53).

Emil Bogen,[7] in response to the reprinting of part of one of Gotthard Deutsch's letters [32] in the *Journal of the American Medical Association,*[33] correctly points out the existence of the 1783 version, which was not known to Deutsch. Bogen agrees with Kroner, who shows the harmony that exists between the other writings of Maimonides and the so-called Prayer of Maimonides in both form and spirit.[36]

Bennigson and his colleagues reprinted the German version in Leipzig in 1931; [22] they briefly trace the history of the prayer from its origin in the *Deutsches Museum.*[1] They erroneously state that it was reprinted in German by Distel in the *Deutsche medizinische Wochenschrift* in August 1904, when they probably mean 1902.[20] This error has been perpetuated by Kagan [13] and Muntner,[23] neither of whom probably had access to the periodical in question. Another, probably typographical, error in Bennigson's paper [22] is the June 1893 date given for Pagel's version of the prayer,[19] an error again perpetuated by Kagan.[13] The correct date is June 1892.

Keller, in 1931, in an essay entitled, "The Ideal Practice of Medicine from the Rabbinical Point of View," compares the Prayer of Maimonides to the Hippocratic Oath and quotes excerpts from both.[8] Maimonides, he says, considers the patient important because he is the creation of the Almighty, so that the responsibility for the outcome of our treatment rests partly with us as an instrument of the Almighty. Hippocrates, on the other hand, considers the preciousness of a human being from the sociological viewpoint.

To commemorate the eight-hundredth anniversary of the birth of Maimonides, in 1935, numerous publications on all aspects of Maimonides appeared in various periodicals, newspapers, journals, and books around the world. Among these are several references to the Prayer. Gershenfeld provides excerpts of the English version.[10] Illevitz and Meyerhof emphatically state that Maimonides did not write the prayer.[37,38] A Spanish version of the prayer also appeared in 1935.[29] The author, E. Singer, states that it was previously published in the *Allgemeine Zeitung des Judenthums* in

1863,[17] in *Sulamit* in 1842, in *Abend Zeitung* in 1840, and in the *Medizinischer Almanach*.

An interesting inquiry by Sir William Osler concerning the authorship of the prayer was answered by the Chief Rabbi of the British Empire, Dr. Joseph H. Hertz, in a letter dated May 23, 1917, but published in the *Canadian Jewish Chronicle* in 1935.[39] The letter reads as follows:

Dear Sir William:

Some 2 years ago you inquired of me as to the "Physician's Prayer" attributed to Maimonides. I can now give you the following information on the subject:

This prayer is the production of Dr. Markus Herz (1747–1802), a friend and pupil of Immanuel Kant and of Moses Mendelssohn. He was a physician to the Jewish Hospital in Berlin. The prayer was composed by him in the German language and was published in a Hebrew translation in the Periodical Ha-Meassef. The current English version seems to be from this Hebrew translation and first appeared in the London paper "Voice of Jacob" on the 24th December, 1841.

Sincerely yours,
J. H. Hertz.

Also in 1935, Münz, in his book on Maimonides,[40] ascribes the prayer to the great medieval physician, although the earlier German edition of his book questions the true authorship.[41]

In 1938 Kagan reprinted excerpts of the English version of the prayer and traced its history.[13] He based his article mainly on two previous papers, those of Bogen [7] and Bennigson et al,[22] as evidenced by Kagan's incorporation of the bibliographical errors in Bennigson's article into his own paper as described above. Kagan concludes with six arguments favoring Maimonides as the true author of the prayer. These arguments can be summarized as follows:

1. The medieval form and style of the prayer conform with Maimonides' other writings.
2. If Marcus Herz was the author, he would have laid claim to its authorship.
3. Dr. Herz, a master of the German language, would have published

the original prayer in German and would only later have arranged for a Hebrew translation.

4. If the later German version omitted Herz's name at his request, he would not have requested Euchel, editor of *Ha-Me'assef,* to mention his name in the Hebrew translation.

5. Herz probably knew of the 1783 German version and sent the document for Hebrew translation to Euchel, who erroneously ascribed the German text to Herz. Herz did not know Hebrew since he did not translate it himself and probably was unaware of the Hebrew editor's note making him the author.

6. All the professional ethics expressed in the prayer are also expressed in some of Maimonides' letters and books.

In 1939 Levinson reprinted the prayer in English as part of a larger review of Maimonides' medical contributions.[12] In 1944 Friedenwald, in his two-volume classic, *The Jews and Medicine,* also reprinted the prayer in English.[14]

A most interesting booklet comparing the prayer of Maimonides to the Oath of Asaph [42] and the physician's prayer of Jacob Zahalon [43,44,14, p. 268–279] was published by Muntner in 1946.[23] In addition to publishing both Hebrew and German versions, Muntner provides us with a brief bibliographical sketch tracing the background of the prayer, a sketch which he found in a 1928 Berlin version of the prayer by Professor Heinrich Levy. The August 1904 date quoted for Distel's version in the *Deutsche medizinische Wochenschrift* is incorrect and should properly be August 1902.[20] Muntner calls attention to the existence of a Hebrew manuscript in the Bibliothèque Nationale de Paris which is entitled "The Prayer of Moses Maimonides." It is Hebrew manuscript no. 873, pt. 7, fol. 98V°, described in the catalogue as follows: [45] "Prayer of Rabbi Moses Maimonides, beginning with *Tefila Lisegulas Eeshim* and terminating by the piece of verse *Galgal Soveiv.*" The great bibliographer Moritz Steinschneider describes an identical Hebrew work as manuscript Warner no. 41, pt. 11, fol. 150, and refers to the Paris Hebrew manuscript as no. 285 (perhaps an error or perhaps an earlier different numbering system).[46] In addition, this medieval Hebrew manuscript version of the "Prayer of Maimonides" was published in 1867 in the weekly Hebrew newspaper *Hakarmel* [47].

Muntner correctly points out that this manuscript version of the prayer is a forgery and could not possibly have been written by Maimonides,[23] since the numerous references to astrology are not in keeping with Maimonides' vehement opposition to the "pseudoscience" of astrology.[48]

Muntner further claims that the versions of the prayer, beginning with the 1783 German edition,[1] although written in the spirit and form of Maimonides, omitting any reference to astrology, are also forgeries and can all be traced back to Marcus Herz.

Probably the most comprehensive review of the subject to date is the one published in Hebrew by Leibowitz in 1954.[2] A photocopy of the 1783 original German version [1] is presented, as well as the first page of the 1790 Hebrew version.[24] Leibowitz must have consulted the original sources, since the bibliographical errors described above first made by Bennigson et al.[22] and later perpetuated by Kagan [13] and others are absent from Leibowitz's paper. A new Hebrew translation, made directly from the 1783 German version, is also provided in this article.

A second French edition of the prayer appeared in 1956,[26] and a short English version was reprinted in 1957.[16] A brief version of "The Oath and Prayer of Maimonides" was published in the *Journal of the American Medical Association* in 1955,[15] in which Maimonides is falsely called an Islamic philosopher, an error that was corrected by Lanzkron and Berner in two separate letters to the editor.[49]

The most recent version of the prayer that I have been able to find is a 1962 French one.[27] Only parts of the prayer are translated into French, according to the author, Dr. J. Pines, from the Paris Hebrew manuscript no. 837 described above.[45]

I have been fortunate in being able to obtain copies of every reference enumerated in the bibliography of this paper. There are undoubtedly other versions, editions, and printings of the prayer in numerous languages in various newspapers, periodicals, and books throughout the world. The popularity of the prayer is attested to by its frequent quotation and publication. Whether Maimonides actually wrote the prayer or not remains an open question. Certainly most of those who are of the opinion that Maimonides did not write it, including Illevitz,[37] Meyerhof,[38] Simon,[26] Hertz,[39] Seeligmann,[28] and others, base their remarks on the statements of Deutsch [32,34] and Schwab,[30,31] although "Medicus" had already attributed authorship of the prayer to Marcus Herz in 1841.[3] As has already been pointed out, both Deutsch and Schwab were probably unaware of the 1783 German version of the prayer, which antedated Herz by seven years, and thus they have perpetuated the concept that Marcus Herz composed the prayer. This thesis may or may not be valid.

Other writers, such as Bogen,[7] Kagan,[13] and perhaps Wolff,[25] agree with Kroner [36] that the prayer was probably truly composed by Maimonides, since it conforms completely with the ideals, medical ethics, and spirit of Maimonides; they believe that the original will yet be found. Pagel also supports this viewpoint.[50] Certainly, at this point in history, this suggestion is no more than wishful thinking. However, it is conceivable that Marcus Herz saw an original manuscript in Hebrew; he may have based his version, in which he does not claim authorship, on such an original. This proposal seems unlikely. Alternatively, Herz may have seen the 1783 German version and asked his friend Isaac Euchel to translate it into Hebrew. The latter may have erroneously ascribed the German to Herz, as Kagan postulates.[13] This theory, too, seems unlikely. It is also possible that neither Maimonides nor Herz wrote the prayer, but that a twelfth-century astrologer wrote it in what became the Paris Hebrew manuscript, from which was extracted an abbreviated German version. A further possibility is that Maimonides did indeed write the prayer, but that an astrologer amended it and only the amended versions are extant today. These two latter possibilities are extremely remote.

It seems clear that the manuscript version of the prayer in Paris [45-46] and Oxford,[47] mentioned above, is a forgery and was not written by Maimonides. This is proved by Muntner,[23] who states that the numerous references to astrology in this work make it impossible to ascribe authorship to Maimonides, who was vehemently opposed to this "pseudoscience." [48]

The question remains whether the 1783 *Deutsches Museum* edition of the prayer,[2] upon which many versions in numerous languages are based,[1-29] was truly written by Maimonides or not. As already mentioned, Kroner,[36] Pagel,[50] Wolff,[25] Bogen,[7] and Kagan [13] support the former view, whereas Leibowitz,[2] Muntner,[23] Schwab,[30-31] Deutsch,[32,34] Illevitz,[37] Meyerhof,[38] Seeligmann,[28] "Medicus," [3] and Hertz [39] believe the prayer to be spurious.

The most potent arguments favoring the rejection of Maimonides as the author come from Professor Leibowitz,[2] who states that no prominent medical historian supports the view of Maimonides' authorship. Furthermore, in Euchel's Hebrew version of 1790,[24] it is specifically stated that the prayer was composed by Marcus Herz and translated from German into Hebrew at his request. The confusion arose from the discovery of an earlier German edition [1] bearing the unfortunate title ". . . From the Hebrew Manuscript of a Renowned Jewish Physician in Egypt from the Twelfth Century." This title leads logically to the supposition that Maimonides is the renowned physician referred to. However, if one carefully reads the text of 1783, one notes that contrary to what Kagan states,[13] style, phrasing, and concepts are not compatible with a medieval dating. A phrase such as "art is great, but the mind of man is ever expanding" is typical and characteristic of eighteenth-century Europe and is at variance with Maimonidean medieval thinking. Here, according to Leibowitz,[51] is the idea of progress, which became even more popular in the nineteenth century.

Further evidence for an eighteenth-century author lies in the phrase "that act unceasingly and harmoniously to preserve the whole in all its beauty." This concept of "beauty," or *das Schöne,* is characteristic of German literature of the Enlightenment. Moreover, a phrase such as "ten thousand times ten thousand organs hast Thou combined" presupposes knowledge of the newer sciences of anatomy, biology, and microscopy. The tensions between colleagues discussed in the prayer are also products of a more modern period and dictated by the new academic hierarchy.

Leibowitz further writes:

> Markus Herz probably wrote the Prayer as a contribution to medical ethics and as a comment on prevailing low standards of the practice. It was usual to insert in almanachs anonymous short contributions. Markus Herz was a warm Jew, proud of the history of his people; he clad his literary piece into the colorful frame indicated in the caption, probably indeed meaning Maimonides, but not based on a manuscript, which did not exist, but as belonging to the belles-lettres. Editions of Hebrew medical manuscripts began only in 1867 [Steinschneider's Donnolo].[51]

One of the greatest authorities on the medical writings of Maimonides was Suessman Muntner. His book on the subject of Maimonides' prayer has already been mentioned earlier in this paper.[23] Muntner also strongly believed[52] that Marcus Herz composed this prayer in beautiful German and that a very poor translation into Hebrew was produced by Euchel.[24] Furthermore, an anonymous or unknown writer added the confusing caption to this earliest (1790) Hebrew version. Muntner further states that Herz based his version of the prayer on the earlier Prayer of Jacob Zahalon,[43,44,14 pp. 268–279] which was written in the seventeenth century, and was greatly influenced and stimulated by it.

From all the foregoing discussion, the evidence overwhelmingly favors the concept that the physician's prayer attributed to Maimonides is a spurious work, not written by Maimonides but composed by an eighteenth-century writer, probably Marcus Herz. Absolute proof that this is so is, however, lacking and may never be discovered.

Recently, in a comparative and historical study of the Jewish religious attitude to medicine and its practice,[53] Dr. Immanuel Jakobovits, Chief Rabbi of the British Commonwealth, emphasized the ethical and moral responsibilities of the physician as a divine agent in the alleviation of human suffering. Deeply pious and moving prayers of gratitude for divine help, such as those of Asaph,[42] Judah Halevy,[14 p. 27] Jacob ·Zahalon,[43,44,14 pp. 268–279] and Abraham Zacutus,[14 pp. 295–321] as well as the Physician's Prayer attributed to Maimonides,[1–29] says Jakobovits, all recognize God as the ultimate healer of disease, while also asserting "the indispensable part played by the physician, his art and his medicines" in the preservation of health.

The Physician's Prayer attributed to Maimonides contains moral and ethical standards by which a physician should conduct his professional life. The daily recitation of this prayer serves to remind the physician of these standards which have been set up for him and which he should attempt to live up to. Physicians should constantly carry with them the highest code of medical philanthropy and professional ethics. Such noble philosophy and high aspirations of the profession are embodied in the Physician's Prayer.

There follows below the English version of the "Daily Prayer of a Physician" by Dr. Harry Friedenwald, reprinted from the *Bulletin of the Johns Hopkins Hospital* 28 (1917): 256–61, with kind permission from the editors and publishers.

Daily Prayer of a Physician

Almighty God, Thou hast created the human body with infinite wisdom. Ten thousand times ten thousand organs hast Thou combined in it that act unceasingly and harmoniously to preserve the whole in all its beauty— the body which is the envelope of the immortal soul. They are ever acting in perfect order, agreement and accord. Yet, when the frailty of matter or the unbridling of passions deranges this order or interrupts this accord, then forces clash and the body crumbles into the primal dust from which it came. Thou sendest to man diseases as beneficent messengers to foretell approaching danger and to urge him to avert it.

Thou hast blest Thine earth, Thy rivers and Thy mountains with healing substances; they enable Thy creatures to alleviate their sufferings and to heal their illnesses. Thou hast endowed man with the wisdom to relieve the suffering of his brother, to recognize his disorders, to extract the healing substances, to discover their powers and to prepare and to apply them to suit every ill. In Thine Eternal Providence Thou hast chosen me to watch over the life and health of Thy creatures. I am now about to apply myself to the duties of my profession. Support me, Almighty God, in these great labors that they may benefit mankind, for without Thy help not even the least thing will succeed.

Inspire me with love for my art and for Thy creatures. Do not allow thirst for profit, ambition for renown and admiration, to interfere with my profession, for these are the enemies of truth and of love for mankind and they can lead astray in the great task of attending to the welfare of Thy creatures. Preserve the strength of my body and of my soul that they ever be ready to cheerfully help and support rich and poor, good and bad, enemy as well as friend. In the sufferer let me see only the human being. Illumine my mind that it recognize what presents itself and that it may comprehend what is absent or hidden. Let it not fail to see what is visible, but do not permit it to arrogate to itself the power to see what cannot be seen, for delicate and indefinite are the bounds of the great art of caring for the lives and health of Thy creatures. Let me never be absent-minded. May no strange thoughts divert my attention at the bedside of the sick, or disturb my mind in its silent labors, for great and sacred are the thoughtful deliberations required to preserve the lives and health of Thy creatures.

Grant that my patients have confidence in me and my art and follow my directions and my counsel. Remove from their midst all charlatans and the whole host of officious relatives and know-all nurses, cruel people who arrogantly frustrate the wisest purposes of our art and often lead Thy creatures to their death.

Should those who are wiser than I wish to improve and instruct me, let my soul gratefully follow their guidance; for vast is the extent of our art. Should conceited fools, however, censure me, then let love for my profession steel me against them, so that I remain steadfast without regard for age, for reputation, or for honor, because surrender would bring to Thy creatures sickness and death.

Imbue my soul with gentleness and calmness when older colleagues, proud of their age, wish to displace me or to scorn me or disdainfully to teach me. May even this be of advantage to me, for they know many things of which I am ignorant, but let not their arrogance give me pain. For they are old and old age is not master of the passions. I also hope to attain old age upon this earth, before Thee, Almighty God!

Let me be contented in everything except in the great science of my profession. Never allow the thought to arise in me that I have attained to sufficient knowledge, but vouchsafe to me the strength, the leisure and the ambition ever to extend my knowledge. For art is great, but the mind of man is ever expanding.

Almighty God! Thou hast chosen me in Thy mercy to watch over the life and death of Thy creatures. I now apply myself to my profession. Support me in this great task so that it may benefit mankind, for without Thy help not even the least thing will succeed.

REFERENCES

1. "Tägliches Gebet eines Arztes bevor er seine Kranken besucht—Aus der hebräischen Handschrift eines berühmten jüdischen Arztes in Egypten aus dem zwölften Jahrhundert," *Deutsches Museum* 1 (1783): 43–45.
2. J. O. Leibowitz, "The Physician's Prayer Ascribed to Maimonides," *Dapim Refuiim* 13 (1954): 77–81.
3. Medicus [pseud.], "Daily Prayer of a Physician," *Voice of Jacob* (London), 1, no. 7 (1814): 49–50.
4. M. C. Peters, *Justice to the Jew: The Story of What He Has Done for the World* (London and New York: Neely, 1899), pp. 173–75.
5. W. W. Golden, "Maimonides' Prayer for Physicians," *Transactions of the Medical Society of West Virginia* 33 (1900): 414-15.
6. H. Friedenwald, "The Ethics of the Practice of Medicine from the Jewish Point of View," *Bulletin of the Johns Hopkins Hospital* 28 (1971): 256–61.
7. E. Bogen, "The Daily Prayer of a Physician," *Journal of the American Medical Association* 92 (1929): 2128.
8. H. Keller, "Comparison between Hippocratic Oath and Maimonides' Prayer in the Ideal Practice of Medicine from the Rabbinical Point of View," in *Modern Hebrew Orthopedic Terminology and Jewish Medical Essays* (Boston: Stratford Co., 1931), pp. 142–46.
9. D. Roman, "Maimonides' Prayer," *Hahneman. Monthly* 67 (1932): 244–50.
10. L. Gershenfeld, "The Medical Works of Maimonides and His Treatise on Personal Hygiene and Dietetics," *American Journal of Pharmacology* 107 (1935): 14–28.
11. "Physician's Prayer by Maimonides," *Medical Leaves* 1 (1937): 9.

12. A. Levinson, "Maimonides, the Physician," *Medical Leaves* 2 (1939): 96–105.

13. S. R. Kagan, "Maimonides' Prayer," *Annals of Medical History* 10 (1938): 429–32.

14. H. Friedenwald, *The Jews and Medicine* (Baltimore: Johns Hopkins Press, 1944), 1:28–30.

15. "The Oath and Prayer of Maimonides," *Journal of the American Medical Association* 157 (1955): 1158.

16. J. S. Minkin, *The World of Moses Maimonides: With Selections from His Writings* (New York: Yoseloff, 1957), pp. 149–50.

17. L. Philippson, "Tägliches Gebet eines Arztes vor dem Besuch seiner Kranken (Aus der hebr. Handschrift eines berühmten jüdischen Arztes aus dem zwölften Jahrhundert)," *Allgemeine Zeitung des Judenthums* 27, no. 4 (1863: 49–50.

18. L. Philippson, *Weltbewegende Fragen in Politik und Religion aus den letzten dreissig Jahren,* Zweiter Theil: Religion (Leipzig: Baumgärtner, 1869), pp. 159–60.

19. J. Pagel, "Das Gebet des Arztes," *Allgemeine Zeitung des Judenthums* 56, no. 25 (1892): 294–95.

20. Th. Distel, "Gebet eines jüdischen Arztes im 12. Jahrhundert," *Deutsche medizinische Wochenschrift* 28, no. 32 (1902): 580.

21. "Gebet eines jüdischen Arztes im 12. Jahrhundert," *Cor.-Bl. f. schweiz Aerzte* 32, no. 19 (1902): 611–13.

22. W. Benningson et al., *Des Moses Maimonides Morgengebet bevor er seine Kranken besuchte* (Leipzig, 1931), p. 6.

23. S. Muntner, *The Deutero Prayer of Moses: With an Introduction about the History of the Prayer, Attributed to the Physician Maimonides and a Contemplation on the State of the Praying and on the Valour of the Prayer in General* (Jerusalem: Geniza, 1946), p. 57.

24. I. Euchel, "Prayer for the Physician as He Pours Out His Anxieties Before God Prior to Visiting the Sick: Composed by Sir Hofrat Professor Herz," *Ha-Me'assef* 6 (1790): 242–44.

25. J. Wolff, "Prière d-un médicin juif á l'usage de ses confrères," *Univers israélite* 58 (1903): 753–55.

26. I. Simon, "L'oeuvre médicale de Maimonide," *Revue d'histoire de la médecine hébraïque,* no. 31 (1956): 107–20.

27. J. Pines, "La contribution juive à la médecine arabe au moyen âge," *Scalpel* (Brussels), 115 (1962): 207–18.

28. S. Seeligmann, "Morgengebed van den arts naar Maimonides," *Vrijdagavond* 5, no. 1 (1928): 404–6.

29. E. Singer, "Maimonides, Medico," *Semana méd.,* 2 (1930): 1960–65.

30. M. Schwab, *Répertoire des articles relatifs à l'histoire et à la littérature juives parus dans les périodiques de 1783 à 1898* (Paris: Durlacher, 1899), p. 167.

31. M. Schwab, "La prière d'un médecin juif," *Univers israélite* 58 (1903): 818–19.

32. G. Deutsch, "Maimonides' Prayer," *American Israelite,* March 19, 1908, p. 5, cols. 5–6.
33. "The 'Prayer of Maimonides' and Its True Author," *Journal of the American Medical Association* 92 (1929): 836.
34. G. Deutsch, *Scrolls,* vol. 3, *Jew and Gentile: Essays on Jewish Apologetics and Kindred Historical Subjects* (Boston: Stratford Co., 1920), pp. 93–95.
35. H. Haeser, *Lehrbuch der Geschichte der Medicin und der epidemischen Krankheiten,* 3d ed. (Jena: Dufft, 1875), vol. 1.
36. H. Kroner, "Arzt und Patient in der Medizin des Maimonides," *Ost. u. West, Illus. Monatschr. f. modernes Judent.* 12 (1912): 745–50.
37. A. B. Illevitz, "Maimonides the Physician," *Canadian Medical Association Journal* 32 (1935): 440–42.
38. M. Meyerhof, "The Medical Work of Maimonides," in *Essays on Maimonides: An Octocentennial Volume,* ed. S. W. Baron (New York: Columbia University Press, 1941), pp. 265–99.
39. J. H. Hertz, letter to Sir William Osler, *Canadian Jewish Chronicle,* 22 (April 12, 1935): 7.
40. I. Münz, *Maimonides (The Rambam): The Story of His Life and Genius,* trans. and ed. H. T. Schnittkind (Boston: Winchell-Thomas, 1935), p. 191.
41. I. Münz, *Moses ben Maimon (Maimonides): Sein Leben und seine Werke* (Frankfurt a.M.: Kauffmann, 1812), pp. 267–68.
42. F. Rosner and S. Muntner, "The Oath of Asaph," *Annals of Internal Medicine* 63 (1965): 317–20.
43. H. Savitz, "Jacob Zahalon and His Book, *The Treasure of Life,*" *New England Journal of Medicine* 213 (1935): 167–76..
44. I. Simon, "La prière des médecins, 'Tephilat Harofim,' de Jacob Zahalon, médecin et rabbin en Italie (1630–1693), *Revue d'histoire de la médecine hébraïque,* no. 8 (1955): 38–51.
45. Bibliothèque nationale, *Catalogues des manuscripts hébreux et samaritains de la Bibliothèque impériale* (Paris, 1866), p. 142.
46. M. Steinschneider, *Catalogus codicum hebraeorum Bibliothecae academiae Lugduno Batavae* ([Leiden]: E. J. Brill, 1858), p. 188.
47. R. Meshash, "The Prayer of Rabbi Moses Attributed to Rabbi Moses ben Maimon (Maimonides)," *Hakarmel* 6 (1867): 350.
48. A. Marx, "The Correspondence between the Rabbis of Southern France and Maimonides about Astrology," *Hebrew Union College Annual* 3 (1926): 311–58.
49. J. Lanzkron and H. Berner, "Maimonides: Physician, Astronomer, Philosopher, Talmudist," *Journal of the American Medical Association* 157 (1955): 1637.
50. J. Pagel, *Maimuni als medizinischer Schriftsteller* (Frankfurt a.M.: Kauffmann, 1908), p. 17.
51. J. O. Leibowitz, personal communication.
52. S. Muntner, personal communication.
53. I. Jakobovits, *Jewish Medical Ethics* (New York: Bloch, 1959), pp. 15–18.

Therapeutic Efficacy of Prayer

Two recent papers, "The Efficacy of Prayer: A Triple-Blind Study" [1] and "The Objective Efficacy of Prayer: A Double-Blind Clinical Trial," [2] both begin with the following quotation from Francis Galton:

> It is asserted by some that men possess the faculty of obtaining results over which they have little or no direct personal control by means of devout and earnest prayer, while others doubt the truth of this assertion. The question regards a matter of fact, that has to be determined by observation and not by authority; and it is one that appears to be a very suitable topic for statistical inquiry. . . . Are prayers answered or are they not? . . . Do sick persons who pray, or are prayed for, recover on the average more rapidly than others? [3]

In an earlier paper, Galton had suggested that the efficacy of prayer seems to be a simple and perfectly appropriate and legitimate subject of scientific inquiry.[4] Roland believes that Galton's century-old essay is one of the earliest modern applications of statistics to science.[5]

Galton attempted to answer the simple question of whether persons who pray, or who are prayed for, recover, on the average, more rapidly than others. He collated the mean age attained by members of various classes who had survived their thirtieth year from 1758 to 1843. He considered clergy to be a far more prayerful class than either lawyers or physicians. Yet when examining distinguished members of these three classes, he found the mean life span to be 66.4, 66.5, and 67.0 years respectively for clergy, lawyers, and physicians. Hence, concluded Galton, the prayers of the clergy appeared to be futile. He also cited a similar study by Guy, in which sovereigns were found to be the shortest-lived of all classes of persons examined, thus proving that prayer has no efficacy. Galton did not, however, negate the fact that the mind may be relieved

141

by the utterance of prayer. He admitted that the impulse to pour out feelings in sound is not peculiar to man, and that a confident sense of communion with God rejoices and strengthens the heart.

Galton's plea for a scientific inquiry into the efficacy of prayer was approached by two recent studies. Joyce and Welldon "selected" forty-eight patients with "chronic stationary or progressively deteriorating psychological or rheumatic diseases" in two London hospital outpatient clinics. They obtained a "tolerable match" for nineteen pairs. Hence ten patients were immediately eliminated from the study because they could not be paired or matched. In the results section of their paper, the authors write that two pairs of the nineteen originally formed were eliminated because one member of each was found at the end not to satisfy the criteria for admission to the trial. Furthermore, one member of a third pair failed to attend despite repeated requests. The analysis of the data, then, "ignores the effect of pairing," by the authors' own admission. The conclusions of the authors are as follows:

> The first six valid and definite results available all showed an advantage to the "treated" group [for whom prayers were recited]. Five of the next six showed an advantage to the "control" group. These results may be due solely to chance.[6]

The foregoing highly unorthodox and unacceptable statistical maneuvers, I believe, invalidate the entire study. In addition, the study itself concluded with "negative" results, failing to prove (or disprove) the efficacy of prayer.

The second "scientific" study of the efficacy of prayer is that of Collipp. He studied eighteen leukemic children (below age twenty). The names of ten of these children were randomly selected and sent to a prayer group in another city. The group was asked to offer daily prayers for the children. Why ten children rather than nine were allocated to the prayer group is not stated; nor were the two groups matched for age, sex, race, type of leukemia, type of treatment, or other factors. The observation that after fifteen months of prayer seven children in the prayer group were still alive, whereas only two of the control group were, is said by the author to represent a difference in survival at the 90 percent level of significance. But the author fails to take into account the fact that two of the patients in the control group, though none in the treatment group, had acute myelogenous leukemia, a highly malignant type of leukemia in which survival is much shorter than with acute lymphatic leukemia. In fact, these two patients had the shortest survival of all the patients in both groups. Furthermore, survival in acute leukemia is known to be age-dependent, a fact confirmed by Collipp's data, in which the two nineteen-year-old patients (one in the prayer group and one in the control group) had the shortest survival of all the patients with acute lymphatic leukemia. The variety of treatment regimens also makes the two groups of patients incomparable. The author's suggestion of deleting an "atypical child in the control group who survived eleven years" is another unorthodox and unacceptable statistical approach. For all the above reasons, the conclusions of Collipp supporting the concept that prayers for the sick are efficacious are invalid.

What is the biblical and talmudic "religious" evidence supporting the concept that prayers are efficacious? The patriarch Abraham prayed for the recovery of Abimelech (Gen. 20:17) and God healed him. David prayed for the recovery of his son (2 Sam. 12:16) but his son died. Elisha prayed for the recovery of the Shunammite woman's son (2 Kings 4:33) and the boy recovered. King Hezekiah prayed for his own recovery (2 Chron. 32:24) and God added fifteen years to his life. These incidents are anecdotal and hence do not constitute "scientific, statistical proof" of the efficacy of prayer, but they are certainly worthy of mention.

The main function of prayer, from a modern psychiatric viewpoint, is the prevention of despair and despondency. Depression, a very common disorder in our society, may be ameliorated, or possibly prevented, by prayers. Although prayer is desirable in its own right, it may also serve as a preparation or mobilization for action. When the Patriarch Jacob anticipated difficulties with his brother, Esau, Jacob prepared himself "for prayer and for battle" (*le-tefillah u-le' milḥamah*). Prayer may thus set the groundwork for the actions a person must take. Prayer sets a psychological frame of mind to allow the body's psyche to be at rest with itself. The sages of old used to tarry an hour before praying so that they would not pray by rote, and their prayers would have meaning and significance.

There are, of course, different types of prayers. The Bible is replete with descriptive prayers (Ps. 6:3, 30:13, 38:1–10, 102:4–6, 107:6), figurative prayers (Ps. 13:4, 34:21, 147:1), philosophic prayers (Ps. 39:5), prayers of youth, (Ps. 102:24), and prayers of old age (Ps. 71:9). The shortest prayer on record is the famous prayer uttered by Moses for the recovery of his sister, Miriam, who was afflicted with leprosy. Said

Moses: *"El na refa na la"* (O God, heal her, I beseech Thee), and she recovered (Num. 12:13).

The Talmud describes private prayers (*Shabbat* 30b, *Abodah Zarah* 4b, 7b) and public prayers (*Berakhot* 82, *Baba Batra* 91a), morning prayers (*Berakhot* 6b) and afternoon prayers (ibid.), prayers to be recited on entering a house of worship (*Berakhot* 28b) and on leaving a house of worship (ibid.), on going to the privy (ibid. 60b) and on entering a bathhouse (ibid. 60a), on going to bed (ibid. 60b) and upon arising in the morning (ibid. 28b), and on passing through a city (ibid. 54a, 60a). The Talmud further discusses the prayer shawl (*Hagigah* 14b), the time for prayer (*Shabbat* 118b, *Berakhot* 28b, 29b, 31a), the language of prayer (*Shabbat* 12b), the place for prayer (*Berakhot* 8a, 10b, 34b; *Shabbat* 10a), the position for prayer (*Berakhot* 5b, 6b, 10b, 28b, 39a), preparation for prayer (ibid. 32b, *Shabbat* 10a), washing before praying (*Berakhot* 15a, 22a), and sacrifices which accompany prayers (*Pesahim* 82a, *Taanit* 27b, *Megillah* 3a).

The rapidity with which prayers can be answered is described by the *Midrash Rabbah,* in its interpretation of the biblical phrase "whensoever we call upon Him" (Deut. 4:7).

> The rabbis said: A prayer can be answered after forty days, as can be learnt from Moses, as it is written: "And I fell down before the Lord . . . forty days," etc. [Deut. 9:18]; it can be answered after twenty days, as can be learnt from Daniel, as it is written: "I ate no pleasant bread . . . till three whole weeks were fulfilled" [Dan. 10:3]; and after this he prayed, "O Lord, hear, O Lord forgive" [ibid. 9:19]; and it can be answered after three days, as can be learnt from Jonah, as it is written: "And Jonah was in the belly of the fish three days and three nights" [Jon. 2:1], and after that [Scripture says], "Then Jonah prayed unto the Lord his God out of the fish's belly" [ibid. 2]; it can be answered after one day, as can be learnt from Elijah, as it is written: "And it came to pass at the time of the offering of the evening sacrifice, that Elijah the prophet came near, and said," etc. [1 Kings 18:36]; and it can also be answered at its time of utterance, as can be learnt from David, as it is written: "But as for me, let my prayer be unto Thee, O Lord, in an acceptable time" [Ps. 69:14]; while sometimes God answers a prayer even before it is uttered, as it is said: "And it shall come to pass that, before they call, I will answer" [Isa. 65:24].

Regarding the specific question of the efficacy of prayer, the following passage in the Talmud can be cited:

> R. Eleazar said: "Prayer is more efficacious even than good deeds, for there was no one greater in good deeds than Moses our teacher, and yet he was answered only after prayer." . . . R. Eleazar also said: "Prayer is more efficacious than offerings." . . . R. Eleazar also said: "From the day on which the Temple was destroyed the gates of prayer have been closed, as it says: 'Yea, when I cry and call for help He shutteth out my prayer' [Lam. 3:8]. But though the gates of prayer are closed, the gates of weeping are not closed, as it says: 'Keep not silence at my tears' [Ps. 39:13]." . . . R. Hanin said in the name of R. Hanina: "If one prays long, his prayer does not pass unheeded. . . . But is that so? Has not R. Hiyya ben Abba said in the name of R. Yohanan: 'If one prays long and looks for the fulfillment of his prayer, in the end he will have vexation of heart.' . . . There is no contradiction; the latter statement speaks of a man who prays long and looks for the fulfillment of his prayer, whereas the former speaks of one who prays long without looking for the fulfillment of his prayer." R. Hama son of R. Hanina said: "If a man sees that he prays and is not answered, he should pray again." [*Berakhot* 32b]

The conclusion to be drawn from the above talmudic passage is that the claim that God *must* answer a prayer is presumptuous and represents a transgression in Judaism (*Baba Batra* 164b).

Another circumstance where prayers are said to be efficacious is the need of the community for the sick person. Thus the Talmud states:

> . . . it once happened that R. Hanina ate half an onion and half of its poisonous fluid and became so ill that he was on the point of dying. His colleagues, however, begged for heavenly mercy and he recovered because his contemporaries needed him. [*Erubin* 29b]

The distinction and righteousness of the person who utters the prayers is also of importance, as evidenced by the following three brief talmudic citations:

> R. Isaac said: "The prayer of the righteous is comparable to a pitchfork; as the pitchfork changes the position of the wheat, so the

prayer changes the disposition of God from wrath to mercy."
[*Yebamot* 64a]

R. Yoḥahan ben Zakkai relied more on R. Ḥanina than on himself
when prayers were needed for his sick child, assuring his wife, "Although I am greater in learning than Ḥanina, he is more efficacious
in prayer; I am indeed the prince but he is the steward who has
constant access to the king." [*Berakhot* 34b]

There were two dumb men in the neighborhood of Rebbe [R. Judah
the Patriarch] . . . and Rebbe prayed for them and they were cured.
[*Ḥagigah* 3a]

Another interesting anecdote in the Talmud concerning the efficacy
of prayer relates to the son of R. Gamliel who once fell ill (*Berakhot*
34b). R. Gamliel sent two scholars to R. Ḥanina ben Dosa to ask him
to pray for him. When he saw them he went up to an upper chamber and
prayed for him. When he came down he said to them: "Go, the fever has
left him." They said to him: "Are you a prophet?" He replied: "I am
neither a prophet nor the son of a prophet, but I learnt this from experience. If my prayer is fluent in my mouth, I know that it is accepted,
but if not, I know that it is rejected." And so it happened: at that very
moment the fever left him and he asked for water to drink.

The very general use of prayer as a modality of treatment for the sick
is not in itself a *prima facie* argument in favor of the efficacy of prayer.
The fact remains, however, that the majority of mankind prays for the
sick at one time or another. The prayers may differ in content, in the
manner in which they are offered, or to whom they are addressed, but
both religious and nonreligious people alike offer prayers for recovery
when they are sick.

It has been well known since ancient times that the state of mind of a
sick person influences his response to treatment and may even play a role
in the *de novo* occurrence of an illness. In the third chapter of his *Regimen
of Health,* Maimonides states his concept of "a healthy mind in a healthy
body," [7, 8] perhaps the first accurate description of psychosomatic medicine. He indicates that the physical well-being of a person is dependent
on his mental well-being, and vice versa. Many classic psychosomatic
conditions, such as ulcerative colitis and asthma, can, in some patients, be
markedly ameliorated and even cured by psychotherapy. Prayer might
accomplish the same as psychotherapy.

This broader and more comprehensive notion of prayer might well explain the well-established relationship between the common cold and depression, that is to say, the reported higher incidence of colds in patients with depression, and the efficacy of prayer in reversing the depression, thus decreasing the incidence of such upper respiratory infections. The somatic symptoms of crying, sighing, and moaning, with their attendant congestion, in a depressed individual may aggravate a common cold, and these symptoms can be reversed by prayer. Many people are exposed to the same virus or bacteria, yet not all develop symptoms; those who do suffer different degrees of illness. The state of the patient's mind, which can be modified by prayer, is one of many host defense factors that accounts for these variations in illness.

A famous modern psychiatrist (Engel from Rochester) states that despondency predisposes to cancer. He further asserts that prayer decreases despondency and therefore the likelihood of cancer occurring is lessened. Such a theory, if carried to its extremes, is obviously absurd. Can praying three times daily prevent cancer? Nonsense.

No scientific study has yet satisfactorily proved the efficacy of prayer. The question one might pose is: Does the efficacy of prayer have to be scientifically proved? For what purpose? Will the majority of mankind change its praying habits on the basis of the results (positive or negative) of such a study?

Nevertheless, prayer in Judaism is thought to be efficacious if offered by the proper person at the proper time with the proper intent under the proper circumstances.

One should never be discouraged from praying even under the most difficult and troublesome conditions. The Talmud tells us that "even if a sharp sword rests upon a man's neck, he should not desist from prayer" (*Berakhot* 10a).

REFERENCES

1. P. J. Collipp, "The Efficacy of Prayer: A Triple-Blind Study," *Medical Times* 97 (1969): 201–4.
2. C. R. B. Joyce and R. M. C. Welldon, "The Objective Efficacy of Prayer: A Double-Blind Clinical Trial," *Journal of Chronic Diseases* 18 (1965): 367–77.
3. F. Galton, *Inquiries into Human Faculty and Its Development* (London: Macmillan, 1883), pp. 277–94.
4. F. Galton, "Statistical Inquiries into the Efficacy of Prayer," *Fortnightly Review* 12 (1872): 125–35.
5. C. G. Roland, "Does Prayer Preserve?" *Archives of Internal Medicine,* 125 (1970): 580–87.
6. Joyce and Welldon, op. cit.
7. H. L. Gordon, *Moses ben Maimon: The Preservation of Youth. Essays on Health.* (New York: Philosophical Library, 1958).
8. A. Bar Sela, H. E. Hoff, and E. Faris, "Moses Maimonides' *Two Treatises on the Regimen of Health,*" *Transactions of the American Philosophical Society,* n.s. 54, pt. 4 (1964).

Part V
Famous Physicians
in the Talmud

Physicians in the Talmud

The Hebrew terms for "physician," are *rofé* (plural *rofim*) and *asya*. In the Talmud, these terms do not denote a profession in the modern sense. Rather, *rofé* means "healer," not necessarily a physician. On the other hand, the expression *rofé umman* (*Sanhedrin* 91a, *Tosefta Makkot* 2:5, *Tosefta Baba Kamma* 6:17, and elsewhere) probably refers either to a learned physician or a certified physician. The physician's divine license to practice medicine is discussed elsewhere in this book.

The term *rofim* is first used in the Bible to denote the Egyptian servants of Joseph who embalmed his father, Jacob (Gen. 50:2). Some of the prophets use the word *rofé* to mean the physician as medical practitioner. Jeremiah thought it unbelievable that no physician lived in Gilead (Jer. 8:22). King Asa consulted physicians regarding the disease in his feet, thought to be gout (2 Chron. 16:12). Job called his friends "physicians of no value," i.e., physicians of vanity (Job 13:4).

The Midrash uses the term in many proverbs: "physician, physician, heal thine own limp" (*Gen. Rabbah* 23:4); "honor thy physician before thou hast need of him" (*Exod. Rabbah* 26:7); "shame on the province whose physician suffers from gout" (*Lev. Rabbah* 5:6); "a gate that is not opened for good deeds will be opened for the physician," i.e., charity and beneficence keep the doctor away (*Num. Rabbah* 9:13, *Song of Songs Rabbah* 6:11:1).

Physicians are cited in parables in many places in the Midrash (*Exod. Rabbah* 30:22, 46:4, 48:5; *Lev. Rabbah* 13:2; *Num. Rabbah* 20:14; *Song of Songs Rabbah* 2:3:2; *Lam. Rabbah* 1:16:51) and Talmud (*Semahot* 14:21 fol. 50a). A single example follows as an illustration: if a man had a seizure, came under the care of his physician, and died, he only died because he was in idleness; i.e., work leads to prosperity but idleness leads to death (*Abot de Rabbi Nathan* 11:1 fol. 22b).

There are also numerous references to God the Healer throughout the Bible (Ps. 6:3, 41:5, 103:3, 147:3; Num. 12:13; Deut. 32:39; Jer. 3:22, 17:14; Isa. 57:18; etc.). God caused drugs to spring forth from the earth, and with them the physician heals all wounds (*Gen. Rabbah* 10:6). A physician of flesh and blood wounds with a knife and heals with a plaster but the Holy One, blessed be He, heals with the very thing with which He wounds (*Lev. Rabbah* 18:5, based on Jer. 30:17). A physician in Sepphoris possessed the secret of the Ineffable Name (*Eccles. Rabbah* 3:11:3).

A recurring phrase in the Talmud is that "the best of physicians are destined for Gehenna" (*Kiddushin* 82a; *Soferim* 15:10 fol. 41a; *Abot de Rabbi Nathan* 36:5 fols. 31b–31a). One explanation is that they are haughty before the Almighty because they are unafraid of sickness. Secondly, a doctor who considers himself "the best" and refuses in his conceit to consult others could be responsible for the patient's death. Thirdly, a physician at the height of his profession may refuse to attend poor patients. It is such physicians, according to the Talmud, who do not conduct their affairs with the utmost sincerity, who are destined to Gehenna and have no portion in the world to come. It is perhaps for a similar reason that the Talmud advises that one should not dwell in a town where the leader of the community is a physician (*Pesaḥim* 113a); he is too busy with his medical practice to devote himself to community affairs. On the other hand, one should not live in a city without a physician (*Sanhedrin* 17b). Jakobovits (*Jewish Medical Ethics* New York: Bloch, 1975 p. 202) points out that the Greeks and Romans and other cultures also had pronouncements critical of physicians. Some statements, such as "optimus inter medicos ad Gehennam," were nearly or completely identical with the taunt in the Mishnah.

A physician applies bandages to the head, hands, and feet of a man who falls from the roof and whose body is bruised (*Exod. Rabbah* 27:9). A qualified physician treats patients with epilepsy (*Lev. Rabbah* 26:5). If a person was bitten by a snake, one may call for him a physician from a distant place even on the Sabbath, since all Sabbath restrictions are set aside in the case of possible danger to human life (*Yoma* 83b). Physicians compound remedies with which they heal snake bites (*Song of Songs Rabbah* 4:5:1). These statements are self-explanatory.

Other assertions seem to have no scientific validity. The following are examples: A physician can diagnose an intestinal ailment by giving a patient a hard-boiled egg to eat and watching it pass out (*Nedarim* 50a). A physician said that hard pumpkins are injurious to the sick (ibid. 49a). A physician can cure a bodily defect in a betrothed woman (*Ketubot* 74b) or man (ibid. 75a). For pain in the heart, the physicians recommended sucking hot milk from a goat every morning (*Baba Kamma* 80a, *Temurah* 15b). Physicians cured a deathly ill Persian king with the milk of a lioness (*Midrash Psalms* 39:2).

The Talmud advises: he who has pain should seek a physician (*Baba Kamma* 85a). A physician who heals for nothing is worth nothing (ibid.). A physician from afar has a blind eye (or may blind an eye); i.e., he is little concerned about the fate of his patient (ibid.).

Patients pay the physician to cure an ailment without any guarantee that they will be healed (*Ketubot* 105a). A physician can paint the eye of his servant with an ointment and drill his teeth (*Kiddushin* 24b). A woman who wept all night until her eyelashes fell out was told by her physician: paint your eyes with stibium and you will recover (*Lam. Rabbah* 2:15). Once again, there seems to be no medical explanation for this epilation secondary to weeping nor for the cure suggested by the Midrash.

Surgical and orthopedic practices, including the instrumentation therefor, are described in the Talmud as follows: A surgeon wears an apron to protect himself from spurting blood (*Kelim* 26:5), straps the patient tightly to the table (*Tosefta Shekalim* 1:6), and uses a special box to keep his instruments (*Kelim* 16:8). Drugs are kept in a different receptacle (ibid. 12:3) and may be dispensed with the physician's ladle (ibid. 17:12). The surgeon opens abscesses skillfully (*Tosefta Eduyot* 1:8) and opens the skull with the physician's small drill or trepan (*Oholot* 2:3, *Bekhorot* 38a). A physician was once called to cut into an abscess of Joseph ben Piskas (*Semahot* 4:28 fol. 45a). The surgeon cuts away gangrenous parts (*Hullin* 77a) and amputates limbs for leprosy (*Keritot* 15b). He also heals fractures (*Moed Katan* 21b).

Physicians healed R. Zadok, who was near death from fasting (*Gittin* 56b). Expert physicians attended R. Yohanan and R. Abbahu (*Abodah Zarah* 28a). A doctor who can cure a hunchback is considered a "great doctor" and can command large fees (*Sanhedrin* 91a). The sages consulted physicians regarding a woman who was aborting objects like red hairs and pieces of red rind (*Niddah* 22b). The physicians explained that she has an internal sore and is shedding the crust or scab. A physician is consulted in cases of claims for restitution for damages for bodily injuries (*Sanhedrin* 78a) and concerning the ability of a convicted criminal to tolerate disciplinary flogging (*Makkot* 3:11). A sick person is fed even on the Day of Atonement at the word of the physicians (*Yoma* 83a). Even if the patient says he does not need food, we listen to the physicians. Conversely, if the physician says the patient does not need it, whereas the patient says he needs it, we hearken to the patient because "the heart knoweth its own bitterness" (Prov. 14:10). Physicians were consulted in a case where a man had a violent passion for a woman forbidden to him and his heart was consumed by his burning desire and his life was thereby endangered (*Sanhedrin* 75a).

In a town where there is no Jewish physician, the Talmud discusses whether it is preferable for circumcision to be performed by an idolater or a Cuthean (*Abodah Zarah* 26b–27a, *Menahot* 42a). The Talmud also discusses whether or not one is permitted to follow the advice of a heathen physician (*Abodah Zarah* 27a–28b).

There are specific individuals cited in the Talmud with the title "physician": Minyami, Theodos, Tobiya, Benjamin, Bar Girnte, R. Ammi, and R. Nathan. Minyami the physician said that any kind of fluid is bad for pain in the ear except the juice from kidneys (*Abodah Zarah* 28b). No modern medical concept supports such a statement. Theodos the physician said that no cow or pig leaves Alexandria of Egypt without its uterus being cut out to prevent it from reproducing (*Sanhedrin* 93a, *Bekhorot* 28b). The Alexandrians maintained a monopoly on the excellent breed of cows and pigs they had, thus compelling buyers to come to Alexandria. Theodos the physician could also distinguish human from animal skeletons (*Nazir* 52a, *Tosefta Oholot* 4:2). Tobiya the physician is mentioned in the Talmud (*Rosh Hashanah* 1:7) but no medical pronouncement is attributed to him. The same is true of R. Nathan the physician (*Pesahim* 52a).

Abaye described a salve for all pains. The ingredients are not specified. Rabba expounded the recipe in public in Mehoza, whereupon the family (or disciples) of Benjamin the physician tore their garments in despair, fearing their medical practice would diminish (*Shabbat* 133b). Competition among physicians in those days may have been keen. These disciples of Benjamin the physician were thought to be disbelievers, in that they said, "Of what use are the rabbis to us?" (*Sanhedrin* 99b). The Jerusalem Talmud cites Bar Girnte the physician (J. T. *Bezah* 1:60) and R. Ammi the physician (J. T. *Berakhot* 2:4).

There are other individuals in the Talmud who certainly had medical expertise although they are not cited as "physicians." The most illustrious of these is Mar Samuel. The next chapter of this book is devoted to an in-depth discussion of the medical aspects of Mar Samuel. Others include R. Hiyya, who felt the pulse of his sick colleague (*Berakhot* 5b), and R. Ishmael and his disciples, who performed an autopsy on a female corpse. Mar Bar Rav Ashi performed plastic surgery on the penis (*Yebamot* 75b). R. Ḥanina was knowledgeable in healing remedies (*Yoma* 49a). Ben Aḥiya gave remedies to priests with intestinal ailments (*Shekalim* 5:1–2). Rab spent eighteen months with a shepherd to learn eye diseases of animals (*Sanhedrin* 5b). R. Yoḥanan described a remedy for *zafdina* which he had learned from a Roman woman (*Abodah Zarah* 28a). Although it is impossible to ascertain with certainty whether the above talmudic sages were physicians, they do demonstrate a considerable knowledge of medicine.

Jewish law has the advantage of being heir to a rich millennial tradition of intimate partnership between Judaism and medicine. Many of the principal architects of Jewish law, and some of the most outstanding authorities of the Talmud, codes, commentaries, and other rabbinical writings, were themselves medical practitioners. The literary depositories of Jewish law, from the Bible and Talmud to the medieval and modern rabbinical literature, are replete with discussions of religious and moral problems raised in the practice of medicine, and the conclusions reached frequently reflect practical experience in medicine no less than respect for the medical profession, and the infinite regard for human life and health inculcated by Jewish teachings.

Mar Samuel the Physician

This chapter represents a detailed analysis of the medical expertise of one of the sages of the Talmud. Mar Samuel, perhaps the most renowned physician in the Talmud, was probably as great a physician as he was a rabbinic scholar. His knowledge of medicine spans many specialties, including ophthalmology, gynecology, pediatrics, anatomy, toxicology, urology, gastroenterology, bloodletting, therapeutics, and more. His eye-salve was in great demand because of its efficacy. As with other physicians of antiquity, Samuel considered bloodletting to be a universal panacea, prescribing it even as a prophylactic measure. His recommendations in hygiene and general therapeutics were legion. He was physician to R. Judah the Patriarch, and probably also to King Shapur I.

His familiarity with astronomy was no less profound than his knowledge of medicine and his expertise in talmudic law. Further investigation into the statements of Mar Samuel and other physicians in the Talmud may provide the twentieth-century physician with a clearer understanding of ancient medicine and its impact upon our present techniques of diagnosis and therapy of disease.

Mar Samuel, rabbi, physician, and astronomer, one of the most important Babylonian talmudists,[1-6] was born in the town of Nehardea in Babylon around 180 C.E. (according to some sources 174 C.E. or as early as 160 C.E.) and died around 254 C.E. His birth, like his name, was glorified by legend.[2] Physically, he was probably puny and unsightly,[3] and was described as "short and big stomached, black and large teethed" (*Nedarim* 50b). He was modest, humble, and honest in character.[4] Intellectually he was a giant. He received his early education from his father, Abba bar Abba, himself a learned talmudic sage and rich silk merchant. Samuel continued his studies at the rabbinical academy of R. Judah ben Betera in Netzivim (Nisibis), capital city of the Armenian kings. Netzivim was endowed with a medical school, and it is probably here that Samuel obtained his medical instruction. Later he returned to Nehardea and studied under R. Levi ben Sisi. Afterwards he went to Palestine with his father and studied both theology and medicine with R. Ḥanina bar Ḥama in Tzipori (Sepphoris). The latter was considered "an expert in medicine," and his and Samuel's names are frequently encountered together in joint medical statements. It was at this time that Mar Samuel was physician to R. Judah the Patriarch, and later, when he returned to Babylon, he became friendly with and probably the personal physician of King Shapur I (vide infra).

Mar Samuel's Names

Mar Samuel's real name was Shmuel ben Abba Hakohen (lit. Samuel, son of Abba the Priest). He was also called *Yarhinah* (*Baba Meẓia* 85b), meaning astronomer, because of his knowledge of astronomy and astrology. He was named Mar Shmuel (Master Samuel) rather than Rabbi Samuel because he was never ordained, perhaps because R. Judah the Patriarch was ill and unable to assemble the ordination board (*Baba Meẓia* 85b). Mar Samuel consoled the Patriarch by saying that it was most likely foretold even before Adam that he was destined to be a wise man but not an ordained rabbi (ibid.). However, in the Jerusalem Talmud, Mar Samuel is called Rabbi on three occasions (*Peah* 4:5, *Shekalim* 4:4, *Nedarim* 2:2).

Mar Samuel was nicknamed *Ariokh* (*Kiddushin* 39a, *Menahot* 38b, *Shabbat* 53a, *Ḥullin* 76b), a Persian word variously translated as "king," "judge," "powerful," "tall," "lion." He was also called *Shakud,* meaning "industrious scholar" (*Ketubot* 43b). It was said of Mar Samuel that he never ceased studying (*Ketubot* 77a). The verse "No secret troubleth thee" (Dan. 4:6) was applied to Samuel by his contemporary and co-talmudist Rab (Abba Arikha). Mar Samuel was also known as a "great man" (*Hullin* 76a) whose "knowledge was exceptional" (*Niddah* 25b, 64b; *Hagigah* 13b). R. Yohanan used to write to Mar Samuel addressing him with the phrase "Greetings to our learned colleague in Babylon" (*Hullin* 95b). He was also called Mar Samuel of Nehardea (*Abodah Zara* 28b) because he became head of the rabbinical academy of that city after the death of R. Shela. Finally, Mar Samuel was called a physician (*Baba Mezia* 85b), one of the few talmudic sages to whom this designation was specifically applied, although many medical pronouncements throughout the Talmud are attributed to various scholars.

Mar Samuel's Family

Little is known about Mar Samuel's family. His father is mentioned frequently in the Talmud (*Ketubot* 23a, *Pesahim* 103a, *Hullin* 107b, *Bezah* 16b) and was recognized as a learned rabbinic scholar and rich silk merchant. He is referred to in the Babylonian Talmud as *Abuha di Shmuel* ("the father of Samuel"). A brother of Mar Samuel, Phineas, is mentioned, and is said to have suffered a bereavement, and Samuel went to console him (*Moed Katan* 18a). Later, Samuel suffered a bereavement, and his brother came to console him. Although the deceased relative is not identified in the Talmud, it is assumed that it was a son of Samuel who died in order to fulfill Rab's curse.[4] The latter is related in the following incident:

> Samuel and Karna were sitting by the bank of the river and saw Rab coming. Samuel took Rab into his house, gave him barley bread and a fish pie to eat, and strong liquor to drink [i.e., a strong laxative mixture], but did not show him the privy that he might be eased [perhaps as therapy for Rab's stomach ailment]. Rab cursed saying: "He who causes me pain, may no sons arise from him." And thus it was. [*Shabbat* 108a]

Whether Samuel had one or more sons who died early, or whether he had no sons at all, is not clear. Rabbah, son of Samuel, a talmudic sage known for having made both medical and astronomical pronouncements (*Yoma* 84b, *Rosh Hashanah* 20a), may be the son of another Samuel.

Mar Samuel had at least two daughters, as evidenced by a talmudic passage which states that "daughters of Mar Samuel were taken captive" and were brought to the land of Israel (*Ketubot* 23a). Their captors stood outside. Both daughters claimed not to have been violated in captivity, whereupon R. Ḥanina said to R. Shaman ben Abba: "Go and take care of thy relatives," that is, marry one of them. The relationship of R. Shaman to Mar Samuel is not specified.

Elsewhere in the Talmud we hear of Mar Samuel's nephew, or "the son of my father's brother" (*Baba Kamma* 83a). Finally, one passage mentions his daughter Rachel, his son-in-law Issur, and his grandson R. Mari (*Yebamoth* 45b). Rachel was one of Mar Samuel's captive daughters who, while in captivity, was married to an idolater and gave birth to Mari. Issur, the father of the child, embraced Judaism while Rachel was still pregnant, and he is several times referred to in the Talmud as Issur the proselyte (*Baba Bathra* 149a). Mari was declared to be a legitimate Israelite (*Yebamot* 45b).

Mar Samuel the Astronomer

Mar Samuel was very friendly with a non-Jewish astrologer named Ablat, who is mentioned in the Talmud several times (*Shabbat* 156b, *Abodah Zarah* 30a). With his friend Ablat, Samuel studied astronomy. The cradle of this science extended between the Euphrates and Tigris rivers. Astronomy soon degenerated into the pseudo-science of astrology. Samuel once argued with Ablat that Israelites are immune from planetary influences, and, in fact, a case occurred where a man was saved from a fatal snakebite by prayer (*Shabbat* 156b). By reason of his Jewish education, "Samuel attached no importance to the art of casting nativities, and only occupied himself with astronomy under its most elevated aspect," [6] repudiating all astrological superstitions.

The Talmud asks: "What are *zikin?*" (shooting stars), to which Samuel answers: "A comet" (*Berakhot* 58b). He further said: "I am as familiar with the paths of heaven as with the streets of Nehardea, with the exception of the comet, about which I am ignorant" (ibid.). The Talmud also queries: "What is meant by *Kunah?*" Samuel said: "About a hundred stars" (ibid.).

Mar Samuel turned his knowledge of astronomy to practical use. He drew up a calendar "designed to make Babylonian Jewry independent of Palestine in determining the time of the appearance of the New Moon and the days when the holidays were to be celebrated." [1] Samuel himself stated: "I am quite able to make a calendar [Heb. leap years] for the whole of the Diaspora" (*Rosh Hashanah* 20b); and elsewhere the Talmud relates that Samuel sent to R. Yoḥanan the calculation for the intercalation of months for sixty years (*Ḥullin* 95b). Furthermore, Samuel said that the year must not be declared a prolonged or leap year on the thirtieth of the month of Adar "since that day may probably belong to the [next month], Nissan" (*Berakhot* 10b).

Mar Samuel the Talmudist

Mar Samuel developed and enriched Jewish law in all its branches. In matters of civil law, his decisions received final legal validity (*Bekhorot* 49b). The most significant of his decrees was the one in which he declared that *dina demalkhuta dina,* or "the law of the land is the final law" (*Gittin* 10b, *Baba Bathra* 54b). This principle created the theoretical basis for the existence of the Jews in the Diaspora.[1] The object of this precept was not to bring about a compulsory toleration of foreign legislation, but to obtain its complete recognition as a binding law.[6] On the one hand, it reconciled the Jews to being in the country into which fate cast them. On the other hand, the enemies of the Jews, who, throughout the centuries, took as their pretext the apparently hostile spirit of Judaism, could be referred to this "three-worded Jewish law" to invalidate their contention.

Samuel insisted that Jews be as honest with non-Jews as with their own co-religionists (*Ḥullin* 94a). He also introduced the principle that the burden of proof lies with the plaintiff in monetary cases (*Baba Kamma* 46a). He set the maximum margin of profit in sales of items at one-sixth of the price; more than that is considered exorbitant and the transaction is invalid (*Baba Meẓia* 40b, *Baba Batra* 90b). Samuel also invalidated forced divorces in cases where there was no compulsion at the time of the marriage (*Gittin* 88b). He further established humanitarian laws for widows (*Ketubot* 54a, *Gittin* 96a) and orphans (*Ketubot* 100b, *Baba Meẓia* 70a). Numerous other Jewish legal innovations and pronouncements by Mar Samuel are beyond the scope of this essay.[4]

Mar Samuel and King Shapur I

Mar Samuel favored friendly relations with non-Jews. He possessed a particular affection for Persian customs and, as a result, was in exceedingly good repute at the Persian court.[1,6] He was on intimate terms with Shapur I (241–272 C.E.), king of Persia and Babylonia, who ascended the throne after the death of King Artaban and his successor, Ardeshir.[4] Mar Samuel was himself referred to in the Talmud as King Shapur (*Baba Batra* 115b), possibly in jest, because of his loyalty to the king,[1] or perhaps as a mark of honor.[6] Samuel was also called *Ariokh* (vide supra), perhaps meaning Aryan or partisan of the neo-Persians.

The Talmud relates that Mar Samuel used to juggle with eight glasses of wine before King Shapur without spilling their contents (*Sukkah* 53a). A conversation between Mar Samuel and the king (*Sanhedrin* 98a) has the latter saying, "Ye maintain that the Messiah will come upon an ass. I will rather send him a white horse, [this is more fitting]" (*Sanhedrin* 98a). It is further related in the Talmud that when Samuel was informed that King Shapur had slain twelve thousand Jews at Caesarea-Mazaca, capital of Cappodocia, a vital military post on the main roads leading to the East, Samuel did not rend his clothes in mourning, for he was of the opinion that the Jews deserved the defeat because of their sins (*Mo'ed Katan* 26a).

Mar Samuel the Physician

Mar Samuel's knowledge of medicine seems to have been all-encompassing. His medical pronouncements in the Talmud cover a wide range of areas in medicine, including ophthalmology, anatomy, obstetrics and gynecology, therapeutics, embryology, dermatology, wound healing, bloodletting, toxicology, pediatrics, cardiology, urology, gastroenterology, otolaryngology, and general medicine. By far the most renowned of Samuel's remedies is his eye-salve, which is repeatedly mentioned in the Talmud. There follows one such passage:

> Samuel Yarḥina'ah was Rebbe's physician. Rebbe [R. Judah the Patriarch] contracted an eye disease. Samuel offered to bathe it with a lotion but he [Rebbe] said, "I cannot bear it." He [Samuel] said, "Then I will apply an ointment to it." He [Rebbe] objected, "This too I cannot bear." So he [Samuel] placed a phial of chemical under his [Rebbe's] pillow, and he was healed. [*Baba Meẓia* 85b]

Apparently the vapor was sufficiently powerful to penetrate to the eye, though not applied directly. Elsewhere, when someone asked Mar Ukba to send some of Mar Samuel's eye-salve, he replied, "Samuel also said that a drop of cold water in the morning, and bathing the hands and feet in hot water in the evening, is better than all the eye-salves in the world" (*Shabbat* 108b). Perhaps Samuel was recommending a prophylactic regimen to avoid eye infections. Samuel further stated that all liquids used for dissolving collyrium or eye-salves heal eye sicknesses but dim the eyesight, except water, which heals without dimming (*Shabbat* 78a). Elsewhere, Samuel promulgated that fish heal the eyes when ingested at the end of an illness, but are injurious if eaten at the beginning of the eye ailment (*Nedarim* 54b), and that thick saliva is a remedy for eye ailments (J.T. *Shabbat* 14:4), and that the eyes recover from the weakening effect of tears until one is forty years old, but not thereafter (*Shabbat* 151b). There seems to be no modern medical validity to these various pronouncements concerning eye disorders.

Finally, Samuel's ophthalmological expertise is noted in the following passage: "Mar Samuel propounded that if one's eye gets out of order it is permissible to paint it [i.e., apply medication] even on the Sabbath, the reason being because eyesight is connected with the mental [or cardiac] faculties" (*Abodah Zarah* 28b). The Talmud describes what type of eye ailment Samuel is referring to: "discharges, pricking, congestion, watering, inflammation, or the first stages of sickness" (ibid.).

Mar Samuel's understanding of the genito-urinary system is evidenced by two talmudic passages. Firstly, Samuel recognized that a person with "punctured testicles so that the semen issues like a thread of pus" is incapable of procreation (*Yebamot* 75b). Secondly, Samuel said that if an infant's penis, after circumcision, is overgrown with flesh, he must be examined: "as long as he appears circumcised when he forces himself [i.e., performs a Valsalva maneuver, or moves his bowels], it is unnecessary to recircumcise him, but if not he must be recircumcised" (*Shabbat* 137b).

In the field of pediatrics, Mar Samuel discusses the stages of childhood leading up to puberty (*Niddah* 65a), and describes the secondary sex characteristics of a *bogeret* (girl from the age of twelve and one-half years onwards) when he states: "What are the physical signs of a *bogeret*? Samuel said that when she puts her hands behind her, a wrinkle appears beneath the breast . . ." (*Niddah* 47a).

Mar Samuel the toxicologist said that all reptiles have poisonous venom (*Abodah Zarah* 31b). The venom of a serpent is fatal, while that of other reptiles has no lethal effects. Samuel also conceded that onion leaves may be poisonous, and therefore he recommends eating only the bulbs of onions (*Erubin* 29a).

Tachycardia seems to be described when Samuel said that if one is bled and then eats fowl, his heart will palpitate like a fowl's (*Nedarim* 54b). In the area of otolaryngology, Samuel said that if a man has his esophagus and trachea slit, he will die (*Gittin* 70b). Adenoids may be the pathologic entity referred to in the following talmudic citation: "One who has a polypus must divorce his wife. What is polypus? Samuel said: one who suffers from an offensive nasal smell" (*Ketubot* 77a).

Five pronouncements by Samuel in gastroenterology are recorded in the Talmud. He claimed that if an animal swallowed liquid asafoetida, it will develop perforated internal organs (*Hullin* 58b). He also said that "the change in one's regular diet is the beginning of digestive trouble" (*Nedarim* 37b). He further stated that "sleep at dawn is like a steel edge to iron, and evacuation at dawn is like a steel edge to iron" (i.e., beneficial) (*Berakhot* 62b), and "insufficiently cooked vegetables are bad for the bowels" (*Berakhot* 44b). Finally, Samuel used to investigate his own digestive tract, as described in the following incident:

> Samuel said that if one has intestinal ulcers and swallows a small, well-boiled egg, and passes it out per rectum intact, the doctor knows what medicine is required, and how to treat him. Samuel used to examine himself with *kulkha* [the stalk of a certain plant], which caused him so much pain and weakened him so much that his household tore their hair in despair. [*Nedarim* 50b]

In the field of therapeutics, Samuel said that for a man wounded by a poisoned Persian lance, there is no hope (*Gittin* 70a). However, the patient should be given fat roast meat and strong wine, as this may keep him alive long enough to enable him to give his last instructions. It was said in Mar Samuel's name that *alin* (leaves) have no healing properties (*Shabbat* 109a), and that all kinds of cuscuta have no healing properties except *teruza* (a kind of melon or cucumber possessing medicinal properties). Also said in Samuel's name was the edict that if a man is seized by a ravenous hunger on the Day of Atonement, when eating is prohibited, one should give him a tail with honey to eat. Otherwise he might die (*Yoma* 83a). Elsewhere, Samuel said that all medicinal potions taken between Passover and Pentecost are beneficial (*Shabbat* 147b), and "the law is that one may reset a fracture on the Sabbath" because of the possibility of danger to life (*Shabbat* 148a). Samuel also said that a certain ailment is caused by the wind, and were it not for the wind, an ointment could be compounded which would cause the severed parts to grow together and the patient would recover (*Baba Meẓia* 107b). Perhaps the ointment refers to *samtre,* a herb reputed to have the power of uniting severed parts (*Baba Batra* 7b). The following talmudic passage speaks for itself:

. . . if one has intercourse standing, he has attacks of trembling ['*ahilu*]. What is the cure for it? Flour of lentils in wine. Samuel said: "A man should practice all remedies when he is hungry, but this remedy when he is well fed. All remedies should be practiced when standing on the ground, but this remedy, even with one foot on the ground and one foot on the bed." [*Kallah Rabbati* 1:18]

Many of these remedies are based on folk medicine and have no modern medical counterpart.

Apparently Samuel had therapeutic regimens for nearly all ailments. Only in one place in the Talmud does Samuel admit to ignorance. "Samuel said: For all things I know the cure except the following three: eating bitter dates on an empty stomach, girding one's loins with a damp flaxen cord, and eating bread without walking four cubits after it." (*Baba Mezia* 113b).

The specialties of obstetrics, gynecology and fetal development, embryology, and teratology were well understood by Mar Samuel. To examine the uterus, Samuel recommended the use of a "leaden tube [speculum?] whose edge is bent inwards" (*Niddah* 66a). Samuel stated that he knew how one could have repeated sexual connections with a virgin without causing bleeding, that is, without rupturing the woman's hymen (*Niddah* 64b, *Ḥagigah* 14b). In both places, the Talmud comments upon the fact that Samuel's knowledge and capability in medical matters is exceptional. Elsewhere it is related that a certain woman came to Mar Samuel complaining of bleeding occasioned by intercourse. He told R. Dimi ben Joseph to frighten her. If a clot of blood had dropped from her she would have been cured, but since it did not, Samuel said she is "full of blood which scatters [as a result of intercourse] and thus has no cure" (*Niddah* 66a).

Samuel considered a true embryo, as opposed to a clot shaped like a fetus, to have hair on its head (*Niddah* 25a). He also said that in the case of "an aborted sac on which a hair that lay on one side could be seen through the other side," it is not a true embryo, because "if it were in fact a fetus it would not have been so transparent" (ibid.). Samuel further thought that a placenta can be attributed to an embryo as late as ten days after the latter's birth (*Niddah* 26b). For a woman in confinement, as long as the uterus is open, Samuel allows the desecration of the Sabbath (*Shabbat* 128b), including the making of a fire (ibid. 129a). If a woman dies in childbirth on the Sabbath, Samuel requires that one bring a knife and cut open her womb to take out and perhaps rescue the child (*Arakhin* 7a). Samuel's remarkable and accurate knowledge of fetal development is self evident from the following talmudic passage:

> A certain [fetal] sac was submitted to Master Samuel and he said: "This is forty-one days old," but on calculating the time since the woman had gone to perform her ritual immersion [following the conclusion of her menstrual period] until that day and finding that there were no more than forty days, he declared: "The husband must have had marital intercourse during her menstrual period" [an act strictly prohibited in Jewish law]. The man was arrested and confessed. Samuel was different from other people because his knowledge was exceptional. [*Niddah* 25b]

Monster births are also described by Samuel and others (*Niddah* 24a). One such occurrence is thought to represent spina bifida[3] and is called *shesua* in Hebrew.

In the field of dermatology, Mar Samuel propounded that he who washes his face but does not dry it well will develop scabs (eczema?) on his skin (*Shabbat* 133b). The suggested remedy, if these occur, is to wash in beet juice (ibid.). Samuel also said that scabs on the head caused by lack of washing lead to blindness; scabs arising from the wearing of unclean garments cause madness, and scabs due to neglect of the body produce boils and ulcers (*Nedarim* 81a). Since madness is considered the worst of all, it is proved that laundering is of greater importance than bathing.

For wound healing, Samuel said that hot water and oil applied to the wound are beneficial (*Shabbat* 134b). He also stated that an open wound is to be regarded as a dangerous situation for which the Sabbath may be profaned (*Abodah Zarah* 28a). The following remedy is suggested: "for stopping the bleeding, cress with vinegar; for bringing on [flesh], scraped root of cynodon and the paring of bramble, or worms from a dunghill."

The subject of bloodletting, or phlebotomy, is discussed at great length by both Mar Samuel and his contemporary Abba Arikha, known as Rab. There follow some of these discussions:

> Rab and Samuel both say: "He who is bled, let him not sit where a wind can enfold him, lest the cupper drain him of blood and re-

duce his blood to a *rebi'it* [the minimum quantity of blood which can sustain life] and the wind come and drain him still further, and thus he is in danger." [*Shabbat* 129a]

Samuel was accustomed to be bled in a house whose wall consisted of seven whole bricks [each brick is three handbreadths wide] and a half-brick in thickness. One day he was bled and felt himself weak; he examined the wall and found a half-brick missing. [*Shabbat* 129a]

Rab and Samuel both say: "He who is bled must first partake of something and then go out; for if he does not eat anything: if he meets a corpse, his face will turn green; if he witnesses a homicide, he will die; and if he meets a swine, it is harmful in respect of something else [i.e., he may catch leprosy from it]." [*Shabbat* 129a].

Rab and Samuel both say: "He who is bled should tarry awhile and then rise, for a Master said: 'In five cases one is nearer to death than to life. And these are they: When one eats and immediately rises, drinks and rises, sleeps and rises, lets blood and rises, and cohabits and rises.' " [*Shabbat* 129b]

Samuel said: "The correct interval for bloodletting is every thirty days; in middle age [i.e., past forty], one should decrease [the frequency, since the body begins to lose heat at forty years of age and frequent bleedings may be injurious]. At a more advanced age [i.e., past sixty], he should again decrease the frequency." [*Shabbat* 129b]

R. Ḥiyya ben Abin said in Samuel's name: "If one lets blood and catches a chill, a fire is made for him [on the Sabbath] even on the *Tammuz* [summer] solstice. A teak chair was broken up for Samuel [for a fire, other wood being unavailable] . . ." [*Shabbat* 129a]

Rab said: "If one has let blood and has nothing to eat, let him sell the shoes from off his feet to provide the requirements of a meal therewith." What are the requirements of a meal? Rab said meat, while Samuel said wine. Rab said meat: life [i.e., meat] for life, while Samuel said wine: red [wine] to replace red [blood]. [ibid.]

For Samuel on the day he was bled, a dish of pieces of milt was prepared. [ibid.]

Ablat, a Persian sage and friend of Samuel, found Samuel sleeping

in the sun. Said he to him, "O Jewish sage! can that which is injurious be beneficial?" Replied Samuel, "It is a day of bleeding."
[ibid.]

Samuel said: "If one eats a grain of wheat and then lets blood,
he has bled in respect to that grain only [i.e., bleeding immediately
after a meal serves only to lighten one of that meal, but has no
wider effects]. If it is done as a remedy, it is ineffective, but if it is
to ease one from an excess of blood, it does ease [even if performed
immediately after a meal]. When one is bled, drinking is permissible
immediately; eating until one is able to walk half a mile." [*Shabbat*
129b]

This lengthy digression on bloodletting will serve to indicate to the
reader that Mar Samuel was a product of his era. Since the time of
Hippocrates and Galen, bloodletting had been considered to be a panacea
to cure nearly all ailments. Mar Samuel extended this hypothesis and ad-
vocated prophylactic bloodletting to avert illness. He correctly points out
that excessive phlebotomy is harmful and can endanger a person's life.
He also advises a person to eat a little prior to and after bloodletting, to
rest for a while after bloodletting, and to decrease the frequency of blood
donation as one becomes older, particularly when past sixty years of age.
All these suggestions are perfectly reasonable and applicable to this very
day.

There is one modern disease for which the initial treatment of choice
is phlebotomy. This condition is called polycythemia vera and consists
of an overproduction by the body of red blood corpuscles. Such patients
are plethoric, suffer from headaches, have beefy red tongues, conjunctival
suffusion, and occasionally intense itching of the skin. It is likely that
those patients in ancient and medieval times who benefited from bloodletting were afflicted with this disease. Plethora and headache are two of
the signs and symptoms for which phlebotomy was recommended in
talmudic times.

Many of Mar Samuel's assertions regarding bloodletting seem to have
no scientific merit at all. For example: if one is bled and then eats fowl,
his heart will palpitate like a fowl's (*Nedarim* 54b). Furthermore there
are two passages dealing with bloodletting which reflect a mixture of
astrology, medicine, and religion. The hours and the months of the year
were thought to stand under the influence of the planets. Mars represented

war, pestilence, and retribution, while the even-numbered hours of the day were regarded as particularly susceptible to disaster. Hence, bloodletting was forbidden on Tuesdays, as follows:

> Samuel also said: "The correct time for bloodletting is on a Sunday, Wednesday, and Friday, but not on Monday or Thursday. . . . Why not on Tuesday? Because the planet Mars rules at even-numbered hours of the day. But on Friday, too, it rules at even-numbered hours?—Since the multitude are accustomed to it [bleeding on Friday], 'the Lord preserveth the simple' [Ps. 116:6]." [*Shabbat* 129b]

> Samuel said: "The fourth day of the week [i.e., Wednesday] which is the fourth of the month, or a Wednesday which is the fourteenth, a Wednesday which is the twenty-fourth, a Wednesday which is not followed by four [days in the same month]—all are dangerous for bleeding. The first day of the month and the second cause weakness, the third is dangerous. The eve of a Festival causes weakness; the eve of Pentecost is dangerous, and the rabbis laid an interdict upon the eve of every Festival on account of the Festival of Pentecost, when there issues a wind called *Taboaḥ* [lit. slaughter], and had not the Israelites accepted the Torah it would absolutely have killed them." [ibid.]

There is one other large area of medical science where Mar Samuel's pronouncements attest to his vast knowledge, and that is anatomy. R. Judah related in the name of Samuel that the disciples of R. Ishmael once dissected the body of a prostitute who had been condemned to be burnt by the king. They examined and found 252 joints and limbs (*Bekhorot* 45a). The remainder of Samuel's teachings in anatomy center around a talmudic discussion dealing with the subject of *terefah* (lit. torn). *Terefah* refers to an animal suffering from a serious organic disease, whose meat is forbidden even if it has been ritually slaughtered. Such an animal is thought to be nonviable. Thus, Samuel said that if the outer membrane (pleura) of the lung was pierced, the animal is *terefah* (*Ḥullin* 46a). He also stated that if the pharynx was entirely detached from the jaw, i.e., torn away both from the jawbone and the surrounding flesh so that the gullet now hangs loose, the animal is valid, i.e., not *terefah* (ibid. 44a). He further expounded that "the part of the gullet which, when cut opens wide, is the pharynx; but that part which, when cut remains as it was, is the gullet proper" (ibid. 43b).

The sages of the Talmud expounded that if the juncture of the tendons (i.e., the Achilles tendon) was gone, the animal is *terefah* (*Hullin* 76a). Samuel explained: "The juncture of the tendons of which they spoke is the place where the tendons converge, and it extends from the place where the tendons converge up to the place where they part." Samuel further explained that there are three tendons comprising the Achilles tendon (ibid.). He also speaks of fractures of the leg bones.

Elsewhere, the Talmud asks at what point the vitality of the spinal cord ceases, so that any severance of the cord beyond that point would not produce a fatal outcome or render the animal *terefah* (*Hullin* 45b). Samuel said: "Up to the interval between the spinal [sacral] nerves . . ." Severance of the cord at the level of the first sacral nerve renders an animal nonviable, at the third sacral nerve, no harm is done. "As to the second, I do not know," concludes Samuel.

The Talmud asserts that if the membrane of the brain was pierced, even though the inner (pia mater) was not, the animal is *terefah* (*Hullin* 45a). Some say that Rab and Samuel both said that the animal is not *terefah* unless the inner membrane was also pierced. Samuel further mentions that a deficiency of one or two vertebrae (according to Bet Hillel and Bet Shammai, respectively) renders an animal *terefah* (*Hullin* 45b):

> Amemar said in the name of R. Naḥman: "There are three main vessels, one leads to the heart [i.e., aorta], the other to the lungs [i.e., trachea], and the third to the liver [i.e. inferior vena cava]. The one that leads to the lungs is counted as the lungs [and the slightest perforation therein will render the animal *terefah*], the one that leads to the liver is counted as the liver [so that it is *terefah* only if it was gone entirely], but with regard to the one that leads to the heart, there is the above-mentioned dispute [between Rab and Samuel]" . . . R. Ḥiyya ben Joseph went and reported Rab's view to Samuel. Said Samuel: "If this is what Rab said, then he knows nothing about defects in animals."

There are a few general pronouncements by Mar Samuel which pertain to medicine. He considers fasting as a sin (*Ta'anit* 11a), perhaps because it is unhealthy. He explains a seizure of *kordiakos* (*Gittin* 67b)

to mean being overcome by new wine from the vat (delirium tremens?).
He states that only a sick person with fever may be visited (*Nedarim*
41a), thereby excluding those suffering from diarrhea, for whom a visit
from a friend may prove to be an embarrassment, and those with migraine
headaches, because of their need for solitude, and those with eye ailments
who suffer from photophobia. Samuel also said, "Let one who would experience a taste of death put shoes on and sleep in them," a seemingly
unintelligible statement (*Yoma* 78b). He expounded the phrase "heat
expels heat" to mean that in a bathhouse one should open one's mouth to
expel the heat of one's perspiration, and let the heat of the bath enter
(*Shabbat* 41a). Furthermore, he was of the opinion that the removal of
a *sela* size of bone from the skull is incompatible with life (*Bekhorot* 37b).

REFERENCES

1. *Universal Jewish Encyclopedia* (1942), 7: 344–45.
2. D. Margalith, *Ḥakhmay Yisrael Kerofim* [Jewish savants as physicians]
   (Jerusalem: Mossad Harav Kook,) 1962 pp. 62–85.
3. D. Shapiro, "Les Connaissances médicales de Mar Samuel," *Revue des
   études juives* 42 (1901): 14–26.
4. G. Bader, *The Jewish Spiritual Heroes* (New York: Pardes, 1940), 3:
   78–90.
5. J. Preuss, *Biblisch-Talmudische Medizin* (Berlin: S. Karger, 1923), pp.
   21 ff.
6. H. Graetz, *History of the Jews* (Philadelphia: Jewish Publication Society,
   1967), 2:518–22.

Part VI
General Subjects of Interest

Sex Determination as Described in the Talmud

The American public was startled with the publication of a book entitled *Your Baby's Sex: Now You Can Choose*.[1] This book achieved instant fame by being featured on the cover of the April 21, 1970 issue of *Look* magazine. Gynecologist Shettles, author of the book, claims that X and Y spermatozoa can be identified by their different sizes and shapes. The larger, oval-shaped, female-producing sperm are resistant to an acid environment, whereas the smaller, round-headed, but more numerous male-producing sperm succumb in an acid environment. Thus, to insure a female offspring, Shettles recommends a variety of technics to increase the acidity of the cervical and vaginal secretions. If a boy is desired, procedures are described which increase alkalinity in the female lower genital tract.

The original observation of Shettles in 1960,[2] upon which most of his subsequent work is based,[3] was strongly criticized by two eminent embryologists,[4] and thus its validity remains in doubt. Be that as it may, Shettles may have provided twentieth-century man with a possible solution to the age-old desire to choose the sex of one's offspring. However, the secret of determining one's baby's sex was already known to the sages of the Talmud, thus fulfilling the claim of King Solomon that "there is nothing new under the sun" (Eccles. 1:9). The key passage is found in the Babylonian Talmud (*Niddah* 31a):

> R. Isaac, citing R. Ammi, stated: "If the woman emits her semen first* she bears a male child; if the man emits his semen first she bears a female child; for it is said: 'If a woman emits semen and bear a man-child' [Lev. 12:2]." Our rabbis taught: At first it used to be said that "if the woman emits her semen first she will bear a male, and if the man emits his semen first she will bear a female,"

---

* The intent of the biblical term is "to conceive," although the literal translation implies some kind of emission, and therefore the rabbis interpreted the verse as referring to the woman coming to orgasm first.

but the sages did not explain the reason, until R. Zadok came and explained it: "These are the sons of Leah, whom she bore unto Jacob in Paddan-Aram, with his daughter Dinah" [Gen. 46:15]. Scripture thus ascribes the males to the females [i.e., sons of Leah] and the females to the males [i.e., his daughter Dinah].

"And the sons of Ulam were mighty men of valor, archers; and had many sons, and sons' sons" [1 Chron. 8:40]. Now is it within the power of man to increase the number of "sons and sons' sons"? But the fact is that because they contained themselves during intercourse, in order that their wives should emit their semen first, so that their children shall be males, Scripture attributes to them the same merit as if they had themselves caused the increase of the number of their sons and sons' sons. This explains what R. Kattina said: "I could make all my children to be males."

Although "many sons and sons' sons" could refer to offspring in general, that is, male and female, R. Samuel Edels, known as *Maharsha,* in his commentary on the above talmudic passage, explains that the phrase "men of valor and archers" indicates they were all males. R. Edels further states that both Pentateuchal phrases (Lev. 12:2 and Gen. 46:14) are required for our understanding of the basic principle. For if only the quotation "if a woman emits seed" were written, one would only know that if she emits seed first, a male offspring results, but not the reverse. Hence, the scriptural phrase in Genesis to teach us both sides of the principle. If only the latter phrase were written, one would only know that males are ascribed to the females (i.e., sons of Leah) and females to the males (i.e., his daughter Dinah), but one would not understand that it had anything to do with who emits seed first. So R. Edels.

Two places in the Talmud raise the question of what happens if both man and woman emit seed simultaneously (*Niddah* 25b and 28a). Several possible answers are given: the offspring may be a hermaphrodite (*androginos*), or one whose sex is unknown (*tumtum*), or twins, one male and one female.

Elsewhere the Talmud describes a "village of males" (*Kfar Dikraya*), so called because women used to bear male children first, and finally a girl, and then no more (*Gittin* 57a).

Another talmudic passage states that if a man's wife is pregnant and he supplicates that God grant that his wife bear a male child, this is a vain prayer (*Berakhot* 54a). The Talmud then asks:

Does such a prayer avail? Has not R. Isaac, the son of R. Ammi, said that if a man first emits seed, the child will be a girl; if the woman first emits seed, the child will be a boy? [which shows that it is all fixed beforehand]. With what case are we dealing here? For instance, they both emitted seed at the same time. [Apparently in such a situation, prayer would help issue a male offspring.]

A final talmudic passage concerns one of twelve questions that the Alexandrians addressed to R. Joshua ben Ḥananiah.

What must a man do that he may have male children? He replied: "He shall marry a wife that is worthy of him, and conduct himself in modesty at the time of marital intercourse." They said to him: Did not many act in this manner but it did not avail them? Rather, let him pray for mercy from Him to whom are the children, for it is said: "Lo, children are a heritage of the Lord, the fruit of the womb is a reward" [Ps. 124:3]. [Seeing that one has in any case to pray for mercy], what then does he teach us? That one without the other does not suffice. What is exactly meant by "the fruit of the womb is a reward"? R. Ḥama, son of R. Ḥaninah, replied: "As a reward for containing oneself during intercourse in the womb, in order that one's wife may emit the semen first, the Holy One, blessed be He, gives one the reward of the fruit of the womb." [*Niddah* 70b–71a]

How can we in the twentieth century understand what the Talmud meant fifteen hundred years ago? How are we to interpret "if a woman emits seed"? Does it refer to ovulation? If so, then Shettles's hypothesis [1-3] may, in fact, explain the entire talmudic discussion, in that ovulation represents a time when cervical secretions are alkaline, allowing the male-producing sperm to predominate. Does the phrase "if a woman emits seed" refer to female orgasm? We know that orgasm increases the flow of alkaline secretions, which would also enhance the activity of the male-producing sperm.

It would seem obvious from a number of citations in the preceding pages that the meaning must be orgasm rather than ovulation, for otherwise it would not make sense to speak of the men restraining themselves during intercourse in order to allow their wives to "emit seed" first.

Let us turn to the biblical commentaries for assistance in the interpretation of the key phrase "if a woman emits seed [Heb. *tazria*] and gives birth to a male child" (Lev. 12:2) upon which is based the talmudic pronouncement regarding sex determination.

R. Abraham Ibn Ezra asserts as follows:

> . . . Many say that if the woman emits her seed first she bears a male child . . . the view of the Greek savants is that the woman has the seed and the male seed causes it to jell and the entire son comes from the blood of the woman. Actually, the explanation of the word *tazria* is to give forth seed, because she is like the earth.

The latter phrase "she is like earth" is explained by a later biblical commentary (*Siftei Ḥakhomim*) in that "a woman is like earth which sprouts that which one plants therein, and man was created from earth." The words of Ibn Ezra are amplified and clarified by Naḥmanides, or *Ramban,* who, in his commentary on the pertinent quotation in Leviticus, states as follows:

> When the sages interpreted the phrase "if a woman conceives" to mean that if a woman emits her seed first she bears a male child [*Niddah* 31a], their intention was not to imply that the fetus is formed from the seed of the woman. For even though the woman has eggs [i.e., ovaries] like the eggs of a male [i.e., testicles], either she creates no seed in them at all, or that seed jells and contributes nothing to the fetus. The sages said that "she conceives" refers to the blood of the uterus, which gathers in the mother at the end of intercourse and unites with the male seed because, in their view, the fetus is formed from the blood of the female and the white [semen] of the man, and both are called seed. Similarly, they did state [ibid.]: man has three partners [in his creation]: the father supplies white [semen] from which are formed sinews, bones, and the white of the eye; the mother provides the red [semen] from which are formed skin, flesh, blood and hair, and the black of the eye [and God gives the spirit and the breath, beauty of features, eyesight, the power of hearing, the ability to speak and to walk, understanding and discernment]. And this is also the view of [human] creation of physicians. And, according to the Greek philosophers, the entire body of the fetus comes from the blood of the mother. The father only has the hylic power, that is, he gives form to the matter . . . so too renders *Targum Onkelos* "she carries seed."

Naḥmanides is saying several things. First, a fetus or embryo is initiated from uterine blood, which is called seed. Secondly, the ovaries are considered either not to contain seed or the seed therein is useless. Contrary to Ibn Ezra and the ancient Greeks, who are of the opinion that the entire baby comes from the mother's blood, Naḥmanides asserts that the baby is produced from the contributions of both the mother's uterine blood and the father's seed.

Sixteenth-century R. Obadiah Seforno interprets the phrase in Leviticus as follows:

> The sages have already stated [*Niddah* 31a] that if a woman emits seed first she bears a male child, because in fact it is the seed of the woman. And it is the liquid that emanates from her at times during intercourse which plays no role at all in the formation of the male fetus; rather, her uterine blood jells in the seed of the father. When some of her liquid seed enters her jellied blood, then liquid seed is in excess, and the offspring is a girl.

Seforno seems to be saying that ovarian seed is useless for the production of male offspring but does play a role in the formation of girls. In either case, the essential reproductive force is the woman's uterine blood.

The difficulty in properly understanding the key phrase in Leviticus "and if a woman emits seed and gives birth to a male" continued among biblical commentators even down to the present century. R. Baruch Halevi Epstein, in his commentary *Torah Temimah,* offers the following observation on the predetermination of sex by the one who emits seed first:

> It seems clear that the matter was known to the sages because this is the way it is in nature, because all is reckoned after the first power. Therefore, if the man emits semen first, his strength is finished first and the creation is determined by the last power, which is her seed, and therefore she bears a female child. And so, too, the reverse. There is only an allusion or hint of this fact in this scriptural phrase . . . for this well-known occurrence in nature.

The entire concept can be interpreted ethically,[5] that is, as an encouragement to men to practice restraint during intercourse and allow their wives to come to orgasm, holding out the promise of male issue as a reward.

Man continues to be puzzled by the enigma of choosing one's baby's sex prior to sexual intercourse. Hippocrates said that a boy is born from the right ovary, a girl from the left. Maimonides ridiculed this assertion, saying that a man should be either prophet or genius to know this.[6] The Talmud emphatically states that if a woman emits her semen first, she will bear a male, and if the man emits his semen first, she will bear a female. We have yet to understand what the Talmud means. The secret of sex predetermination remains hidden.

REFERENCES

1. D. M. Rorvik and L. B. Shettles, *Your Baby's Sex: Now You Can Choose* (New York: Dodd, Mead, 1970).
2. L. B. Shettles, "Nuclear Morphology of Human Spermatozoa," *Nature* 186 (1960): 648–49.
3. L. B. Shettles, "The Great Preponderance of Human Males Conceived," *American Journal of Obstetrics and Gynecology* 89 (1964): 130–33.
4. L. Rothschild and D. W. Bishop, "X and Y Spermatozoa," *Nature* 187 (1960): 253–56.
5. E. Rackman, "Health and Holiness," *Tradition* 2 (Fall 1959): 67–81.
6. S. Muntner, ed., *Mosheh ben Maimon: Perush Lepirkei Abukrat* [Commentary on the aphorisms of Hippocrates] (Jerusalem: Mossad Harav Kook, 1961).

Snakes and Serpents in
in Bible and Talmud

Introduction

The biological, physiological, and ecological characteristics of the numerous types of poisonous and nonpoisonous snakes found in Israel are described in a variety of specialized publications.[1,2] Only brief discussions of snakes and scorpions and their bites as found in biblical and talmudic literature are available,[3,4] and most are in foreign languages. The present essay is a detailed presentation of snakes, snake venom, remedies for snakebites, and related subjects as found in the Bible, Midrash, and Talmud. For the purpose of this paper, the terms "snake" and "serpent" are used interchangeably. Scorpion bites and wasp, bee, mosquito, or hornet stings are specifically excluded from this essay.

The Hebrew word *nahash* is a generic name for all snakes or serpents of the suborder of reptiles called *ophidia*. The Palestinian viper is thought to be the Biblical *zif'oni;* the carpet viper, or echis, is the equivalent of the biblical *efah;* the cerastes viper represents the biblical *shefifon;* and the cobra is probably identical to the biblical *saraf* or *peten*. Muntner points out that these and other Hebrew names for various types of snakes contain the sounds "ss" or "pf," probably reminiscent of the ominous hissing and puffing of snakes.[4]

The biblical account of the snake in the Garden of Eden is related to the snake throughout the Bible and Talmud as the symbol of evil and malice.

SNAKES AND SERPENTS IN THE BIBLE

The Talmud (*Abot de Rabbi Nathan* 29:3) states that in the Bible the snake is designated by six Hebrew words: *nahash* (29 times), *saraf* (Num. 21:8, Deut. 8:15, Isa. 30:6), *tannin* (Gen. 1:21, Exod. 7:10–12, Isa. 27:1), *zif'oni* (Prov. 23:32; Isa. 11:8, 14:29, 59:5; Jer. 8:17), *efah* (Job 20:16; Isa. 30:6, 59:5), and *akhshub* (Ps. 140:4). The term *shefifon* is also found (Gen. 49:17). *Saraf* may be identical to *peten*, the Egyptian cobra (Deut. 32:33, Job 20:14–16, Ps. 58:5–7).

Naḥash is the snake or serpent which transmitted its spiritual venom to the first woman in the garden of Eden (Gen. 3:1–14). According to the scriptural account, the snake originally had the power of speech and its intellectual powers exceeded those of all other animals. It was its envy of man that made it plot his downfall.

"And God made the beast of the earth" (Gen. 1:25): this refers to the serpent (*Gen. Rabbah* 7:5). "And God created the great sea monsters" (Gen. 1:21): this refers (*Baba Batra* 74b) to Leviathan the slant (i.e., male) serpent (Job 26:13, Isa. 27:11) and to Leviathan the tortuous (i.e., female) serpent (Isa. 27:1). Elsewhere the Bible speaks of a flying serpent (Isa. 30:6) and a sea serpent (Isaiah 27:1). These seem to represent mythological land, sea, and air dragons.

Moses cast his rod on the ground and it became a snake (Exod. 4:3, 7:15). When Aaron and the Egyptians cast rods, they turned into *tanninim,* which Rashi interprets as snakes (Exod. 7:10–12).

In the Bible, snake venom is the epitome of evil, slander, and drunkenness. "Evil people have sharpened their tongue like a serpent; viper's venom is under their lips" (Ps. 140:4): that is, slander is like a serpent's fang and like the poison bag beneath the viper's tongue. The words which fall from the lips of unjust judges are deadly like a snake's poison (ibid. 58:5). The deadly nature of drunkenness is compared to the bite of a poisonous snake and the sting of a basilisk. Vipers' eggs symbolize wickedness and plunder (Isa. 59:5). The desert through which the Jews wandered for forty years swarmed with "fiery serpents and scorpions" (Deut. 8:15). However, a pillar of cloud journeyed in front of them and two sparks of fire issued from between the two staves of the Ark and devoured the serpents and scorpions in front of them (*Deut. Rabbah* 7:9–10).

The punishment for evil or slander is to be bitten by a serpent (Amos 5:19, 9:30, Eccles. 10:8). There is no advantage in being a slanderer or master of the evil tongue (Eccles. 10:11), for "the vipers' tongue shall slay him" (Job 20:16). Such Jews will lick the dust like a serpent (Mic. 7:17). The serpent eats dust as its food (Gen. 3:14, Isa. 65:25). Impenitence will bring retribution in the form of serpents and basilisks which cannot be charmed but will bite (Jer. 8:17).

God will punish the enemies of Israel in the same way. Assyria, Babylon, and Egypt are compared, respectively, to the slant serpent, the tortuous serpent, and the sea dragon (Isa. 27:1). The sound of the Egyptian armies "will go like the serpents" (Jer. 46:22), that is, like a serpent stealthily crawling away. A snake crawls without feet over rocks (Prov. 30:19).

The Biblical Brazen Serpent

When the Israelites fled from Egypt through the wilderness, they complained about the lengthy journey, the long detour around Edom, and the monotony of the manna. For this slander against God and against Moses, they were punished by being bitten by fiery serpents. The story, including the remarkable cure for the snakebites, is described in Numbers 21:5–9 as follows:

> And the people spoke against God, and against Moses, "Wherefore have ye brought us up out of Egypt to die in the wilderness? for there is no bread, and there is no water; and our soul loatheth this light bread." And the Lord sent fiery serpents among the people, and they bit the people; and much people of Israel died. And the people came to Moses, and said, "We have sinned, because we have spoken against the Lord, and against thee; pray unto the Lord that He take away the serpents from us." And Moses prayed for the people. And the Lord said unto Moses, "Make thee a fiery serpent [*saraf*] and set it upon a standard: and it shall come to pass, that everyone that is bitten, when he seeth it, shall live." And Moses made a serpent of brass, and set it upon the standard: and it came to pass, that if a serpent had bitten any man, when he looked unto the serpent of brass, he lived.

Although the term "fiery serpents" is interpreted to mean that they produced fever in the person who was bitten because of the poison of their fangs, the precise identification of the species of snake which bit the Israelites will probably never be known. The speculation by some modern Bible scholars that it was the Medina worm, which produced filariasis, is quite unlikely.

Even more problematical is the question as to why God punished the Jews through snakebites rather than some other form of death. One answer is given by Rashi, who quotes the *Midrash Tanḥuma:*

> God said, as it were, let the serpent, which was punished for slanderous statements, come and exact punishment from those who utter slander. Let the serpent, to which all kinds of food have one taste

[that of earth; cf. Gen. 3:14 and *Yoma* 75a] come and exact punishment from these ingrates to whom one thing [the manna] had the taste of many different dainties [see Rashi on Num. 11:83 and *Num. Rabbah* 19:22].

A similar reason is given by *Seforno* and *Ba'al Haturim,* who state that God punished the Jews with snakes because they acted like snakes with their mouths, i.e., spoke slander. Samson Raphael Hirsch asserts that the serpent's bite was meant to remind the people of the dangers of the wilderness, from which they had been protected by the miraculous power of God. Finally, *Malbim* asserts that God sent snakes to punish the people for their lack of control over their internal snake (i.e., their evil inclination).

The most interesting aspect, however, of this biblical narrative is the manner of treatment for the snakebites. Moses made a copper snake, placed it on a pole, and whoever gazed at it was cured. Many commentaries, including Rashi, ask: Why did Moses make it of copper? The answer appears in the Midrash:

> R. Judan said in R. Assi's name that Moses reasoned as follows: "If I make it of gold [*zahab*] or of silver [*kessef*], these words do not correspond to the other [viz., *nahash,* meaning serpent]. Hence, I will make it of *nehoshet* [brass] since this word corresponds to the other, viz., *nahash nehoshet*—a serpent of brass [i.e., a play on words]." [*Gen. Rabbah* 31:8]

The commentary *Torah Temimah* indicates that Moses understood from the word *saraf* that it was to be made of a substance that resembles burning fire, which gives off sparks, i.e., copper.

How does gazing at a copper serpent cure someone of a snake bite? The Mishnah asks:

> Did the copper serpent kill or make alive? No! What it indicates is that when the Israelites, in gazing at the serpent, turned their thoughts on high and subjected their hearts to their father in heaven, they were healed; otherwise they perished. [*Rosh Hashanah* 3:8]

The Jerusalem Talmud (*Rosh Hashanah* 3:9) points out that a dog bite enfeebles slowly and hence one glance at the brazen serpent would have been sufficient to heal a person. However, a serpent bite kills rapidly and hence the victim had to gaze intently at the brazen serpent in order to be healed.

Naḥmanides, himself a physician, asserts that ordinarily if someone is bitten by a poisonous animal he becomes even more sick if he looks at the animal; for example, if someone bitten by a mad dog looks into water and sees images of a dog, he dies immediately. Physicians even avoid mentioning the name of the animal for fear of harming the patient. Also, if the urine of a rabid dog is shown to someone bitten by the dog, he sees images of dog puppies in the urine. God, however, specifically told Moses to make a serpent, that is, the same animal that bit the Jews, in order to show them that God kills and God makes alive. Thus a double miracle occurred: they recovered from a poisonous snakebite, and they recovered from the worsening condition of looking at a snake after being bitten by one.

Ibn Ezra asks why the copper snake had to be placed on a pole. His answer is: "to be high so that all could see it." He also points out that many Israelites erred and treated the brazen serpent like a divine object, worshipping it like a God. Because the Jews preserved it as an object of veneration, it was eventually destroyed by King Hezekiah (2 Kings 18:4). The sages highly praised him for this act (*Pesaḥim* 4:9, 56a: *Berakhot* 10b; *Abodah Zarah* 44a).

Snakes and Serpents in the Midrash

The Midrash tells us that in Galilee a serpent is called *aviya* (*Gen. Rabbah* 26:7). A serpent is said to bear offspring after seven years (ibid. 20:4). Some snakes are harmless and can be domesticated. When they live in a house, they are fond of garlic (ibid. 54:1). Some snakes may even be afraid of man (ibid. 34:12). A serpent's eyelid quivers after death (ibid. 98:14). A serpent can be rendered harmless by snake-charmers (ibid. 19:10; *Deut. Rabbah* 6:11, 7:10; *Song of Songs Rabbah* 7:8:1).

The snake as the symbol of evil and of slander is found throughout the Midrash. Even Moses spoke slanderously of the Children of Israel (Exod. 4:1) and followed the example of the serpent which spoke slanderously of its Creator (*Exod. Rabbah* 3:12). The conversion of Moses' staff into a serpent as he threw it on the ground (Exod. 4:3) may have been a sign of God's displeasure, as if to say: "You, Moses, did what this serpent did" (ibid.). Alternatively, the rod was converted into a serpent to symbolize Pharaoh (ibid. and *Exod. Rabbah* 9:4), who is called a serpent (Ezek. 23:3, Isa. 27:1).

The sages compare the kingdom of Egypt to a snake. Just as the serpent hisses and slays, so does the kingdom of Egypt hiss and slay, for they put men in prison and silently plan to kill them. Just as a serpent is twisted, so does the kingdom of Egypt pervert her ways. Just as a serpent is crooked, so is Pharaoh (*Exod. Rabbah* 9:4). Edom (i.e., Rome) is also compared to a serpent (ibid. 15:17). The serpent entices women but not men (*Gen. Rabbah* 98:14).

The Gibeonites acted in the manner of the serpent (*Num. Rabbah* 8:4) and were cursed like the serpent (Josh. 9:23). The curse of the serpent is also described elsewhere (*Gen. Rabbah* 20:5; *Num. Rabbah* 14:12, 18:21, 19:11). Media produced Haman the wicked, who inflamed the Medians like a serpent (*Gen. Rabbah* 16:4, *Lev. Rabbah* 13:5). Haman also hissed at the people like a serpent (*Esth. Rabbah,* proem:5).

Because the wisdom of the serpent was so great, therefore the penalty inflicted upon it was proportionate to its wisdom (*Eccles. Rabbah* 1:18:1). The serpent was once asked: "Why are you generally to be found among fences?" He replied: "Because I made a breach in the fence of the world [i.e., caused man to sin]." Therefore, the serpent has become the executioner of all those who make breaches in fences (based on Eccles. 10:8). The serpent was asked: "Why do you bite? What do you gain thereby? The lion tears his prey and eats it but you simply bite and kill!" He answered: "I receive instructions from on high! [i.e., from God]." He was asked: "How is it that you bite into one limb and your poison travels to all the limbs?" He answered: "A slanderer can live in Rome and slay in Syria [i.e., slander, like the poison of the serpent, spreads]" (*Deut. Rabbah* 5:10, *Lev. Rabbah* 26:2, *Num. Rabbah* 19:2, *Eccles. Rabbah* 10:10).

R. Yannai observed a snake approaching the city, hissing as it went. If the snake was stopped from going in one direction, it went in another direction, and if it was stopped from proceeding in that direction, it moved in another. R. Yannai thought it was on its way to carry out its mission. This suspicion was confirmed when he later heard that so-and-so was bitten by a snake and died (*Lev. Rabbah* 22:4, *Num. Rabbah* 18:22, *Eccles. Rabbah* 5:8:4).

God can carry out His purposes even through a serpent, a scorpion, a flea, or a frog (*Gen. Rabbah* 10:7, *Lev. Rabbah* 22:3, *Eccles. Rabbah*

5:8:3). R. Eleazar ben Dama met his death by a serpent bite for having disobeyed the law about conversing with a *min,* or apostate (*Eccles. Rabbah* 1:8:3, *Abodah Zarah* 27b).

Haughty girls used to have a picture of a serpent on their shoes to entice men (Isa. 3:16). Alternatively, they placed perfume vials between their heels and their shoes and pressed upon them when a man approached so that the perfume went through him like the poison of a snake (*Lam. Rabbah* 4:14:18), that is, the man was instilled with passionate desire (*Shabbat* 62b).

Usury is like someone bitten by a serpent who does not feel the bite until swelling sets in; so, too, usury is not felt until it has grown upon the debtor (*Exod. Rabbah* 31:7, 31:13).

The fright of only seeing a serpent is sufficient to cause one's hair to fall out (*Exod. Rabbah* 24:4). If a person has already been bitten by a snake, even a piece of rope terrifies him because it looks like a snake (*Song of Songs Rabbah* 1:2:3, *Eccles. Rabbah* 7:1:4). A snake may encircle the neck of a man, possibly choking him to death rather than poisoning him (*Lam. Rabbah* 2:2:4). Remedies for snakebites (vide infra) are described (*Song of Songs Rabbah* 4:5:1), including the wearing of a grass wreath on one's head (*Gen. Rabbah* 10:7, *Lev. Rabbah* 22:4).

SNAKES AND SERPENTS IN THE TALMUD

Anatomy and Physiology of Snakes

The eyeball of a serpent is round like that of a man, but the eyes of a serpent are on the side of the head like fishes, whereas man and beasts have eyes in front of the head (*Niddah* 23a). A woman may abort a fetus having the likeness of a serpent (ibid. 24b). All animals copulate with their faces against the back of the female, except three which copulate face to face, and these are fish, man, and a serpent (*Bekhorot* 8a). A viper (or adder) has a seventy-year pregnancy. A serpent has a seven-year pregnancy (ibid.). Serpents have sexual intercourse even after the female is already pregnant (ibid. 8b). A snake was once seen copulating with a toad (or lizard) and a new breed of creature called an *arod* was born (*Hullin* 127a), whose bite is deadly (*Berakhot* 33a). If the white and the yolk of an egg are mixed up, one may be certain that it is a reptile's or serpent's egg (*Hullin* 64a). Three wax stronger as they grow older, viz., a fish, a serpent, and a swine (*Shabbat* 77b).

Habits of Snakes

Snakes are found in houses (*Pesaḥim* 112b) and specifically in holes and crevices (ibid. 8a) or in walls (*Abot de Rabbi Nathan* 17:6). Cats eat snakes and spit out the small bones which may stick in a man's foot and endanger him (ibid. 112b). Apparently cats are immune from snake's venom (*Abodah Zarah* 30b). Snakes consider garlic to be a delicacy (*Gen. Rabbah* 54:1) and hence, if pulverized garlic was left exposed, it becomes prohibited lest a snake ate from it (*Beẓah* 7b). The usual food of a serpent is dust (Gen. 3:14, Isa. 65:25), and even if the serpent were to eat all the delicacies of the world, he would feel therein but the taste of dust (*Yoma* 75a).

Snake Charmers

Snakes and serpents may be charmed on the Sabbath to render them harmless (*Sanhedrin* 101a). A snake charmer can make a snake spit out something it is holding in its mouth (*Pesaḥim* 10b). A snake around a burial vault was once charmed away by the sages' pleas (*Baba Meẓia* 84b, 85a). Other references to snake charmers are found elsewhere in the Talmud (*Keritot* 3b, *Sanhedrin* 65a).

Giant Snakes

Biblical references to sea monsters and dragons are numerous (vide supra). The Talmud describes a frog the size of a fort which was swallowed by a snake. This enormous snake in turn was swallowed by a raven (*Baba Batra* 73b). The credibility of such an occurrence is verified by one of the sages who said: "Had I not been there I would not have believed it" (ibid.). Another incident is described in which a raven bites off the head of a sea-serpent, turning the waters to blood (ibid. 74b).

If a person swears that he saw a serpent as large as the beam of the olive press, his oath is considered to be vain since such a situation is contrary to the facts known to man (*Shebuot* 29a). The Talmud then asks: "Was there not a serpent in the days of King Shapur of Persia which swallowed thirteen hides [or "stables," *var. lec.*] full of straw?" (*Nedarim* 24b, *Shebuot* 29b). Rashi explains that it was a man-eating serpent; hot coals were concealed in the straw and these killed it. This incident is reminiscent of the Apocryphal story of Daniel and the dragon (*Gen. Rabbah* 68:13).

In the Messianic age all animals will assemble and come to the serpent and say to him: "The lion claws its victims and devours him, the wolf tears him and devours him, but as for thee, what benefit dost thou derive?" (*Ta'anit* 8a). He will answer: "What benefit has he who uses his tongue, viz., the slanderer?" (*Arakhin* 15b). There is no healing for the slanderer (*Kallah Rabbati* 3:22). The Omnipresent has many agents of death: demons, bears, leopards, lions, wolves, snakes, serpents, and scorpions (*Semakhot* 8:15, *Kallah* 1:23). Since the abolition of the four types of capital punishment in Jewish law, he who would have been sentenced to burning either falls into a fire (*Ketubot* 30b) or is bitten by a snake (ibid; *Sanhedrin* 37b).

Snake Bites and Snake Venom

Samuel, the most illustrious physician-sage in the Talmud, said that all reptiles have poisonous venom; that of a serpent is fatal while that of other reptiles has no fatal effect (*Abodah Zarah* 31b). His colleague Rab said that obese Arameans who eat abominable and creeping things become immune to snake poison (ibid.). R. Judah says that a snake's poison is lodged in the fangs, which automatically empty on contact with the victim's flesh, whereas the other sages say that the poison must be emitted by the snake's own accord (*Sanhedrin* 78a).

There are three kinds of venoms (of serpents): that of a young one sinks to the bottom of a container of fluid; that of one not quite young drops to about the middle; while that of an old one floats on top. Are we to take it that the older a serpent gets the more his strength diminishes? Its strength may indeed increase, but its venom becomes weaker (*Abodah Zarah* 30b).

In ancient times, outdoor privies resulted in the danger of people being bitten there while not fully clothed (*Berakhot* 62b), for it even wraps itself around the penis (J.T. *Ta'anit* 4:69). He who behaves modestly in a privy is delivered from snakes, scorpions, and evil spirits (*Berakhot* 62a). Snakebites are more common during the wheat harvest (*Yebamot* 116b), and if a woman states that her husband was bitten by a snake in the harvest and died she is believed (*Eduyot* 1:12). If a man falls into a pit full of serpents and scorpions, we assume he will die unless he is a snake-charmer (*Yebamot* 121a). One is cautioned against provoking even a little snake (*Pesaḥim* 113a). If a snake is wound around one's foot, it may not necessarily bite (*Berakhot* 33a). A scorpion is more certain to bite (ibid.), and some sages are of the opinion that a snake is afraid of a sleeping person whereas others disagree (*Abodah Zarah* 30a).

A serpent is killed because of danger (*Parah* 7:9). Even if it looks harmless, one should crush its brain (J.T. *Kiddushin* 4:66). If someone is bitten by a snake he jumps up suddenly (*Soferim* 3:13). The capture of a snake to avoid being bitten is permitted even on the Sabbath and involves no liability. However, to catch it for a remedy (its poison can be used medicinally) involves liability (*Shabbat* 3a, 107a; *Eduyot* 2:5). If someone is bitten by a snake, one may call a physician for him even on the Sabbath or Day of Atonement from one place to another (*Yoma* 83b). If an animal ate poison or was bitten by a snake, and the animal was afterwards slaughtered, it is not forbidden as *terefah* (i.e., non-kosher), but it is prohibited on account of the danger to life (*Hullin* 58b, *Terumot* 8:6). When any food becomes dry it is permitted because serpent's venom, if present therein, would not let it get dry (*Abodah Zarah* 35a).

One should not eat figs, grapes, cucumbers, or gourds that have holes, because of fear that the holes were made by a snake and that these foods, therefore, contain poison (*Terumot* 8:6). In the same vein, it is prohibited from selling a person a pair of sandals made from leather of a dead animal claiming they were made from leather of a slaughtered animal; firstly, because it is untrue, and secondly, because it is dangerous (*Hullin* 94a). The commentaries explain that the danger is the possibility that the dead animal might have been killed by snake poison, and that remnants of the poison might still be found in the leather.

Generally, the bite kills rapidly. However, it also occurs that a person first notices that he was bitten when the wound swells (*Exod. Rabbah* 31:6) and the patient comes home. This swelling is an invariable sign of a snake bite. It once happened in a place called Zalmon that a certain man called out: "I was bitten by a snake and I am about to die"; when they reached him, they could no longer recognize him (*Yebamot* 16:6).

If someone was fortunate enough to have been bitten by a snake but survived, he later fears even a string (or thread) because it resembles a snake (*Eccles. Rabbah* 5:1).

Danger of Drinking From Uncovered Water or Wine

It is prohibited to drink from wine, water, or milk that was left uncovered because a snake may have drunk from it and discharged poison into it (*Terumot* 8:4). How long must they have remained uncovered to become forbidden? As long as it would take a snake to come forth from a place nearby and drink (*Hullin* 10a, 49b). All other liquids are permitted since a snake has no liking for them. For example, uncovered beer in vats and barrels is allowed since it is assumed that serpents do not drink beer. Some say that it is permitted because the bitter taste of the hops counteracts any venom that might be in the beer so that it is harmful only to sick people (*Abodah Zarah* 31b).

The law forbidding the use of liquids left uncovered does not apply to new wine during the first three days of fermentation, because during this time it repels snakes (*Ta'anit* 30a, *Sanhedrin* 70a). Fully matured (i.e., fermented) wine and beer is permitted, for if venom were present, the wine or beer would not have fermented (*Abodah Zarah* 31b). Uncovered water, if filtered through a strainer, is permitted since the venom of a serpent is like a fungus which floats on the surface and remains where it is (*Sukkah* 50a). There is a lengthy discussion in the Talmud as to whether or not diluted wine (the usual proportion is two water to one pure wine) becomes forbidden through being left uncovered as a snake may or may not drink it (*Abodah Zarah* 30a).

R. Joshua ben Levi said: "There are three kinds of wine to which the prohibition through being left uncovered does not apply, namely: strong, bitter, and sweet." "Strong" is the acrid *tila* [a wine with a very pungent taste] which makes the wine-skin burst; "bitter" is wine made of unripe grapes; "sweet" is wine made of grapes sweetened by the heat of the sun. [The taste of any of these being objectionable, a snake would not drink thereof even if left uncovered.] R. Ḥama taught that those three were improved wines: "strong" is wine mixed with pepper; "bitter" mixed with wormwood; "sweet" is sparkling wine. Said R. Simeon ben Lakish: "*Karina* becomes prohibited through being left uncovered." What is *Karina*? Said R. Abbahu: "*Karina* is a sweet wine which comes from Asia." Said Raba: "In its own place, however, it is rendered unfit if left uncovered, the reason being that it is the 'local wine' [and snakes of that locality drink it]" (*Abodah Zarah* 30a).

Chopped cress mixed with wine is not subject to the rules pertaining to uncovered liquids because the vinegar in it deters snakes from tasting it (ibid. 30b). Babylonian *kutah* (a mixture of sour milk, crusts of bread, and salt) is also not rendered unfit if left uncovered, though those in the Diaspora have the practice of forbidding it. R. Manashi said: "If it has traces of biting we must suspect it of being bitten by a serpent." Said R. Ḥiyya ben Ashi in the name of Samuel: "Water that drips into a vessel is not subject to the rules in regard to uncovered liquids [as the noise caused by the dripping would frighten a serpent]." R. Ashi said: "That is if the dripping is continuous" (ibid.).

The Talmud states (ibid.) that the venom of a young snake sinks to the bottom. What practical application has this? That of the following teaching: If a barrel was uncovered, even if nine persons drank of its contents with no fatal consequence, the tenth person is still forbidden to drink thereof. It happened indeed that nine people drank of such and did not die but the tenth one died; and R. Jeremiah said: "It was a case of the venom sinking to the bottom." Likewise, if a cut melon was left uncovered and nine persons partook thereof without fatal consequences, it is forbidden for a tenth person to partake thereof, for it once happened that nine persons ate of such a one and did not die and the tenth one who ate it died; and Rab said that it was a case of venom that sank to the bottom (ibid.).

Water which had been left uncovered should not be poured out in a public road, or used for sprinkling the floor of a house, or for kneading mortar; nor should one give it to his animal or to his neighbor's animal to drink; nor should one wash one's face, hands, or feet therewith. Others said: "Only a part of the body that has an opening [where the poison might penetrate the body] must not be washed therewith but where there is no opening it is permitted" (ibid.).

For baking purposes, it is permitted to use water that was left uncovered, because snake poison is destroyed by fire. For this reason, Mar Samuel only drank warmed water. In general, boiled water was permissible even after it cooled. It was thought that a snake does not drink from this type of water (and, therefore, does not discharge its poison therein) (J.T. *Terumot* 8:45).

Remedies for Snake Bites and Venom

Eupatorium (*abub ro'eh,* lit. shepherd's flute) is said to be a remedy for someone who drank uncovered water (*Shabbat* 109b). If this plant is not available, then let the patient bring five roses and five glasses of strong liquor, boil them together, and drink it. The mother of one of the sages prepared a potion of one rose and one glass of strong liquor for a certain man. She boiled them up, made him drink it, lit the stove and swept it out, placed bricks in it (for the sufferer to sit on), and the poison of the snake issued like a green palm-leaf. R. Avia said, "For someone who drank uncovered water, the remedy is a quarter [*log*] of milk from a white goat." R. Huna ben Judah said: "Let him obtain a sweet citron, scoop it out, fill it with honey, set it on burning embers to boil, and then eat it." R. Ḥanina said: "One drinks urine forty days old [or, of a baby forty days old] as a remedy." R. Yoḥanan said: "*Elaiogaron* [a kind of oil and garum], *kangad* [a kind of chevril], and *theriac* are efficacious against both uncovered water and witchcraft" (ibid.).

If one swallows a snake, he should be made to eat cuscuta with salt and run three *mils*. R. Shimi ben Ashi saw a man swallow a snake; thereupon he appeared to him in the guise of a horseman, made him eat cuscuta with salt and run three *mils* before him, and it issued from him in strips. Others say: R. Shimi ben Ashi swallowed a snake, thereupon Elijah came, appeared to him in the guise of a horseman, made him eat cuscuta with salt and run three *mils* before him, and it issued from him in strips (ibid.).

If one is bitten by a snake, he should procure an embryo of a white ass, tear it open, and be made to sit upon it; providing, however, that it was not found to be *terefah* (non-kosher). A certain officer of Pumbeditha was bitten by a snake. Now there were thirteen white asses in Pumbeditha; they were all torn open and found to be *terefah*. There was another on the other side of Pumbeditha, but before they could go and bring it a lion devoured it. Thereupon, Abaye observed to them, "Perhaps he was bitten by a snake of the rabbis, i.e., as a punishment for disobeying the rabbis" (ibid. 110a). If a person was bitten by a snake and is about to die by divine decree, prayer or a meritorious act might reverse the outcome (ibid. 156b). Prayer might also prevent a snakebite (*Pesaḥim* 111a).

A crushed mosquito is a remedy for a serpent's bite. Also a serpent is a remedy for an eruption! How? One black and one white serpent are brought, boiled to a pulp, and rubbed in (*Shabbat* 77b).

Prevention of Snakebite

If a snake winds itself around a person, let him go down into water, put a basket over its head, and force the snake away from himself, and when it goes on to the basket, he should throw it into the water, ascend, and make off.

If a man is scented by a snake which pursues him, if his companion is with him, he should make him ride four cubits to break the track of the scent. If not, let him jump over a ditch (the water breaks the scent). If not, let him cross a river; and at night place his bed on four barrels and sleep under the stars (so that the snake cannot attack him either from below or above), and bring four cats and tie them to the four legs of the bed. Then he should fetch rubbish and throw it there, so that when they hear a sound the cats will devour it.

If a man is chased by a snake, he should flee into sandy places where the snake cannot follow.

If a woman sees a snake and does not know whether it has turned its attention to her or not, let her remove her garments and throw them in front of it; if it winds itself around them, its mind is upon her; if not, its mind is not upon her. What can she do? She should cohabit with her husband in front of it. Others say, That will even strengthen its instincts. Rather she should take some of her hair and nails and throw them at it and say, "I am menstruous" (*Shabbat* 110a).

Miscellaneous References to Snakes and Serpents

One of the ten miracles that occurred during the time of the Temple was the following: never did a serpent or a scorpion injure anyone in Jerusalem (*Yoma* 21a, *Abot* 5:5). The words of the wise are compared to the hiss of a serpent, that is, they are very potent (*Abot* 2:10). A patient in the throes of hunger is compared to one having been bitten by a snake (*Sanhedrin* 98b).

A serpent that kills is put to death by a court of twenty-three (*Sanhedrin* 2a). According to R. Akiba, it is killed without a trial (ibid. 15b). For an invasion of snakes and scorpions, the people cry (i.e., pray) aloud (*Ta'anit* 14a). If a woman testifies that her husband was killed by a snake or scorpion during such an invasion, she is believed (*Yebamot* 114b). Since a husband cannot always be on the lookout to invalidate the vows of a woman who constantly makes vows and then breaks them, she is compared to a serpent and the following metaphor is used: no one can live with a serpent in the same basket (*Ketubot* 72a, 77a, 86b). The same expression is used in the case of a cantankerous husband, or in any situation of mistrust between husband and wife (ibid.).

The blood of a snake does not cause defilement but is forbidden for eating (*Keritot* 4b). If a serpent drinks from the water of the red heifer (Num. 19:2 ff.), it renders the water invalid (*Parah* 9:3, 11:1). The hind has a narrow womb. When she crouches for delivery, a serpent is allowed to bite her at the opening of the womb and she is delivered of her offspring (*Baba Batra* 16b).

Current Scientific Interpretations

Many of the statements in the Bible and Talmud concerning snakes and serpents have primarily homiletical connotations. Perhaps because of this, only a few of such statements have any scientific validity. The midrashic assertion that a serpent bears offspring every seven years is contrary to scientific fact. Most snakes and serpents have a litter every year. It is possible that the species referred to in the Midrash is now extinct. More likely is the explanation that the seven years is not meant to be taken literally. Rather, the divine punishment on the snake for all times for enticing Eve in the Garden of Eden is to suffer more and for longer during pregnancy and parturition than a woman. Other interpretations are possible.

That snakes are fond of garlic (*Gen. Rabbah* 54:1) and dust (Gen. 3:14, Isa. 65:25) and dislike vinegar (*Abodah Zarah* 30b) is also not to be understood literally. Since snakes are exclusively carnivorous, their diet consists entirely of meat and meat products. For a snake to copulate with a toad or a lizard (*Hullin* 127a) seems impossible from a scientific viewpoint. The venom of young snakes is identical to that of old snakes; hence, the talmudic assertion that the venom of young snakes sinks to the bottom of a container of fluid whereas that of an old one floats on top (*Abodah Zarah* 30b) is unexplained.

The pronouncement of R. Judah that a snake's poison is lodged in the fangs, which automatically empty on contact with the victim's flesh (*Sanhedrin* 78a), is incorrect. In actuality, in 60 percent of snakebites from poisonous snakes, no venom is injected into the victim, thus supporting the view of the sages who argue with R. Judah (ibid.).

The incident of the biblical brazen serpent is described in detail above and seems inexplicable from a purely scientific viewpoint. The danger of drinking from uncovered water or wine is extremely remote and essentially nonexistent. Snakes do not discharge venom into fluid from which they drink. They inject their victims with poison to kill them in order to eat them or fight off an enemy, such as man. Only if a snake has recently discharged venom and still has a few drops of fresh, moist venom on its fangs could it possibly exude poison into fluid from which it drinks. Even then there is no danger to a human being who imbibes such fluid since snake poison is not absorbed through the intestinal tract of man if taken in orally. Only if the person has ulcerations in his mouth or stomach would the remote possiblity of absorption of some of the poison exist. Hence, the fears of the sages concerning the drinking of uncovered water or wine were unfounded.

The use of snake poison to prepare an antidote for a person bitten by a snake (*Shabbat* 3a, 107a; *Eduyot* 2:5) does have scientific merit. Such antidotes were already prepared in the twelfth century and earlier as described by Maimonides.[5] The prevention of snakebites by a variety of means (vide supra) is also a modern concept. To confuse a snake with an unusual scent or object to force the snake away from oneself (*Shabbat* 110a) finds its analogy in present day use of shark repellents.

Further study and analysis is needed to clarify the meaning of statements concerning snakes in classic Jewish sources and to shed light on the possible scientific validity of such statements.

REFERENCES

1. S. Bodenheimer, *Haḥai Be'Eretz Yisrael* [Animals in the land of Israel] (Tel Aviv: Dvir 1953), pp. 370–79.
2. Y. Flikos, *Haḥai Shel Hatanakh* [Animals in the Bible] (Tel Aviv: Sinai, 1954), pp. 102–8.
3. J. Preuss, *Biblisch-Talmudische Medizin* (Berlin: S. Karger, 1911), pp. 224–29.
4. S. Muntner "Al Hakashot Naḥash Ve Akitzoth Be Safrut Hatanakhit Vehatalmudit" [Snakes and scorpions in biblical and talmudic literature], *Dapim Refuiim* (Tel Aviv), 21, 7 (November 1962) [Hebrew and French].
5. S. Muntner, *The Medical Writings of Moses Maimonides: Treatise on Poisons and Their Antidotes* (Philadelphia: J. B. Lippincott, 1966).

"Forensic Medicine" in the Talmud

There is a very interesting passage in the Talmud that deals with the identification of a stain on a garment, as to whether it is blood or dye. The passage in question reads as follows:

> Seven substances must be applied to a stain [to ascertain whether it is blood or dye]: tasteless spittle, the liquid of crushed beans, urine, natron, lye [*borit*], Cimolian earth [*kimonia*], and lion's leaf [*eshlag*]. If one immersed [the garment with the suspicious stain] and . . . applied to it the seven substances and the stain did not fade away, it must be a dye. . . . If the stain faded away or grew fainter [as a result of the application of the seven substances], it must be a blood-stain. . . . What is meant by "tasteless spittle" ?—that of a man who has tasted nothing [on that day]. "The liquid of crushed beans" ?—paste made of crushed beans that were naturally peeled off. "Urine" ? —this refers to such that has fermented. One must scour the stain three times with each of the substances. If they were not applied in the prescribed order, or if the seven substances were applied simultaneously, it is as if he has not done anything. [Mishnah *Niddah* 9:6–7]

These seven substances are discussed at length in the Talmud (*Niddah* 63a ff.) and its commentaries as follows:

Tasteless Spittle

The first principle enunciated in the definition of tasteless spittle is that a person must have eaten nothing since the previous evening, (or midnight, according to one sage), since food sweetens the spit and causes it to lose its strength. This is the explanation given by the talmudic commentary of Rashi. The food, however, that one eats in the early evening before going to bed has no such weakening effect. Elsewhere the Talmud

195

teaches that "if a man slept all day, his is no tasteless spittle and if he was awake all night, it is tasteless spittle," indicating that the night and not sleep is the determining factor. The Talmud concludes that both conditions are necessary for spit to be tasteless: sleep (or dozing) and night. Sleep in the daytime, after one has had some food which sweetens the spit, or night without sleep when the effect of the food has not passed, is not enough. It is intriguing to speculate whether the Talmud is referring to fermentation of food by the action of saliva, thus rendering the food sweet.

A further requirement is that the person not speak after he arises early in the morning because speech also decreases the efficacy of the spit in the latter's action on a (blood or dye) stain.

The Liquid of Crushed Beans

The second of the seven substances to be applied to a stain to ascertain whether it is blood or dye is a paste made from crushed beans that were naturally peeled off. One sage in the talmud says that one should use the boiling liquid of crushed beans before salt is added, since salt would weaken it (*Niddah* 63a). The reason for the weakening effect of salt is not given.

Urine

The Talmud states that the urine must have fermented for three days (*Niddah* 63a). Others state for a minimum of three days but up to forty days. Most commentaries agree that the urine which is necessary to identify a stain as blood or dye refers to urine which has been standing for between three and forty days, not less and not more.

Urine of an old man is considered better (i.e., stronger and more effective) than that of a child; that of a woman better than that of man; that of the summer season better than that of the winter season; and covered urine is better than uncovered urine. The explanation for the efficacy of "fermented urine" is not apparent in the Talmud or in the commentaries thereon.

Natron

The Talmud explains that natron refers to Alexandrian natron and not the Antipatrian one (*Niddah* 62a). Maimonides states that natron is alum (*Commentary on the Mishnah, Kelim* 2:1). Bertinoro considers natron to be "a type of earth; *shib* in Arabic, or alum." R. Israel Lipschuetz, author of *Tiferet Yisrael,* also considers natron a type of earth. Today we identify natron as native sodium carbonate.

Borit

The English version of the Talmud translates the word *borit* as lye. At least one sage in the Talmud says that *borit* means sulphur (*Niddah* 62a). Maimonides, Bertinoro, and others consider *borit* to be a type of plant or grass (*al gasol* in Arabic).

Kimonia

Kimonia is usually translated as Cimolean earth. The Talmud uses another synonym, *shaluf doz,* which is a type of clay used in cleaning garments (*Niddah* 62a). Elsewhere in the Talmud R. Akiba states that *kimonia* is a kind of salt (*Shabbat* 90a). Maimonides identifies it as "alkali salt" (*Commentary on the Mishnah, Niddah* 9:6). Bertinoro claims it is a grass which one dries and pulverizes, and the powder is then used to cleanse one's hands. *Tiferet Yisrael* also agrees that *kimonia* is a type of grass.

Eshlag

Eshlag probably refers to lion's leaf. It was said to be "found between the cracks of pearls, and it was extracted with an iron nail" (*Niddah* 62a). Although *Tiferet Yisrael* avers that *eshlag* is a type of grass, Bertinoro states that he doesn't know what it is. Others (i.e., Jastrow) consider *eshlag* a kind of alkali or mineral used as a soap.

The seven substances described above are mentioned elsewhere in the Talmud (*Sanhedrin* 49b, *Zebahim* 95a), and all but the first two are discussed in *Shabbat* 90a. The efficacy of these substances in being able to distinguish a blood stain from a dye stain is undisputed in the Talmud. In fact, the matter is stated as fact in both the code of Maimonides (*Hil. Issurei Biah* 9:36–38, *Hil. Mishkav Umoshav* 4:13) and the code of Joseph Karo (*Shulḥan Arukh, Yoreh Deah* 190:31). Karo adds, however, that today (he lived from 1488 to 1575) "we are not knowledgeable in some of these names." Apparently Karo wished to put a stain to the test to ascertain whether it was blood or dye but was unable to do so because he was not sure of the exact identity of the seven substances.

Regular soap apparently washes out both blood and dye stains from a garment and would be perfectly suitable to cleanse the garment from the stain, no matter what it be. However, regular soap would not resolve the question of ritual impurity which applies to a blood stain. The question to which the seven substances address themselves is the problem of blood versus dye. The seven substances apparently do not distinguish between different types of blood (i.e., animal versus human blood) since they wash out all types of blood stains.

It might be difficult for the twentieth-century forensic pathologist to make use of the talmudic suggestion to wash a garment with seven substances to ascertain whether a stain is blood or dye. However, the historical interest of such a passage in the Talmud, written in the second century, is relevant to all those involved in the "modern" specialty of forensic medicine.

Suicide in Bible and Talmud

Introduction

Every day in the United States, about sixty people kill themselves by poisoning, hanging, drowning, shooting, stabbing, jumping from high places, or other means. Although nearly twenty-five thousand deaths from suicide are recorded annually in the United States,[1] the actual figure, according to the National Institute of Mental Health, is probably closer to fifty thousand yearly.[2]

Worldwide, more than 500,000 suicides are registered yearly, according to the World Health Organization,[3] and there are approximately eight times as many suicide attempts. The problem of suicide has reached such proportions that the United States Public Health Service created the National Center for Studies of Suicide Prevention in October 1966, headed by Dr. Edwin S. Schneidman. Presently there are ninety regional suicide prevention centers in twenty-six states in this country, whereas in 1965 there were only fifteen such centers.

The medical, psychological, psychiatric, legal, and social literatures are replete with articles, monographs, symposia, and other publications on suicide. Factors such as age, sex, marital status, day of week, month of year, method, religion, race, motivation, living conditions, repetitive attempts, medical and psychiatric histories of patients attempting and committing suicide, are amply covered in these writings as well as the many books published on this subject.[4] A periodical devoted exclusively to suicide is the *Bulletin of Suicidology,* published by the United States Public Health Service since 1967.

Several salient features of the problem deserve mention. Suicides are three times more frequent in men than in women, although there are more attempts by women than men. Twice as many White Americans commit suicide as do Black Americans, and twice as many single people kill themselves as do married individuals. College students have a suicide rate 50 percent higher than non-college-students of comparable age, sex, and race. In industrialized countries, physicians, dentists, and lawyers have a higher rate of suicide than other professionals. Although the suicide rate has remained relatively constant in the United States over the past decade or so, poisoning by drugs, especially barbiturates, has become much more popular as a method of choice.[5]

The age group with the highest suicide rate is that above sixty-five years. Suicide ranks third as a cause of death among teenagers.[6] It has also been estimated that the ratio of suicide attempts to actual successes in adolescents is 100 to 1.

One phase of suicide hardly discussed at all is the religious aspect. This essay attempts to organize and present in a systematic fashion the subject of suicide as found in Jewish sources. The closely related topic of martyrdom will be discussed briefly at the end.

Suicide in the Bible

During the period of the Judges, in approximately the eleventh or twelfth century B.C.E., lived Samson of the tribe of Dan, whose story is known to all. Samson's final effort in bringing down the Philistine temple upon himself as well as his enemies is vividly described in the Book of Judges (16:23–31):

> And Samson said: "Let me die with the Philistines." And he bent with all his might; and the house fell upon the lords, and upon all the people that were therein. So the dead that he slew at his death were more than they that he slew in his life.

At the end of the First Book of Samuel (31:1–7), we read of King Saul's final battle against the Philistines on Mount Gilboa in the eleventh century B.C.E. Here, Saul saw his three sons Jonathan, Abinadab, and Malchishua, and most of his army, slain. Not wishing to flee or to be taken prisoner and exposed to the scorn of the Philistines, King Saul entreated his armor bearer to kill him. The latter refused and so the king fell upon his own sword. The biblical passage concludes: "And when his armor bearer saw that Saul was dead, he likewise fell upon his sword and died with him" (I Sam. 31:5).

From these events it would appear as if Saul committed suicide. However, later on when David is informed of Saul's death, we read as follows:

> And David said unto the young man that told him: "How knowest thou that Saul and Jonathan his son are dead?" And the young man

that told him said: "As I happened by chance upon Mount Gilboa, behold, Saul leaned upon his spear; and lo, the chariots and the horsemen pressed hard upon him. And when he looked behind him, he saw me, and called upon me. And I answered: 'Here am I.' And he said unto me: 'Stand, I pray thee, beside me, and slay me, for the agony hath taken hold of me because my life is just yet in me.' So I stood beside him and slew him, because I was sure that he could not live after that he was fallen . . ." [2 Sam. 1:5–10]

Biblical commentators differ in their interpretation of this passage. R. David Kimḥi explains that Saul did not die immediately when he fell on his sword but was mortally wounded. In his death throes, Saul asked the Amalekite to render the final blow of mercy to hasten his death. Rashi, *Ralbag,* and *Meẓudat David* agree with Kimḥi and consider the death of King Saul a case of euthanasia. Others view the story of the Amalekite as a complete fabrication.

In any event, Saul did attempt suicide. Only the question of his success is debated. As to Saul's armor bearer, no one disputes that he committed suicide.

King David's faithless counsellor, Ahithophel, committed suicide by hanging himself in his native town of Gilo. One of several reasons probably prompted suicide. First, he knew that Absalom's attempt to overthrow David was doomed and that he would die a traitor's death. Second, and less likely, is the disgust of Ahithophel at Absalom's conduct in setting aside his counsel, thus wounding Ahithophel's pride and disappointing his ambition.[7] Finally, David's curse (*Makkot* 11a) may have prompted Ahithophel to hang himself.

And when Ahithophel saw that his counsel was not followed, he saddled his ass and arose, and got himself home unto his city, and set his house in order, and strangled himself; and he died and was buried in the sepulchre of his father.[8]

King Baasha of Israel reigned from 911 to 888 B.C.E. and was succeeded by his son Elah. The latter was addicted to idleness and drunkenness and passed the days drinking in his palace while his warriors were battling the Philistines at Gibbethon.[9] Zimri, a high-ranking officer, took advantage of the situation, assassinated Elah, and mounted the throne. His reign, however, lasted only seven days. As soon as the news of King

Elah's murder reached the army on the battlefield, General Omri was elected king and laid siege to the palace. When Zimri saw that he was unable to hold out against the siege, he set fire to the palace and perished in the flames. It is written in 1 Kings 16:18: "And it came to pass, when Zimri saw that the city was taken that he went unto the castle of the king's house, and he burnt the king's house over him with fire, and he died."

Some biblical commentators, notably *Radak* and *Mezudat David,* to whom the thought of suicide was abhorrent, interpret that Omri burned the house over Zimri. Most commentators, however, interpret the biblical passage literally.

Suicide in the Apocrypha

In the Second Book of Maccabees two acts of suicide are recorded. The first occurred when King Demetrius I of Syria (162–150 B.C.E.) escaped from his imprisonment in Rome and returned home as an invader.[10] Attempting to put down a rebellion of his Judean subjects, King Demetrius sent Nicanor, one of the warriors who escaped with him from Rome, to Judea, to treat the insurgents with the utmost harshness. Nicanor, in order to induce surrender from the Judeans, ordered that the most respected man in Jerusalem, Ragesh (or Razis), be seized. When the arresting soldiers were forcing open the courtyard door to Ragesh's house, "he fell upon his sword preferring to die nobly rather than to fall into the wretches' hands . . ." (2 Macc. 14:41–42). The ghastly tale of his lack of success in the first suicide attempt, his subsequent attempt by throwing himself down from a wall, and his final success by self-disembowelment is vividly described (ibid. 14:43–46).

The second act of suicide is that of Ptolemy, an advocate of the Judeans at the Syrian court, who was called a traitor before King Antiochus Eupator. Unable to maintain the dignity of his office, Ptolemy poisoned himself (2 Macc. 10:12).

Other Suicides and Near Suicides in Ancient Jewish Writings

All the suicides mentioned in the Bible and Apocrypha are psychologically understandable. Each knew what lay ahead if he remained alive, namely, a prolonged, torturous martyrdom and/or disgrace to the God of Israel. All were prominent people. Except, perhaps, for King Saul, none could be accused of having experienced temporary insanity to excuse his act of self-destruction. Perhaps Ragesh and Ptolemy were influenced by the Greek philosophy of their times, in which suicide was highly acceptable.

There are several individuals mentioned in the Bible, Apocrypha, and other ancient Jewish writings who considered suicide and perhaps wished to attempt it, but did not.

Job, during his quest for an explanation of his wretchedness, speaks of suicide: "And my soul chooseth strangling, and death rather than these my bones" (Job 7:15). He did not attempt suicide, perhaps out of either love or fear of God, as he himself states: "Though He slay me, yet will I trust in Him " (ibid. 13:15). Possibly Job did not mean to even consider suicide, but was remarking that he would prefer death to life. This question remains unresolved.

One of the most famous "near suicides" is Flavius Josephus, who failed to commit suicide at Jotapata in the year 69 C.E. when all the other Zealots there did so in a mass suicide pact. Flavius Vespasian, successor to Nero as emperor of Rome, had come to conquer Judea. Strong resistance was offered at the fortress of Jotapata. After a forty-day siege, the fortress fell. Many chose suicide by flinging themselves over the walls or falling on their weapons. Josephus, however, sought concealment in a huge cistern in which he found forty of his own soldiers. They all swore to die by their own hand in a mass suicide pact. When his turn came, Josephus reneged and surrendered to the Romans.[11] In Josephus' *Antiquities of the Jews,* there are numerous examples cited of suicide, including the mass suicide at Masada.

Suicide in the Talmud

The Talmud is replete with stories concerning suicide and martyrdom as well as discussions relating to the laws of burial and mourning for the deceased.

Abodah Zarah 18a describes R. Ḥanina ben Teradion's death by burning at the hands of the Romans. He was wrapped in a Scroll of the Law, bundles of branches were placed around him, and these were set ablaze. The Romans also brought tufts of wool, which they had soaked in water, placing them over his heart to prevent a quick death. When his disciples pleaded with him to open his mouth so that the fire consume him more quickly, he replied that one is not to accelerate one's own death. The executioner asked him: "Rabbi, if I raise the flame and remove the tufts of wet wool from your heart, will I enter the life to come?" Yes, was the reply. The executioner did as he proposed and the rabbi died speedily. The executioner then jumped into the fire and was burned to death. A voice from heaven exclaimed that R. Ḥanina ben Teradion and his executioner had been assigned to the world to come.

Another case of suicide is related in *Baba Batra* 3b. Herod, a slave of the Hasmonean house of the Maccabees, had set his eyes on a certain maiden of that house. One day he heard a voice from heaven saying that every slave that rebels now will succeed. So he killed the entire household but spared the maiden. When she saw that he wanted to marry her, she ran up to the roof and cried out: "Whoever comes and says that he is from the Hasmonean house is a slave, since I alone am left of it, and I am throwing myself down from this roof." Herod loved her so much that he preserved her body in honey for seven years.

The suicide of the Roman officer who saved the life of R. Gamliel is portrayed in tractate *Ta'anit* (fol. 29a). When Turnus Rufus the wicked destroyed the Jewish Temple, R. Gamliel was condemned to death. A high officer came to the house of study to search for him, but R. Gamliel hid. The officer found him and asked him secretly: "If I save you, will you bring me into the world to come?" The answer was affirmative. The officer made R. Gamliel swear to it, then mounted the roof and threw himself down and died. The Romans annulled the decree against R. Gamliel according to their tradition that the death of one of their leaders (i.e., the officer's suicide) was a punishment for an evil decree. Thereupon a voice from heaven was heard saying that this high officer was destined to enter the world to come.

Two nearly identical stories are told in tractates *Ḥullin* (94a) and *Derekh Ereẓ Rabbah* (chap. 9, 57b). Because of an incident that once occurred, it was decreed that guests may not give any of the food that is set before them to the host's son or to his servent or deputy unless they have received the host's permission to do so. The incident was that in a time of scarcity a man invited three guests to his house and only had three eggs, which he set before them. When the host's (hungry) child entered and stood before them, one of the guests took his portion and gave it to him; the second guest did the same, and so did the third. When the father came in and saw his son with one egg in his mouth and holding two in his hands he picked him up to his full height and flung him to the ground so that he died. When the mother saw her child dead, she went up to the roof, threw herself down, and died. On seeing this, the father also went up to the roof, threw himself down, and died. R. Eleazar ben Jacob said: "Because of this, three souls perished."

A related incident that terminated in suicide is told in tractate *Ḥullin* (94a). A man had sent his friend a barrel of wine and there was oil floating at the mouth of the barrel, leading the recipient to believe that the whole barrel contained oil. He invited some guests to partake of it. When he came and found that it was only wine, he went and hanged himself out of shame because he had nothing else prepared to set before his guests. As a result, it was decreed that a man should not send to his neighbor a barrel of wine with oil floating on top of it.

Another talmudic episode of suicide is found in the commentary of Rashi on *Abodah Zarah* 18b. R. Meir is said to have fled to Babylon. One of the reasons given is "because of the incident of [his wife] Beruria." The incident concerns the fact that R. Meir's wife once taunted him regarding the rabbinic adage that women are temperamentally lightheaded. He replied that one day she would testify to its truth. Subsequently she was enticed by one of her husband's disciples, proving she was too weak to resist. She then committed suicide by strangulation.

A mass suicide is described in tractate *Gittin* (57b), where four hundred boys and girls are said to have been carried off for immoral purposes. They guessed what they were wanted for and said to themselves that if they drowned in the sea they would attain the life in the future world, as portrayed in Psalms 68:23. The girls leaped into the sea first and the boys followed.

In *Gittin* 57b is related the story, from the Second Book of Maccabees, of the woman and her seven martyred sons. The sons were killed one by one by Emperor Antiochus Epiphanes for refusing to serve an idol. As the last son was being led away to be killed, his mother said to him: "My son, go and say to your father Abraham: Thou didst bind one [son to the altar, i.e., Isaac] but I have bound seven altars." Then she went up on a roof and threw herself down and was killed. A voice thereupon came forth from heaven saying, "A joyful mother of children" (Ps. 113:9).

Another incident is related in tractate *Berakhot* (23a). A certain student once left his phylacteries on the side of the road in a hole before entering a privy. A harlot passed by and took them. She came to the house of learning and said: "See what so and so gave me for hire." When the student heard this, he went to the top of a roof and threw himself down and killed himself.

The rules and regulations governing suicide are discussed in at least two tractates of the Talmud. In *Baba Kamma* 61a is found the following: "No Halakhah may be quoted in the name of one who surrenders himself to meet death for the words of the Torah." Further in the same tractate (91b) we find: ". . . who is the Tana that maintains that a man may not injure himself? It could hardly be said that he was the Tana of the teaching: 'And surely your own blood of your souls will I require' [Gen. 9:5], which R. Eleazer interpreted to mean that I will require your blood if shed by the hands of yourselves [i.e., suicide], for murder is perhaps different . . ." Rashi interprets this scriptural verse to mean that even though one strangles onself so that no blood flows, still I will require it.

The major talmudic discussion of rules governing suicide is found in chapter 2 of tractate *Semahot*. Here we are told that we do not occupy ourselves at all with the funeral rites of someone who committed suicide willfully. R. Ishmael said: we exclaim over him "Alas for a lost [life]. Alas for a lost [life]." R. Akiba said to him: "Leave him unmourned; speak neither well nor ill of him." Further, "we do not rend garments for him, nor bare the shoulder [as signs of mourning], or deliver a memorial address over him. We do, however, stand in a row for him [at the cemetery after the funeral to offer condolences] and recite the mourner's benediction for him because this is respectful for the living [relatives]. The general rule is that we occupy ourselves with anything that is intended as a matter of honor for the living . . ."

The Talmud (*Semahot* 2:2) defines an intentional suicide. It is not he who climbed to the top of a tree and fell down and died, nor he who ascended to the top of a roof and fell down and died, as these may have been accidents. Rather, a willful suicide is one who calls out: "Look, I am going to the top of the roof or to the top of the tree, and I will throw myself down that I may die." When people see him go up to the top of the tree or roof and fall down and die, then he is considered to have committed suicide willfully. A person found strangled or hanging from a tree or lying dead on a sword is presumed not to have committed suicide intentionally and none of the funeral rites are withheld from him.

The Talmud (ibid., 4 and 5) next relates two childhood suicides and considers neither an intentional suicide. One case concerns the son of Gornos of Lydda, who ran away from school, and the other case is that of a child in Bnei B'rak, who broke a bottle on the Sabbath. In each case, the father threatened to punish the child, and out of fear each child destroyed himself in a pit. R. Tarfon in the former case, and R. Akiba in the latter case ruled that these were not willful suicides and therefore none of the funeral rites should be withheld.

Suicide in the Midrash

In the Midrash, *Ecclesiastes Rabbah* (chap. 10, 7; fol. 26b), the story is told of R. Akiba walking (barefoot) to Rome when met by a eunuch officer of the emperor riding on a horse. The officer asked him whether he was the famous rabbi of the Jews, and he answered yes. In order to embarrass R. Akiba, the eunuch said three things: "He who rides on a horse is a king, he who rides on a donkey is a free man, and he whose feet have shoes on is a human being; he who has none of these is worse than a dead person." R. Akiba replied saying three things: "One's beard is one's majestic countenance, happiness of heart is one's wife, and the inheritance of God is to have children; woe is the man who is lacking all three. Not only that but Scripture states, 'I have seen servants upon horses and princes walking as servants upon the earth' [Eccles. 10:7]." When the eunuch officer heard these words, he knocked his head against a wall until he died.

Another case of intentional suicide is related in *Genesis Rabbah* (65: 22; fol. 130b). The case is that of Yakum of Zerorot, nephew of R. Yose ben Yo'ezer of Zeredah. Yakum taunted R. Joseph Meshita and, as self-punishment, subjected himself to the four modes of execution inflicted by the courts: stoning, burning, decapitation, and strangulation. He took a post, planted it into the earth, raised a wall of stones around it, and tied a cord to it. He made a fire in front of it and fixed a sword in the middle of the post. He hanged himself on the post, the cord was burned through, and he was strangled. The sword caught him while the wall of stones fell upon him and he was burned.

Suicide in the Codes of Jewish Law

In his *Mishneh Torah* Maimonides states:

> For one who has committed suicide intentionally we do not occupy ourselves at all [with the funeral rites], and we do not mourn for him or eulogize him. However, we do stand in a row for him and we recite the mourner's benediction, and we do all that is intended as a matter of honor for the living. [*Hil. Evel* 1:11]

Maimonides then defines an intentional suicide exactly as defined in tractate *Semaḥot*.

The commentators on Maimonides' code, R. David ben Zimra (*Radvaz,* 1479–1598), R. Joseph Karo (*Kesef Mishneh,* 1488–1575), and R. Abraham di Boton (*Leḥem Mishneh,* 1560–1609), all point out that Maimonides considers mourning an honor for the dead and therefore prohibited.

Code of Jacob ben Asher (Tur)

R. Jacob ben Asher (*Yoreh Deah* 345) codifies the section of the Talmud from tractate *Semaḥot* (vide supra) nearly verbatim. He states that we do not rend garments, bare the shoulder, or eulogize the willful suicide victim. However, we do stand in a row to offer condolences to the family at the cemetery and we utter the mourner's benediction, for these are intended as a matter of honor for the living relatives. R. Jacob ben Asher then continues by saying that the prohibition of rending the garments refers only to distant relatives, but the immediate relatives who have to mourn the deceased should rend their garments as a sign of mourning. This is diametrically opposed to Maimonides. The *Shulḥan Arukh* follows Maimonides.

R. Jacob ben Asher (*Tur*) defines a willful suicide as it had been defined in *Semaḥot*. However, a child who committed suicide even willfully is not considered to have attained his full measure of intelligence. Similarly, he continues, anyone who commits suicide in unusual circumstances, such as King Saul, is not considered a willful suicide, and he is entitled to all funeral rites. According to R. Joseph Karo (*Bet Yosef*) and R. Joel Sirkes (*Bet Ḥadash*) in their commentaries on Jacob ben Asher, the latter statement in the *Tur* is based upon Naḥmanides' work entitled *Sefer Ha'adam.*

Code of Joseph Karo (Shulḥan Arukh)

Karo's code is based primarily upon the earlier codes of Alfasi, Maimonides, and Asher ben Yeḥiel (father of Jacob ben Asher). Karo seems to combine the talmudic (tractate *Semaḥot,* vide supra) and Maimonidean regulations regarding suicide. He states that we do not occupy ourselves at all for anyone who has committed suicide willfully (*Yoreh Deah* 345). We do not mourn for him (contrary to Jacob ben Asher, but in agreement with Maimonides) or eulogize him or rend garments for him or bare the shoulder. However, all that is in honor of the living, such as standing in a row to offer condolences to the relatives of the deceased, is performed.

Several commentators on Karo, including R. Shabtai Hakohen (*Siftei Kohen*, 1621–1662), R. Zechariah Mendel of Kracow (*Be'er Hetev*, 17th cent.), and R. Abraham Zvi Eisenstadt (*Pithei Teshuvah*, 1813–1868), point out that Jacob ben Asher's code differs from Karo in that the former does require garment rending and mourning of close relatives of the deceased. R. Shabtai Hakohen also quotes R. Solomon ben Abraham Adret (*Rashba*), who, in one of his several thousand responsa (no. 763), explains that "we do not occupy ourselves at all," as cited from the Talmud and Maimonides, does not refer to the burial itself. Rather, only the rites surrounding the funeral are withheld but the deceased must be buried.

Suicide in Recent Rabbinic Writings

Responsa literature on suicide is rather sparce. R. Moses Schreiber was asked concerning a person found drowned in a river (Responsa *Hatam Sofer, Yoreh Deah* 326). R. Schreiber defines in great legal detail what a willful suicide is in Jewish law. He seeks legal technicalities, such as fear, anger, emotional instability on the part of the victim, which, if present, would remove the deceased from being considered an intentional suicide. He thus justifies the actions of Saul and Ahithophel. R. Schreiber concludes that laws of mourning, including the recitation of the Kaddish prayer, are observed even for an intentional suicide victim.

R. Yehiel Michael Toktzinski, in his two-volume work entitled *Gesher Hahayyim* (Jerusalem, 1960), devotes an entire chapter (no. 25) to a discussion of suicide. The person who commits willful suicide is considered a murderer. It matters not whether he kills someone else or himself since his own soul is not his, just as someone else's soul is not his. Would we be able to bring this man to justice in this world, he would be adjudicated as any murderer. In fact, he may be so judged in Heaven above.

The thirteenth-century *Sefer Hasidim*, written by R. Judah the Pious One, states (no. 675) that even one who neglects the preservation of his health is guilty of partially murdering himself. R. Toktzinski states that it may even be a graver sin to commit suicide than to murder someone else for several reasons. First, by killing himself, a person removes all possibility of repentance. Secondly, death in most circumstances is the greatest atonement for one's sins (*Yoma* 86); however, in a suicide's death there has been committed a cardinal transgression rather than expiation. A third reason why Judaism abhors suicide is that the person who takes his own life asserts by this act that he denies the divine mastery and ownership of his life, his body and his soul. The willful suicide further denies his divine creation. Our sages compare the departure of a soul from a human body to a Torah Scroll which has been consumed by fire. Thus, a person who commits suicide can be likened to one who burns a Sefer Torah.

He who takes his own life is also one who denies the Judaic teaching of the immortality of the soul and the eternal existence of Almighty God. Such a person will have to answer to heavenly judgment in the world to come, as our rabbis of blessed memory stated: "He who willfully destroys himself has no share in the world to come."

Martyrdom in Judaism

The subject of suicide is intertwined with the topic of martyrdom, since many suicides are committed as an act of martyrdom. The Jewish attitude toward martyrdom is based upon the following passage: "Ye shall therefore keep my ordinances and my judgments which, if a man do, he shall live in them: I am the Eternal" (Lev. 18:5). The rabbis deduce from the words "he shall live" that martyrdom is prohibited save for idolatry, adultery, and murder (*Sanhedrin* 74a). All other commandments may be transgressed if life is in danger in order that "he shall live." Martyrdom includes both the ending of one's own life for the sanctification of the name of God (Lev. 22:32) and allowing oneself to be killed in times of religious persecution rather than transgress biblical commandments. Perhaps the best known examples of martyrdom in Jewish life are the ten famous scholars executed or martyred by the Roman state at different times for their insistence on teaching the Torah.

The topic of martyrdom is vast, and there is a great deal of literature on it, especially from the Responsa during and after the Holocaust. This subject is mentioned here only for purposes of "touching all bases," since martyrdom might be considered a special form of suicide.

Suicide and Modern Psychiatry

The preponderance of modern psychiatric thinking on the pathology of suicides is that the act of suicide, whether or not successful, is, with rare exceptions, *prima facie* evidence of mental illness. Most often the illness is depression or despondency, but occasionally it may manifest itself as a psychosis or schizophrenia. The rare exception can be illustrated by a person who has lived a full and good life and who feels he (or she) has nothing to look forward to. If this type of person attempts or commits suicide, it is not a sign of despondency.

Suicide may represent the act which expresses the fantasy reunion of a person with a departed loved one or a fantasy reunion with God. Such a psychiatric aberration of a person's mind cannot be classified as anything other than pathological. Suicide can accompany virtually all psychiatric illnesses or may occur during periods of life crisis and stress in persons without discernible mental illness.

Although physicians daily witness profound despair and tragedy in their patients, suicide attempts are an unusual event, and successful suicide is rarer still. The clinician should recognize the painful states of bitterness and desperation which so often raise the suicidal impulse.

At the other extreme of modern psychiatric thought is the American psychiatrist Thomas Szasz, who claims that suicide is rarely, if ever, a sign of mental illness. He further asserts that a person should have the right to commit suicide just as a person has many civil rights. Halakhah would not condone such an approach, because in Judaism we believe that the human body is not ours to do with as we please. Man was created in the image of God and was entrusted with his body, to guard it and to watch over it. This is the philosophy behind Judaism's abhorrence of suicide. Since the vast majority of suicides are assignable to emotional stress or psychiatric illness, lenient rabbinic rulings are usually enunciated (*Gesher Haḥayyim,* loc. cit.).

Summary and Conclusions

Judaism regards suicide as a criminal act and strictly forbidden by Jewish law. The cases of suicide in the Bible, as well as in the Apocrypha, Talmud, and Midrash, took place under unusual and extenuating conditions.

In general a suicide is not accorded full burial honors. The Talmud and the codes of Jewish law decree that rending one's garments, delivering memorial addresses, and other rites of mourning which are an honor for the dead are not to be performed for a suicide victim. The strict definition of a suicide for which these laws apply is one who had previously announced his intentions and then killed himself immediately thereafter by the method he announced. Children are never regarded as deliberate suicides and are afforded all burial rites. Similarly, those who commit suicide under extreme physical or mental strain, or while not in full possession of their faculties, or in order to atone for past sins, are not considered as willful suicides, and none of the burial and mourning rites are withheld.

These considerations may condone the numerous acts of suicide and martyrdom committed by Jews throughout the centuries, from the priests who leaped into the flames of the burning Temple to the martyred Jews in the time of the Crusades, from the Jewish suicides during the medieval persecutions to the martyred Jews in recent pogroms. Only for the sanctification of the name of the Lord would a Jew intentionally take his own life or allow it to be taken as a symbol of his extreme faith in God. Otherwise intentional suicide would be strictly forbidden because it constitutes a denial of the divine creation of man, of the immortality of the soul, and of the atonement of death.

REFERENCES

1. P. Solomon, "The Burden of Responsibility in Suicide and Homicide," *Journal of the American Medical Association* 199 (1967): 321–24.
2. B. Nelson, "Suicide Prevention: NIMH Wants More Attention for 'Taboo' Subject," *Science,* 161 (1968): 776–77.
3. "Campaign Against Suicide," *Medical World News* 10 (January 3, 1969): 7.
4. See E. S. Shneidman and N. L. Farberow, ed., *Clues to Suicide* (New York: McGraw-Hill, 1957): E. A. Morielli, *Suicide: An Essay on Comparative Moral Statistics* (New York: D. Appleton & Co., 1903): P. Bohannan, ed., *African Homicide and Suicide* (Princeton: Princeton University Press, 1960); J. D. Douglas, *The Social Meanings of Suicide* (Princeton: Princeton University Press, 1967); L. Yochelson, ed. *Symposium on Suicide* (Washington: George Washington University 1967); P. M. Yap, *Suicide in Hong Kong with Special Reference to Attempted Suicide* (Hong Kong University Press, 1958); E. Stengel, and N. G. Cook, *Attempted Suicide: Its Social Significance and Effects* (London: Chapman & Hall, 1958); P. Sainsbury, *Suicide in London: An Ecological Study* (London: Chapman & Hall, 1955); H. Hendin, *Suicide and Scandinavia: A Psychoanalytic Study of Culture and Character* (New York: Grune & Stratton, 1964); C. U. Leonard, *Understanding and Preventing Suicide* (Springfield, Ill.: Charles C. Thomas, 1967): E. Durkheim, *Suicide: A*

Study in Sociology (Glencoe Ill.: Free Press, 1951); N. L. Farberow, and E. S. Shneidman, *The Cry for Help* (New York: McGraw-Hill, 1961); G. E. Murphy, and E. Robins, "Social Factors in Suicide," *Journal of the American Medical Association* 199 (1967): 303–8; "The Burden of Responsibility," ibid. 199 (1967): 334; "Changing Concepts of Suicide," ibid. 199 (1967): 752; "Suicide and Suicidal Attempts in Children and Adolescents," *Lancet* 2 (1964): 847–48; "Of Suicide and Folly," *Canadian Medical Association Journal* 96 (1967): 1167–68.

5. F. M. Berger, "Drugs and Suicide in the United States," *Clinical Pharmacology and Therapeutics* 8 (1967): 219–23.

6. H. Bakwin, "Suicide in Children and Adolescents," *Journal of Pediatrics* 50 (1957): 749–69; H. C. Faigel, "Suicide Among Young Persons: A Review of Its Incidence and Causes, and Methods for Its Prevention," *Clinical Pediatrics* 5 (1966): 187–90; H. Jacobziner, "Attempted Suicides in Adolescence," *Journal of the American Medical Association* 191 (1965): 7–11.

7. H. Graetz, *History of the Jews*, 6 vols. (Philadelphia: Jewish Publication Society), 1:143.

8. 2 Sam. 17:23.

9. Graetz, *History of the Jews*, 1:192.

10. Ibid., 1:482–85.

11. Ibid., 2:276–90.

12. See also *Abodah Zarah* 17b: *Ta'anit* 18b, 29a; *Berakhot* 61b; *Pesaḥim* 50a; *Baba Batra* 10b; *Sanhedrin* 11a, 14a, 74a, 74b, 110b; I. Y. Unterman, *Shevet Miyehudah* (Jerusalem, 1955), pp. 38 ff.; I. Jakobovits, *Jewish Medical Ethics* (New York: Bloch, 1959), pp. 52–54.

Miscellaneous Items

1. *Artificial Respiration in Biblical Times*

Current understanding of the physiology of respiration began with the discovery of the circulation of the blood by William Harvey in the seventeenth century. The completion of the modern theory of respiration was dependent on the discovery of the different atmospheric gases: carbon dioxide by Black in 1759, hydrogen by Cavendish in 1766, nitrogen by Rutherford in 1772, and oxygen by Priestley and Scheele in 1771 and Lavoisier in 1775.

Life cannot exist in a human being if breathing stops. The only way to sustain the life of an individual in whom respiration has ceased is to produce movement of air into the lungs. Early attempts at artificial respiration included breathing or blowing into the victim's nostrils with a small bellows, rolling a drowned person over a cask, or suspending him by the heels.

The principle of artificial respiration by pressure on the thoracic cage was introduced by Hall in 1856. The Hall method consisted of rolling the patient from a prone to a side position combined with pressure on the back. The following year, Silvester modified this technic by placing the victim on his back and applying pressure to the anterior side of the chest wall.

In 1893 Schafer published his method of resuscitation. This prone pressure technic of artificial respiration was introduced into the United States shortly after the turn of the century and was the method of choice for many years. The Schafer technic of resuscitation was superseded by the back pressure–arm lift method and most recently by the mouth-to-mouth technic. Mechanical devices designed to restore or aid in respiration are, of course, desirable when available and applicable to the situation at hand, but as an emergency first aid measure nothing can replace mouth-to-mouth breathing or other manual technics to move air into the lungs.

Perhaps the earliest accounts of the application of the mouth-to-mouth method of resuscitation can be found in two incidents related in the

Bible. In chapter 4 of 2 Kings are described some of the wonderful acts of
Elisha the prophet. One of these acts was to promise the birth of a son
to a barren woman from the town of Shunam who gave hospitality to
Elisha. The prophecy of Elisha was fulfilled but was followed by the tragic
death of the boy. The latter's revival by Elisha has already been described
above in the chapter on sunstroke.

Another incident nearly identical to that of Elisha and the Shunammite woman's child is described in the seventeenth chapter of 1 Kings.
Here prophet Elijah, the predecessor of Elisha, warns King Ahab of Israel
(reigned 876–854 B.C.E.) of a drought which will last for several years.
To escape the drought, Elijah traveled to Zarephath, where he received
hospitality from a sinful widow who had an only son. The Bible then
relates:

> And it came to pass after these things that the son of the woman,
> the mistress of the house, fell sick; and his sickness was so sore,
> that there was no breath left in him. And she said unto Elijah:
> "What have I to do with thee, O thou man of God? Art thou come
> unto me to bring my sin to remembrance and to slay my son?" And
> he said unto her: "Give me thy son." And he took him out of her
> bosom, and carried him up into the upper chamber, where he abode,
> and laid him upon his own bed. And he cried unto the Lord, and
> said: "O Lord my God, hast Thou also brought evil upon the widow
> with whom I sojourn, by slaying her son?" And he stretched him-
> self upon the child three times, and cried unto the Lord, and said:
> "O Lord my God, I pray thee, let this child's soul come back into
> him." And the Lord hearkened unto the voice of Elijah, and the
> soul of the child came back into him, and he revived. [1 Kings
> 17:17–22]

The phrase 'there was no breath left in him" is interpreted by Josephus
(*Antiquities* 8, 13:3) to mean that he appeared to be dead. Most biblical
commentators, however, including Rashi, *Ralbag, Mezudath David,* and
Radak, consider the boy actually to have died. *Mezudath David* remarks
that the verse "and he stretched himself upon the child" means that
Elijah placed his mouth on the child's mouth and his eyes on the child's
eyes just as Elisha did to the son of the Shunammite woman. *Radak*
again states that this was done to breathe onto the boy and warm him
with Elijah's natural body warmth. *Ralbag* also supports this viewpoint,

and further remarks that it was as if the prophet wished to transfer the breath of his limbs to the limbs of the child.

These two biblical narratives seem to describe accurately and vividly the mouth-to-mouth method of resuscitation. It seems entirely plausible and reasonable to interpret these anecdotes in this fashion without denying one's faith in the miraculous divine intervention on behalf of the two victims. In these two instances, a most unique method of resuscitation was perhaps first utilized, which only now, twenty-eight hundred years later, is fully recognized and universally adopted.

2. Anesthesia in the Bible and Talmud

Soporifics of various kinds have been used since the earliest times.[1] Among these are Homer's nepenthe, fumes of Indian hemp, Dioscorides' potion, mandrakes, the soporific sponge of Salerno, and many others. Probably the earliest mention of anesthesia is that found in the Bible, in the description of the creation of woman from a rib of Adam. In Genesis 2:21, we find the following statement: "And the Eternal God caused an overpowering sleep [Heb. *tardemah*] to fall upon the man and he slept; and He took one of his ribs and shut in flesh instead thereof."

Although this overpowering sleep occurred by divine intervention, it embodies the concept of anesthesia. In fact, some Jewish Bible commentaries specifically interpret the above Pentateuchal phrase to refer to anesthesia. R. Meir Loeb ben Yeḥiel Michael, known as *Malbim*, states that *tardemah* is "a deep sleep in order not to feel the pain." The biblical commentary of R. Samson Raphael Hirsch uses the expression *bewegungslosigkeit,* which literally means "motionlessness." Thus, Hirsch may not be trying to convey the concept of lack of pain but lack of motion. It is possible that the English translation of Hirsch's commentary, "something like anesthesia," is a mistranslation for the concept of anesthesia. Elsewhere (Gen. 15:12), *Malbim* interprets *tardemah* to be "a state of deep sleep and cessation of body powers because of mental anguish" (lit. distress of the heart). The word *tardemah* is found in twelve additional places in the Hebrew Bible.[2]

The value of alcohol as an anesthetic is described in the Babylonian Talmud, where we find the following ruling: "When one is led out to execution, he is given a goblet of wine containing a grain of frankincense in order to benumb his senses, for it is written: 'Give strong drink unto him that is ready to perish and wine unto the bitter in soul' [Prov. 31:6]" (*Sanhedrin* 43a).

Rashi explains that the benumbing of the senses is an act of compassion to minimize or eliminate anxiety of the accused during his execution (loc. cit.). The Talmud also states that the noble women of Jerusalem used to donate the wine and bring it (ibid.). If they did not, it had to be provided from public funds.

Elsewhere the Talmud has a similar pronouncement: "the condemned are given wine containing frankincense to drink so that they should not feel grieved" (*Semaḥot* 2:9). Maimonides, in his code, goes one step further by stating that "after the condemned has confessed, he is given a cup of wine to benumb his senses and *to intoxicate him* [emphasis added], and then he is executed by the mode of death prescribed for the offense of which he is guilty" (*Hil. Sanhedrin* 13:2).

An unknown anesthetic sleeping potion is also mentioned in the Talmud in relation to an abdominal operation performed upon R. Eleazar, the son of R. Simeon: "He was given a sleeping draught [Heb. *samma deshinta*], taken into a marble chamber [perhaps an operating theater], and had his abdomen opened . . ." (*Baba Meẓia* 83b). The type of drink used is not indicated nor do the commentaries on the Talmud specify what it may have been.

There is yet a fourth talmudic mention of an anesthetic: "a man whose arm had, by a written decree of the government, to be taken off by means of a drug, would require that it should be cut off by means of a sword . . ." (*Baba Kamma* 85a). Preuss, in his classic work on biblical and talmudic medicine, assumes that the amputation was to be performed using the same anesthetic sleeping draught as mentioned above.[3]

REFERENCES

1. A. Castiglioni, *A History of Medicine* (New York: Alfred A. Knopf, 1941).
2. Judg. 4:21; 1 Sam. 26:12; Ps. 76:7; Prov. 10:5, 19:15; Dan. 8:18, 10:9; Jon. 1:5, 1:6; Isa. 29:10; Job 4:13, 33:15.
3. J. Preuss, *Biblisch-Talmudische Medizin* (Berlin: S. Karger, 1923), p. 277.

3. *The Biblical Quail Incident*

The biblical story of the consumption of quails by the Israelites in the desert, as described in the sixteenth chapter of Exodus and the eleventh chapter of Numbers, continues to intrigue medical historians as well as biblical scholars. The subsequent sudden death of the Israelites is explained by various medical writers to have been due to some form of food poisoning. A recent paper by Ouzounellis postulates that the biblical quail incident was, in fact, an epidemic of myoglobinuria.[1]

An alternate explanation of the quail affair is that the entire happening was an act of God. Some biblical commentators, in fact, state that many of the people who died had not consumed any quail at all but were stricken as soon as they raised the meat to their mouths. This is the interpretation of the phrase "while the meat was yet between the teeth, before it was consumed" (Num. 11:33). It is conceivable to attribute the deaths to both divine intervention as well as organic food poisoning if we interpret that God punished the people by medical means.

Further reference to the quail incident is found in the Psalms (78:26–31, 106:13-15) and in the Babylonian Talmud (*Yoma* 75b, *Sanhedrin* 17a, *Abot* 5:4, *Ḥullin* 27b, *Arakhin* 15a).

Moses Maimonides, in his monumental medical work, *The Aphorisms of Moses,* makes two interesting comments regarding quail consumption. In chapter 13 he states: "Many people who indulge greatly in eating quail meat develop cramps in the muscles because of the hellebore [a Veratrum alkaloid] which is the nourishment of the quail,"[2] Maimonides may, in fact, be describing myoglobinuria, but he attributes it not to the quail meat itself but to the hellebore which quails feed upon.

In chapter 20 of his medical aphorisms, Maimonides states as follows: "The quail acts similar to the nature of birds in that it helps the healthy as well as those convalescing from illness, its flesh is fine, it dissolves [lit. opens] a kidney stone and stimulates urine flow."[3] Here Maimonides describes the efficacy of quail and other fowl meat for diuresis and the dissolution of renal calculi. Perhaps a controlled study to confirm or reject this medieval proposition might someday be performed. In the interim, medical historians and biblical scholars will continue to dispute the true nature of the quail incident.

REFERENCES

1. *Journal of the American Medical Association* 211 (1970): 1186.
2. F. Rosner, S. Muntner, *The Medical Aphorisms of Moses Maimonides* (New York: Yeshiva University Press, 1970), Vol. 1, p. 255.
3. Ibid., 1971. Vol. 2, p. 78.

4. *Dolphins in the Talmud*

The Hebrew or Aramaic word *dolfanim* is variously translated as "dolphins, a fish about which many fables were circulated among the ancients,"[1] "dolphins,"[2] "a type of whale,"[3] "dolphins,"[4] and "a big sea fish."[5] The term probably corresponds to the Greek *delphinus*.

There is a most unusual passage in the Babylonian Talmud concerning the possible cohabitation of dolphins with human beings. The text in question reads as follows: "Dolphins [Heb. *dolphanim*] are fruitful and multiply *like* human beings [Heb. *kibnei adam*]. What are dolphins? Said Rab Judah: 'living beings [lit. children] of the sea' " (*Bekhoroth* 8a). Rashi has a variant textual reading in which he states that dolphins are fruitful and multiply *from* human beings (Heb. *mibnei adam*); that is to say, if a human being has intercourse with a dolphin, the latter becomes pregnant therefrom. "Living beings of the sea" are explained by Rashi as follows: "there are fish in the ocean which have half the features of human beings and half the features of fish, and in Old French *syrene.*" A commentator called *Hametargem,* who translates all the Old French words in Rashi, considers *syrene* to be a mermaid (*meervaybshen*).

Tosafot adopt the textual reading of Rashi that dolphins multiply *from* human beings. *Tosafot* further state that their view is supported by the *Tosefta,* where it states that "dolphins are born and raised *from* human beings." Later talmudic commentators, such as *Maharsha* and *Shitah Mekubezet* (Bezalel Ashkenazi, 17th cent.), also agree with the textual variant "dolphins are fruitful and multiply *from* human beings." A seemingly lone dissenting viewpoint is that of Jacob Emden, who asserts that the original textual reading "dolphins are fruitful and multiply *like* human beings" is correct.

If one consults the *Tosefta* directly, one finds a discussion as to whether or not various types of animals can crossbreed with one another (*Bekhorot* 1:5). The *Tosefta* then states that a human being cannot breed with them or they with humans. The key phrase then follows: "dolphins reproduce and grow up *like* human beings." It is thus apparent that Rashi and all the subsequent talmudic commentators either misquoted the

Tosefta or, more likely, possessed manuscripts of the *Tosefta* different from the printed editions of today. A single Hebrew letter makes the difference between the word *kibne* ("like") and *mibne* ("from"). Scribes in antiquity and the Middle Ages frequently made inadvertent errors in copying manuscripts. They sometimes even took the liberty of intentionally adding, deleting, or modifying a letter, word, or phrase on their own. Be that as it may, how does one explain the entire talmudic passage and, in particular, the statement of Rashi that there are fish in the ocean which have half the features of human beings and half the features of fish?

Kohut provides one possible interpretation.[3] He points out the correct textual reading of the *Tosefta* that dolphins are fruitful and multiply like human beings. He also asserts that the intent of the Talmud is to teach us that dolphins have sexual intercourse like human beings and that the female gives birth to live offspring and suckles its young and does not lay eggs. Thus, Rashi means to say that female dolphins have breasts like humans and suckle their young like humans, yet dolphins resemble fish because they live in the sea. This interpretation seems correct in view of the fact that the talmudic text regarding dolphins is preceded by a discussion of which fish breed and which fish lay eggs (*Bekhorot* 7a). The Talmud states: "Whatsoever gives birth gives suck, and whatsoever lays eggs supports its young by picking up food for it." Today we know that dolphins are mammals and thus have some features resembling human beings and others resembling fish. Kohut further asserts that dolphins are compared in the Talmud to human beings because they are extremely devoted to humans and are therefore called *philantropon zoon* in Greek, meaning a philanthropic animal.

The reason Rab Judah calls dolphins "living beings of the sea," continues Kohut, is well known from Greek writings where the dolphin is characterized as a creature which does not live on land. In Hebrew, the expression is *ein le'dolphanim memshalah ba-yabashah,* meaning "dolphins have no dominion on dry land," and because they live in the sea, they are called "rulers of the sea."

One of the major commentaries on the *Tosefta* called *Minḥat Bikkurim* (Samuel Avigdor of Slonimo), raises the possibility that dolphins can be raised by suckling from human beings.

What remains difficult to explain is the original statement of Rashi that dolphins are fruitful and multiply from human beings, meaning that if a human being has intercourse with a dolphin, the latter becomes pregnant therefrom.*

REFERENCES

1. M. Jastrow, *A Dictionary of the Targumin, the Talmud Babli and Yerushalmi, and the Midrashic Literature* (New York: Pardes, 1950), 1:286.
2. R. Alcalay, *Milon Ivri-Angli Shalem* [Complete Hebrew-English Dictionary] (Hartford, Conn.: Prayer Book Press, 1965), p. 417.
3. A. Kohut, *Arukh Hashalem* (New York: Pardes, 1955), 3:72–73.
4. I. Epstein, ed., *The Babylonian Talmud: Seder Kodoshim,* vol. 3, *Tractate Bechoroth* (London: Soncino Press, 1948), p. 47.
5. R. Grossman, *Milon Ivri-Angli* [Hebrew-English dictionary] (Tel Aviv: Dvir, 1951), p. 69.

---

*The editor of the *Jewish Press* (Sept. 26, 1975, p. 5) proposes that "Rashi apparently was trying to portray a mythical creature, a mermaid, of which many people believed to have existed." He further points out that the Aramaic term *dolfanim,* recorded in the Talmud over fifteen hundred years ago, may not be the true meaning of what we today call a dolphin. He also states that one of the ten sons of the wicked Haman (Esth. 9:7) was called Dolphon. Finally, he states that the talmudic passage in question might be interpreted allegorically; that is to say, a person who associates with Dolphon, a symbol of evil, may produce a half and half person, one who is evil but hides behind a pious face.

GLOSSARY OF RABBINIC AUTHORITIES AND COMMENTATORS

Adret, Solomon ben Abraham, See *Rashba*.
Akedat Yizḥak. Isaac Arama (1420–1494). Bible commentator.
Alfasi Isaac (1013–1103). First codifier of talmudic law.
Altschul, David. See *Mezudat David*.
Arukh Hashulḥan. Yeḥiel Michael Epstein (1829–1908). Codifier of Jewish law.
Asher ben Yeḥiel. See *Asheri*.
Asher, Jacob ben. See *Tur*.
Asheri. Asher ben Yeḥiel (1250–1327), also known as *Rosh*. Codifier of Jewish law.
Ashkenazi, Beẓalel. See *Shitah Mekubezet*.
Azulay, Ḥayyim Joseph David. See *Birkei Yosef*.
Ba'al Haturim. See *Tur*.
Baḥ. Joel Sirkes (1561–1640). Talmudic commentator, also wrote commentary on *Asheri*.
Be'er Hetev. Zechariah Mendel of Kracow (17th cent.). Commentator on Karo's *Shulḥan Arukh*.
Bertinoro, Obadiah (1470–1520). Mishnah commentator.
Bet Ḥadash. Joel Sirkes' commentary on Jacob ben Asher's *Tur*.
Bet Yosef. Joseph Karo's commentary on Jacob ben Asher's *Tur*.
Birkei Yosef. Ḥayyim Joseph David Azulay (1727–1806). Commentator on Karo's *Shulḥan Arukh*.
Edels, Samuel. See *Maharsha*.
Eger, Shlomo. See *Gilyon Maharsha*.
Eisenstadt, Abraham Zvi Hirsch. See *Pitḥei Teshuvah*.
Elijah of Vilna. See *Hagra*.
Epstein, Barukh Halevi. See *Torah Temimah*.
Epstein, Yeḥiel Michael. See *Arukh Hashulḥan*.

224

Fraenkel, David. See *Korban Ha'Edah.*

Gerondi, Nissim. See *Ran.*

Gilyon Maharsha. Shlomo Eger (1769–1842). Commentator on Karo's *Shulḥan Arukh.*

Hagra. Elijah of Vilna (1720–1797), also known as the Vilna Ga'on. Commentator on Karo's *Shulḥan Arukh.*

Halevi, Judah. See *Kuzari.*

Halevy, David ben Samuel. See *Turei Zahav.*

Heller, Yom Tob Lippman. See *Tosafot Yom Tob.*

Hirsch, Samson Raphael (1808–1888). Bible commentator.

Iba Ezra, Abraham (1092–1167). Bible commentator.

Isserles, Moses. See *Ramah.*

Karo, Joseph. See *Shulḥan Arukh, Beth Yosef,* and *Kesef Mishneh.*

Kesef Mishneh. Joseph Karo's commentary on Maimonides' *Mishneh Torah.*

Kimḥi, David. See *Radak.*

Korban Ha'Edah. David Fraenkel (1704–1762). Commentator on Jerusalem Talmud.

Kuzari. Apologetic book written by Judah Halevi (1075–1141).

Landau, Ezekiel. See *Noda Biyehudah.*

Leḥem Mishnah. Abraham di Boton (1560–1609). Commentator on Maimonides' *Mishneh Torah.*

Lipschuetz, Israel. See *Tiferet Israel.*

Luria, Solomon. See *Maharshal.*

Maharsha. Samuel Edels (1551–1631). Talmudic commentator.

Maharshal. Solomon Luria (1510–1573). Talmudic commentator.

Maimonides, Moses. See *Rambam.*

Malbim. Meir Leib ben Yeḥiel Michael (1809–1879). Bible commentator.

Margolis, Moses. See *Penei Moshe.*

Mekhilta. Extra-talmudic collection of biblical interpretation.

Mezudat David. David Altschul (18th cent.). Bible commentator.

Midrash, Midrash Rabbah. Extra-talmudic collection of homiletical biblical commentary and interpretation (6–11th cent.).

Minḥat Bikkurim. Samuel Avigdor of Slonimo. *Tosefta* commentator.

Mishneh Torah. Code of Jewish Law of Moses Maimonides. See *Rambam.*

Nachmanides, Moses. See *Ramban.*

Noda Biyehudah. Ezekiel Landau (1737–1793). Author of Responsa.

Onkelos. Second-century Aramaic translation-paraphrase of the Bible.

Penei Moshe. Moses ben Simon Margoliot (d. 1781). Commentator on Jerusalem Talmud.

Pithei Teshuvah. Abraham Zvi Hirsch Eisenstadt (1813–1868). Commentator on Karo's *Shulhan Arukh.*

Radak. David Kimhi (1160–1235). Bible commentator.

Radvaz. David ben Zimra (1479–1598). Commentator on Maimonides' *Mishneh Torah.*

Ralbag. Levi ben Gerson (1288–1344). Bible commentator.

Ramah. Moses Isserles (1510–1572). Foremost commentator on Karo's *Shulhan Arukh,* for which he wrote his famous *Glosses.*

Rambam. Moses Maimonides (1135–1204). Physician and talmudist. Author of the *Commentary on the Mishnah,* the *Guide for the Perplexed,* and the authoritative code of Jewish law, *Mishneh Torah.*

Ramban. Moses Nahmanides, or Moshe ben Nahman (1194–1268). Bible and Talmud commentator and author of *Torat Ha'adam.*

Ran. Nissim Gerondi (1320–1380). Talmudic commentator.

Rashba. Solomon ben Abraham Adret (1235–1310). Author of Responsa and Novellae.

Rashi. Solomon ben Isaac, or Shlomo ben Yitzhak (1040–1105). Foremost and greatest commentator of Bible and Talmud.

Reischer, Jacob. See *Shevut Yaakov.*

Rosh. See *Asheri.*

Sefer Hasidim. Judah the Pious (13th-cent.). Philosophical and ethical writer.

Shakh. See *Siftei Kohen.*

Shevut Yaakov. Jacob ben Joseph Reischer (1670–1733). Author of Responsa.

Shiltei Gibborim. Joshua Boaz Baruch (16th cent.). Talmudic commentator.

Shitah Mekubezet. Bezalel Ashkenazi (1520–1598). Collection of talmudic commentaries.

Shulhan Arukh. Joseph Karo (1488–1575). Author of the authoritative code of Jewish law, *Shulhan Arukh. Also* wrote commentaries on the *Tur* and *Mishneh Torah.*

Siftei Hakhamin. Commentary on *Rashi.*

Siftei Kohen. Shabtai ben Meir Hakohen (1621–1662), also known as *Shakh.* Commentator on Karo's *Shulhan Arukh.*

Sirkes, Joel. See *Bah.*

Taz. See *Turei Zahav.*

Tiferet Yisrael. Israel Lipschuetz (1782–1860). Mishnah commentator.

Torah Temimah. Baruch Halevi Epstein (1860–1942). Bible commentator.

Tosafot. Talmudic commentary of various 12–13th century Franco-German rabbis.

Tosafot Rid. Isaiah ben Mali di Trani (1200–1260). Talmudic commentator.

Tosafot Yom Tob. Yom Tob Lippman Heller (1579–1654). Mishnah commentator.

Tur. Jacob ben Asher (1269–1343). Codifier of Jewish law. Also known as *Ba'al Haturim.*

Turei Zahav. David ben Samuel Halevy (1586–1667) also known as *Taz.* Commentator on Karo's *Shulḥan Arukh.*

Yad Abraham. Abraham Maskil Le'Aytan. Talmudic commentator.

Zohar. Book of Jewish mysticism ascribed to the talmudic sage R. Simeon ben Yoḥai.

Indices

Compiled by Robert J. Milch, M.A.

I. Pasages Cited
1. HEBREW BIBLE

2. APOCRYPHA AND PSEUDEPIGRAPHA

3. RABBINICAL WRITINGS

Bab. = Babylonian Talmud.　　Jer. = Jerusalem Talmud.
　　M. = Mishnah.　　Tos. = Tosefta.

3A. MIDRASH

4. CLASSICAL WRITINGS

II. Names and Subjects

Aaron, 69, 180
Abaye, 51, 56, 83, 108, 191
Abba Arikha. *See* Rab
Abba Shaul, 18
Abbahu, R., 117, 153, 189
Abdominal disorders, 218
Abihu, 69
Abimelech, 8, 143
Abimi, 117
Abinadab, 200
Ablat, 159, 166
Abner, 93
Abortifacients, 34
Abortion, 34
Abraham, xi, 6, 11, 31, 113, 143, 205
Absalom, 201
Abscesses, 153
Absinthium, 9
"Account of an Hemorrhagic Disposition . . . , An" (Otto), 43
Acne, 10
Adders, 185
Adonijah, 88
Adret, R. Solomon b. Abraham, 94, 209
Aetius of Amida, 14, 50
Aḥa b. Ammi, R., 56
Aḥa b. Jacob, R., 73
Ahab, 67, 215
Ahithophel, 35, 201, 209
Air pollution, xii
Akedat Yiẓḥak. See Arama, R. Isaac
Akhshub, 179
Akiba, R., 80, 101, 114, 192, 197, 206, 207
Albucasis, 43
Alcoholism and drunkenness, 10, 35, 64. *See also* Delirium tremens
Alfasi, R. Isaac, 44, 46, 57, 208
Alopecia, 10
Al Tasrif (Albucasis), 43
Altschul, R. David, 67, 68, 201, 202, 215
Alum, 196
Amaurosis, 7
Amemar, 82
Ammi, R., 30, 154, 173
Amnon, 34
Amputations, 16, 31, 153. *See also* Surgeons and surgery
Amulets, 13
Anatomy and anatomical studies, 10, 12, 16, 17, 81, 154, 168. *See also* names *of individual organs*

Androginos, 174
Anemia, xii, 30, 44, 47, 64, 70, 72
Anesthesia, x, 16, 217–18
Antiochus Epiphanes, 205
Antiochus Eupator, 202
Anus, 16
Aorta, 82
Apoplexy, 32
Arama, R. Isaac, 111
Ardeshir, 160
Aretaeus, 64
Ariokh. *See* Samuel, Mar
Aristotle, 17, 50
Artaban, 160
Arteries, 16
Arthritis, xii
Artificial respiration, xii, 9, 67, 214–16
Arukh Hashulḥan. See Epstein, R. Yeḥiel Michael
Asa, 7, 59, 60
Asafetida, 80, 83, 163
Asahel, 93
Asaph, xii, xiii, 14, 22, 27, 89, 119–23, 136
   Oath of Asaph, xii, xiii, 121–23, 132
Asher b. Yeḥiel, R., 46, 57, 94, 208
Asheri. *See* Asher b. Yeḥiel, R.
Ashi, R., 27, 56, 189
Ashkenazi, Beẓalel, 221
Askara, 30
Assi, R., 182
Asthma, 146
Astrology and astronomy, 30, 132, 134, 158, 159, 167–68. *See also* Intercalation
Asya, 13, 29, 151
Autopsies, 13, 17, 154
Avia, R., 83, 190
Aviya, 183
'Aẓevet, 10
Azulay, R. Ḥayyim Joseph David, 45, 46, 111

Ba'al Haturim. See Jacob b. Asher, R.
Baasha, 201
Baba ben Buta, 16
Baḥ. See Sirkes, R. Joel
Baheret, 10
Baldness, 10
Balm, 15
Balsamodendron, 9
Bandages, 7, 9
Bar Ginte, 30, 154

DATE DUE